The Interior Distance

Born in Belgium, Georges Poulet received doctorates in both law and literature at the University of Liège and has taught at the University of Edinburgh and The Johns Hopkins University. He is now the Professor of French literature at the University of Zurich, Switzerland, where he is completing a book on the subject of the Infinite Circle.

The
Interior
Distance

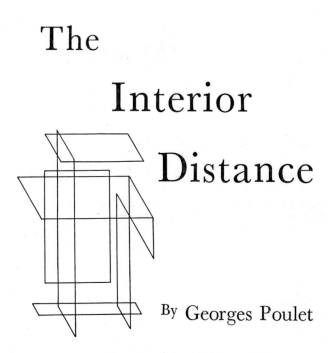

By Georges Poulet

Translated by Elliott Coleman

Baltimore: The Johns Hopkins Press

Distributed in Great Britain by Oxford University Press, London

Printed in the United States of America by H. Wolff
Book Manufacturing Company, Inc., New York

Library of Congress Catalog Card Number 59-10766

This book has been brought to publication with the
assistance of a grant from The Ford Foundation.

Translator's Note

The first volume by Georges Poulet to be translated from French into English appeared in 1956 under the title *Studies in Human Time*. The Paris edition (*Études sur le temps humain*) had in 1950 been awarded the *Prix Sainte-Beuve*. The American translation of it contains a specially written Appendix entitled "Time and American Writers."

The Interior Distance, the second and final volume in this particular series, now presented in English in collaboration with the author, was published in France in 1952 (*La distance intérieure*) and won both the *Grand Prix de la Critique littéraire* and the French Academy's *Prix Durchon* in Philosophy.

Born in Belgium, Georges Poulet received doctorates in both law and literature at the University of Liège and has taught at the University of Edinburgh and The Johns Hopkins University. He is now the Professor of French Literature at the University of Zurich, Switzerland, where he is completing a book on the subject of the Infinite Circle.

With the present publication of *The Interior Distance,* there has been brought to readers of English an entire critical work of the highest order.

Baltimore   *Elliott Coleman*
April 27, 1959

Author's Preface

Every thought, to be sure, is a thought *of* something. It is turned invincibly toward the somewhere else, toward the outside. Issuing from itself, it appears to leap over a void, meet certain obstacles, explore certain surfaces, and envelop or invade certain objects. It describes and recounts to itself all these objects, and these accounts or these descriptions constitute the inexhaustible objective aspect of literature. But every thought is also simply a thought. It is that which exists in itself, isolatedly, mentally. Whatever its objects may be, thought can never place them, think them, except in the interior of itself. If it is necessary for it to go searching through the exterior spaces for one or another of the thousands of objects which offer themselves there, it is no less necessary for it to constitute itself as a sort of interior depth which the images from outside will come to populate. My thought is a space in which my thoughts take place, in which they take their place. I watch them arrive, pass on, wander aside or sink out of sight, and I distinguish them at spatial and temporal distances which never cease to vary. My thought is not made up solely of my thoughts; it is made up also, even more perhaps, of all the *interior distance* which separates me from, or draws me closer to, that which I am able to think. For all that I think is in myself who think it. The distance is not merely an interval; it is an ambient milieu, a field of union. Thus there is revealed another aspect of literature, a hidden aspect, the invisible face of the moon. Objectively, literature is made up of formal works the contours of which stand out with a greater or lesser clarity. They are poems, maxims, and novels, plays. Subjectively literature is not at all formal. It is the reality of a thought that is always particular, always anterior and posterior to any object; one which, across and beyond all objects, ceaselessly reveals the strange and natural impossibility in which it finds itself, of ever having an objective existence. The studies which follow, like those which were published last year,[1] seek to bring to light that interior vacancy in which the world is redisposed.

GEORGES POULET

[1] Under the title *Études sur le temps humain*. Paris. Plon. 1950. [*Studies in Human Time*. Translated by Elliott Coleman. Baltimore: The Johns Hopkins Press, 1956.]

Contents

The Interior Distance

Chapter I

Marivaux

I

An Author is a man who in his idleness feels within himself a vague desire to think about something; and this could be called reflecting on nothing.[1]

A mere nothing reflected in a mind which also is nothing: a reflection in a mirror, such is Marivaudian literature.

It is the literature of an eighteenth-century Mallarmé.

Before anything occurs in such a mind, if indeed anything ever does occur there, nothing as yet exists except a state of emptiness and indolence, the preliminary state of the person who, existing only by means of his feelings, has as yet no feeling; the state, in short, of Adam before the Creator had breathed into him, the state of Condillac's statue before it became odor of rose. A state of psychological nothingness, like paralysis or sleep:

> Without the spur of love and pleasure, our hearts are veritable paralytics: we are waters that must wait a mover, to be moved.[2]

Such an existence, never beginning or always ending, returns to its primitive inertia; for of itself it never arrives at anything active or conscious; it never transforms itself into action, into words, and into wit:

> If I have any wit, I am sure nobody knows it; for I have never taken the pains to keep up a conversation, and that because of an invincible laziness.[3]

The essentially lazy person is incapable of sustaining a conversation, a thought, or any activity whatsoever. It is troublesome to renounce this permanent negation of existence which is fundamentally sloth:

> Yes, my dear friend, I am lazy, and I enjoy this blessing in spite of the fortune which could not rob me of it . . . Ah, Holy sloth! Wholesome indolence![4]

> . . . I know some people who, waking up in their bed in the morning, feel nothing but regret at having to leave it; and I swear to you . . . that the pleasure of finding oneself warm, snug, and at rest is a pleasure I renounce with the greatest difficulty.[5]

At its extreme, this pleasure is no different from despair. In a youthful letter written at a time when he was experiencing intensely the feeling of the brevity and nullity of life, Benjamin Constant recalled the remark of the poet Young, who, having lost all incentive to live, refused to get up: 'I see no reason to rise, man." Extreme unhappiness, extreme indifference, extreme laziness end in the same vacuity. Like the Mallarmean lifelessness, the Marivaudian laziness is that negative, paralyzing, indefinitely prolongable state that is the result of the absence of any hope.

But also the absence of any truth. Like Mallarmé, Marivaux begins by being unable to feel anything. And he can feel nothing because there is nothing to feel, except that thing which comes to nothing and is called illusion. One recalls the story of the seventeen-year-old Marivaux having surprised his lover practicing in her mirror the airs she was going to use with him: "It turned out that her expressions, which I had thought so naive, were, to describe them correctly, only a bag of tricks."[6] In that mirror, as later Mallarmé in his, Marivaux saw truth dissolved, or at least that truth to which alone he attached any value, veracity of feeling, human sincerity. And perhaps this is the reason why fundamentally in Marivaux's work there is such a sorrowful note. One would not be wrong to compare it with that of Watteau, provided one does not imply by that in the one or the other any romantic nostalgia. Those who embark for Cythera set out neither toward the past nor toward love. They set out for nonbeing. They are comedians who play their comedy, who parade their illusion. In parading it they reveal and dissolve it. Their departure is the disappearance of the factitious in its own smoke. Thus all existence is brought either to nothing at all or else to that vapour which is the illusory creation of our vanity. There is only the choice between idleness and illusion. And the one gives us nothing, while the other gives us less than nothing:

> Here are a thousand mere nothings for something which is truly nothing.[7]

In the first place, *as first place,* one must see in Marivaux's mind just this nothing, made of vacancy and vapour. And this place is also a time, if one can call time the permanence of inertia. It is a time that does not even flow, and which, like the "stagnant water," will continue not to flow, unless, only unless, something makes it move! A single chance stroke, an intervention from outside, can rouse this nothing, can fill this void.

II

—I don't know what is happening to me.[8]

—What does it mean . . . Who can protect oneself from such a happening? [9]

—Is what is happening to me conceivable? What an adventure! O Heavens! What an adventure! Must my reason perish in it? [10]

Here we see the Marivaudian being rising up out of non-existence in undescribable astonishment. He *is* this astonishment. Without the slightest moment of gradation, in a lightning flash, he has passed from his negative state of habitual stupor, which is the state of sloth, to an entirely different sort of stupor, an essentially active stupor which is the stupor of being. What has happened to me? I have come to be. But I still know nothing about the event which has happened except that it has happened, that I cannot distinguish it from myself, and that it now forms a part of my very existence. More than that, when confronted with this event, I forget everything except this event and myself, and that this event is myself. I am that which is happening, although I am also the one to whom it is happening. I feel and apprehend myself in this instant in which unquestionably I unite my consciousness of being to this event's being. Yet all this only increases my astonishment, for I know that if what is happening to me is I, myself, on the other hand I know less than ever what is happening. My consciousness of being is at one and the same time a knowledge and an ignorance. What I know is that I am. What I do not know is what I am.

The Marivaudian astonishment is thus an admirably concrete form of the *Cogito* which situates the feeling of existence well before the moment of the Cartesian *Cogito,* at a sort of original point in which being is not even yet thought, in which it is barely its own event. This astonishment is like a pause of the reflective activity, a momentary disappearance of the intelligible universe in which one situated his own being. One no longer knows where one is, one is lost, one no longer comprehends, one is at his wit's end, one knows not what to decide and feels as if he were struck stupid. This is an astonishment which allows us no margin for reflection. In contrast to the Cartesian *Cogito,* the Marivaudian *Cogito* is purely negative. I do not know what I think, nor even if I think. And if I spontaneously recognize that something is happening to me, that is very simply because it is happening to me. I cannot get out of this. It is given to me to be the one to whom something happens. It is given to me to be, that is all.

My thought is nothing but bewilderment.

The bewilderment of being what happens to me.

But for this wonder to be absolute, for the discovery of being what is happening to me to exert its full force, it is necessary that what happens to me be the thing least foreseen, most stupefying, or most new. It is necessary that the consciousness of being what I feel myself to be catch me by complete surprise. Such is the "surprise of love":

—Yes, I love him; it is a partiality that has surprised me.[11]

—You, a lover, I exclaimed, dropping my eyes; you, sir, I never expected it. —Alas! nor I, he replied; this is a complete surprise.[12]

Thus love surges up in me, in order to be me, without my being able to connect it with anything else besides its action and my passion. It is both myself and the cause of myself. From myself to it I can indeed proceed by some kind of induction, but not as one retravels in the mind the course of a duration. This cause which forms me does not precede me, since it is me; and if I situate it behind me, I must place myself there too—imagining by a sort of infinite regression an unknown being which was me, produced by a love unknown to me, which still was me. Immediate and quasi-formal cause of my being, love is at each instant only that actual force which ensures that I am and that I love, that I am a being who loves. And so the bewildered consciousness does not discern in its present the effect of an antecedent and efficient cause. What it is, is not explained by what it has been. Nothing in its prior state determined that it would necessarily be what it now discovers itself to be. Precisely, it knows neither why nor how it is, and neither why nor how it is what it is:

—Ah! I know not where I am; let us breathe a sigh. *Whence comes* that sigh? Tears brim my eyes; I feel seized with the deepest sadness, *and I know not why*.[13]

It happens all the time that people act in consequence of confused ideas which *come they know not how,* which move them, and upon which they do not reflect at all.[14]

If I am what I am, it is thus without knowing *why* or *how,* it is all simply a matter of chance. It is not at all a creative, transcendent force which in forming my being would form the rationality of my being. At any rate I have no consciousness of it as such. Nor is it an immanent, determining force within myself, by reason of which I should decide to be what I am:

> I can only come upon thoughts which chance makes spring up within me, and I should be sorry to contribute anything of my own to them.[15]

> Vainly we should attempt to hinder our own hearts
> From feeling the sweetness of a love unforeseen.
> They have come there by chance, to which the soul is subdued,
> And of which we can without shame experience the surprise.[16]

> I assign no character to my ideas; chance gives them their tone.[17]

But this chance which forms everything and which forms me is not different from me. Love is a sort of self that I give myself, without knowing it or willing it. I create myself by chance. And this creation puts me suddenly in the presence of an unknown, astonishing, incomprehensible being, with whom I do not know what to do, who is my present being, who is myself:

> Is it not chance that makes everything? [18]

> —Oh! I am lost, Madam, I no longer understand anything.

> —No more I: I no longer know where I am, I don't know how to unravel myself . . .[19]

> There it is, I love you, that is decided, and I understand nothing of it.[20]

III

> —Of what are you dreaming, fair Silvia?
> —I dream of myself, and I understand nothing.
> —What then do you find in yourself that is so incomprehensible?

—I wished to take revenge on those women, you know that?
All that is past . . . *I loved* Arlequin . . . Ah, well! I believe
I love him no longer.[21]

I wished, and I wish no longer. I love, but I no longer love what
I loved. The Marivaudian personage is incomprehensible to himself only because he is at one and the same time his past and his
present; and because from his past to his present there is no road.
His bewilderment is that of being lost.

—I am lost, my head whirls, I know not where I am.[22]

—I wish to find myself and I lose myself.[23]

—I lose myself! It's like a fairy tale.[24]

— . . . In the confusion of ideas which all that gives me, it
happens, in very truth, that I lose sight of myself.[25]

To lose sight of oneself is to lose sight of the spread of one's
own existence. The latter is no longer a temporal continuity,
analogous to and perhaps identical with the spatial continuity; it
is on the one hand a confused and multiple actuality in which
(as Joubert will demonstrate) one sees nothing because one is too
close to things, and it is on the other hand so radical a nonactuality that it is instantaneously relegated to an infinite distance.
Nothing connects this present with that past, unless it be the
feeling of the utmost difference between them. Moreover, we have
precisely *passed* from one to the other. How can that have happened?

There is in the work of Marivaux a short sentence that keeps
perpetually recurring, and which, under a spatial form, marvelously expresses this exactly temporal perplexity: "Where am I?"
—"I do not know where I am."—"I don't know where I can be."—
"I no longer know where I am."—with a thousand more variations
or variants. Of all Marivaux's phrases, there is none more significant, none more appropriately Marivaudian. None is more
universally or continually applicable. This is so true that if,
perchance, one Marivaudian character makes such a remark,
another immediately takes it up and applies it to himself:

> —I ask you, what have I come to?
> —I don't know the word for it; you tell me, what have I myself come to? I am in the same case as you . . .[26]

or again if some person inadvertently refers to the matter, another immediately agrees and adds: "Ah! you are in the right key; mind you keep to it." [27]

The Marivaudian being is always keyed in the same way; of himself, he can hardly sing any other song. The tone of these novels and comedies is always, in effect, the tone at once exclamatory and interrogative of one's being astray and of searching for the way that leads from his being to his being. "Where am I?" That means in brief: It is necessary that I be somewhere, but how can I connect this place with the place I have left, and with the one at which I intend to arrive? How can I trace the route and set my bearings? There is neither road nor route. There is only darkness and worry:

> —Do not ask me what I think, I am confused, I don't know where I am.[28]

> —I no longer know where I am, I wouldn't know how to unravel myself, I feel as if I were dying! What is this state? [29]

Indeed, in one way, this state is a kind of death. For it is the consciousness of a rupture with being. One is suddenly a being who is broken off from what he felt himself to be. One lives his death. Then one tries to pull himself together again. *Where am I?* Is not this the question which would be asked by somebody who has lost the thread of his discourse, of his thought? And the very question he would raise, if it were the thread of his existence which had snapped? This is precisely the essential experience of a Marivaudian character. He has lost the thread of his very existence. He wants to recover it, to renew it; he feels he must regain his vital continuity. He cannot. Ariadne's clue is broken. He is no longer an habitual being, he is nothing more now than an actual being, lost among the turnings of the labyrinth:

—I want to find myself and I lose myself.[30]

—Do not leave me, save me! I no longer know myself.[31]

—My mind is completely disordered; I no longer know where I am; let me recognize myself.[32]

Supplication or cry for help, it is inevitably in vain that such a one in his essential disorder appeals to his fellow-creature. For it is not at all a question here of the external relation which creates love between two persons, but of that internal relation with oneself, which precisely the love for another has profoundly shaken and perhaps destroyed.

"Let me recognize myself."—"I no longer recognize myself."— "I saw you, and from that instant I was no longer the same." [33] As the Princess of Clèves had already realized, love makes one lose one's identity. One is no longer the one that one was. But one is. And thus, detached from oneself, different from oneself, one discovers some part of oneself left behind—strange, dissimilar, therefore unimportant. Memory is of no avail. It is much better to be disencumbered of it, and to be rid at the same time of those lapsed images of the self which have become impostures. Of every single Marivaudian character, one can say what Lubin says of the countess: "Ah! sir, what would you have her do with a memory?" [34]

What would you have them do with a duration? Without a past to sustain them, without identity, without temporality, Marivaudian beings know neither who they are nor where they are. Yet they must be some place, they must occupy some space. What is that space?

IV

Had I *fallen from the skies,* I could not have have been more giddy.[35]

I should not know how to tell you what I felt upon seeing this great city, with its bustle, its people and its streets. For me it was *the Empire of the Moon;* I was no longer myself, I no longer remembered anything; I moved, I opened my eyes, I was astonished, and that was all.[36]

Without identity, without memory, without origin, fallen from the skies, the Marivaudian being lands upon an indescribable world. Nothing in it is recognizable; consequently nothing in it is intelligible. Nothing within it is related to anything else. It is the Empire of the Moon and the Kingdom of the Actual. For perceptible and affective reality is, in itself, nothing else; it is what is presented to us before we can relate it to memories and ideas. It constitutes a double space, exterior and interior, made up of a disconcerting plurality of motions and forms. Each detail therein exists for itself. It occupies a place, it catches the eye, it produces its particular sensation. It suggests nothing, recalls nothing, signifies nothing. It has number, but only discrete number, which no one can add up. Without as within, it multiplies and sparkles. The space occupied by the purely actual being is nothing but a delicious disorder.

> Everything about it was as if *cast at random:* disorder reigned there indeed, but the pleasantest disorder in the world, which made a charming effect, and one could neither have disentangled it nor explained its cause.[37]

It is the realm of *"Je ne sais quoi."* Sprung from "I know neither how nor why," it is indelibly stamped with its origin. The play of love and chance can only engender a chaos. Marivaux himself said so (if indeed he is the author of Part Six of the *Paysan parvenu*): "The heart is only a chaos when it begins to feel love." [38]

A chaos of images, sensations, desires, even thoughts, into the multiplicity of which one finds himself transported as if by magic, little knowing what he feels or where he is going:

> I was lost in a chaos of motions to which I abandoned myself gently but not without some uneasiness.[39]

I would not know how to define for you what I felt. It was a mixture of disturbance, pleasure, and fear.[40]

A mixture of pleasure and confusion, that was my state.[41]

The actual being seems less a being than a plurality, a *mêlée* of beings. It has not only lost identity, but also unity, simplicity: it is a sort of aggregate of things and of motions which mingle without coalescing:

> I felt so many motions, so much confusion, so much vexa-tion, that I knew not where to begin to *speak;* moreover it was an entirely new situation for me, the *mêlée* I found myself in. I had never experienced anything like it before.[42]

Pleasure, fear, love, pain, vexation, movements of all sorts im-mediately spring forth from all sides to entangle their threads within a mind which they stun with their agitation and number. Everything is present at once, a swarm of things, composed of an infinity of small, particular existences. All these elements come together at the same time and yet do not form an ensemble. They fill up the whole, without ever becoming a whole. A staggering mixture that invades the mind, that is the mind. A mixture *in which* one is and *which* one is, a state in which one can neither isolate anything nor embrace anything. Pure confusion.

v

Instantaneous confusion:

> I went to shut myself up in my room, and there anxiety, pleasure, fear, shame, and finally a thousand different motions agitated me at once.[43]

> Everything I said came to my mind in a flash.[44]

> Everything that then came to my mind on the subject, though it takes some time to tell, *required only an instant to be thought.*[45]

But before that instant in which all is thought and felt, there was nothing; or at least nothing that remains actually thought and felt. This fullness conceals a void. The Marivaudian being, without identity, without past, without habits, suddenly opens his eyes and sees all at once what he sees for the first time. It seems that this existence is given to him, not little by little as temporal existence is, but simultaneously and at a single stroke. Thenceforth in this confusion there is revealed a profusion. By the wonderful action of love and chance, a disconcerting but fascinating world surges up out of absentness, a new world for a new Adam. At any moment some caprice of feeling can lay hold of the Marivaudian being and, amidst a superabundance of disorder, give him an existence as multifarious as that of a jungle. Thus the "Indigent Philosopher," abandoning himself to the whimsical and fecund company of a troupe of comedians:

> An hour after having been with them, it was as if I had known them ten years: they sang along the way, they drank, they ate, they made love. Ah! the good life! Kings could not lead such a life! it is too happy a one for them, and they are too lordly for it. Deuce take it! my friend, *I was like a child at the breast,* I opened my eyes, my heart swelled; *I lived, for I had never lived before.*[46]

A return to a pristine moment when the consciousness of living is unaccompanied by the consciousness of having lived. With Marivaux, as with all the writers of the eighteenth century, one finds continually a haunting preoccupation with a primitive being seized in the initial moment of its existence. It is the whole subject of *La Dispute,* perhaps the most subtly metaphysical piece of this "metaphysical theatre." There Marivaux undertakes to bring to life again before the spectators the "first age of the world":

> —Yes, the men and women of that time, the world and its first loves, are going to reappear before our eyes as they were, or at least as they ought to have been. Not the same adventures perhaps, but the characters will be the same; you are going to see the same state of heart; *souls as new as the first creatures;* newer still, if that is possible.[47]

Now, since chance does not cease to be chance, it does not cease to create; and consequently, thanks to its continuous creation, we are always "new souls" and each moment at the "first age of the world." In the allegory of the *Miroir,* in which, as Sainte-Beuve says, Marivaux expounded his philosophy of history, one finds the following thesis: Nature is not at all in its decline. It is still very young in us. Perhaps it is ageless. And thus it is with humanity. There are formed there, periodically, convulsions of all sorts—wars, invasions, epidemics—by means of which there appear new modes of existing. In short, for Marivaux (as for Fontenelle), if the world is always young, it is because it periodically returns to chaos. It is a world that only exists and survives by shocks:

> Each of these (political) states brought forth a new spirit and provided the earth with one more experience.[48]

> Sesostris, Cyrus, Alexander and his successors, and especially the Romans, did not disturb and shake the earth or give it such violent shocks without venting their new ideas, without causing new developments in man's capacity for thought and feeling.[49]

Humanity as a whole is therefore no different than Marianne or Silvia; and Sesostris or Alexander do not play in history a role any different from that which love plays in the existence of a lover. At random, haphazardly, they beget the troublous and the new. Thanks to them, man can be reborn and life begin again.

A philosophy of history which rigorously ends in the destruction of all history, since one always sets out again into the new. Neither Nature, therefore, nor humanity, nor the individual being ever grows old:

> I am seventy-four years old, as I write this: I have lived a long time, then: a long time indeed, alas! I am wrong: properly speaking *I live only in this instant that passes;* there was another which already is no longer, in which I have lived, it is true; but in which I no longer exist; and it is as if I had not been; thus *could I not say that my life does not last; that it is*

always beginning? thus, young and old, we would all be of the same age. A child is born as I write, and, as I see it, aged as I am, he is already as old as I. That is how it seems to me; and on this basis what is life? a perpetual dream, except for *the instant one possesses,* and which *in its turn becomes dream.*[50]

In all the literature of the eighteenth century it would be difficult to find a page in which the consciousness of the ephemeral is more clearly expressed. Perhaps La Fontaine and Keats, in other centuries, have been the only ones along with Marivaux who have had at one and the same time enough courage and suppleness to seize the slightest furtive instant of their existence and place in it all their faith, all their desire, all their spiritual exigencies. On the other hand, it would be a grave mistake to confuse the thought of Marivaux with the banal *Carpe diem* of the imitators of Chaulieu and Horace. It is not a question here of profiting from the moment because the moment is the place of our pleasures. It is a question of recognizing in the instant which lives and dies, which surges out of nothingness and which ends in dream, an intensity and a depth of significance which ordinarily one attaches only to the whole of existence. For Marivaux, as for Aristippus, Pater, and Gide, the instant is all, for it is only within itself, and not in time, that something happens and ceases to be, which is all our destiny. Our being is a rapid sketch, an immediate gesture, a cry of astonishment that mounts to our lips. It is the inexpressible state in which all at once there are confusedly revealed within us and to us certain feelings heretofore unknown. Suddenly a thousand forms are glimpsed in the shadows of the mind. At the same time a thousand thoughts traverse the troubled waters of our soul. All that is us; and it is only that which could be true and could be us. Let us receive it, let us live it in the instant in which one can live it. Let us refresh ourselves with this drop of time which encloses the only true and good time, and upon which our being so easily floats. Let us concern ourselves first of all with the moment in which we are; for man never is, except in the moment; he is never in time:

You are going to think that the object which occupied me at first was the unhappy situation in which I was left: no, *that situation had regard only to my life; what occupied me had regard to me, myself.*

You will say that I dream, to make such a distinction: not at all, *our life, so to speak, is less dear than us, than our passions.* To see sometimes what happens instinctively in us, one would say *that in order to be, it is not necessary to live;* that it is only by accident that we live; but that it is naturally that we are.[51]

VI

If it is naturally that we are, it is naturally also that we enjoy our being. In the interior of the instant there is so gentle a motion from feeling to enjoying that it seems to happen of itself, without conscious effort:

Disquieted by love and fear, she lost herself within her own emotions, reflected on nothing, felt nothing distinct within her mind, except a dangerous sweetness which she dared not enjoy, and which she enjoyed in spite of herself.[52]

This insidious enjoyment, this confused consciousness, how are we to avoid confounding them with their cause? Since we cannot distinguish our passions from our being, how should we be able to distinguish from among our feelings the feeling we have of our feelings? And there is also the fact that with Marivaux consciousness of self is never a reflective consciousness. A momentary reflection of a momentary event, it appears in the instant only as the highest scintillation of the instant. And if consequently it is exact to say with Marivaux that his creatures "reflect on nothing," it is no less exact to say that they are thus spontaneously *reflected,* and that the feelings which bring them to birth bring to birth in them at the same time, as in a mirror, the charming image of those feelings. At the extremity of every emotion there is always in Marivaux a fresh apparition of oneself to oneself. Thus Marianne, losing and finding herself again amidst the bustle of the streets of Paris:

I was no longer myself, I no longer recalled anything. I moved, I opened my eyes, I was astonished, and that was all.
I found myself again, however, along the course of my walk, *and then I enjoyed my complete surprise: I felt my movements . . .*[53]

Or again, Églé discovering herself in the Mallarmean mirror of a brook:

The brook showed all my expressions, and all of them pleased me . . . I could pass my life in looking at my face. How I am going to love myself now![54]

So that, for Marivaux, if love makes us leave ourselves, it brings us back to ourselves. For the love which one experiences for another human being finds its rapid perfection only in becoming the love which one experiences for oneself. It attains its completion only in the moment in which it becomes, beyond the discovery of the other, a knowledge of self. The fairy who lies in wait for Harlequin knows well the miraculous mutation of love into intelligence:

—Sometimes he looks at me, and every day I long for the moment when he can be conscious of me, *and conscious of himself.*[55]

To love is to be conscious; and to be conscious is to be conscious of self; it is therefore to love oneself.

This is found agreeably expressed, in bad enough verse, in the *Divertissement* of *l'Amour et la Vérité:*

Happy the lover all akindle.
He who has never loved at all
Lives not, or at least life ignores;
Lacking the pleasure of being charmed
By a lovable object whom one adores
Could one be aware of being born?

Awareness of self, confused knowledge but knowledge, thought thus bursts out with Marivaux at the apex of emotion. If the latter is at first an anxiety, a giddiness in which all rational knowledge disappears, it is through this disturbance that the

human being has the chance of discovering what he really is, that
is to say, what he is spontaneously. There are two kinds of minds:
the first being that which "can never learn anything but reason-
ing," [56] and that "only with time." [57] It avails little if we want
to know ourselves, because we are instantaneous beings who could
never be overtaken by a discursive and consequently slow-moving
thought. But to this slow and clumsy intellectual knowledge,
there is opposed another, agile and prompt; it is more exactly
to *feel* than to *know:*

> —I did not know the difference between *knowing* and *feeling.*
> —*Feeling,* Madam, is the style of the heart . . .[58]

But once again, the style of the heart is absolute instantaneity:

> . . . There are instants in which passion furnishes man with
> sudden views impossible to resist, bewildering as they may
> be, and which must prevail upon all he had previously re-
> solved to do, and what he had believed most wise . . . ; and
> perhaps one never is more in his right sense, nor has more
> vitality, than in moments like these.[59]

For Marivaux then, as for Pascal, true knowledge is a knowledge
of the heart.

> As for me, I think that feeling alone can give us unfailing
> intelligence of ourselves . . .[60]
> . . . And what is this feeling? It is an instinct that leads us
> and makes us act without reflection, in presenting us with some-
> thing that touches us . . .[61]

Intelligence, therefore, is not something superimposed upon
the heart. It does not analyze the passions in order to extract from
them, by no one knows what operation, some essence. Strictly
speaking, there is no possible rational knowledge of being. At
least for ourselves. There is only an immediate experience in
which one is conscious of what one feels:

> —One puts nothing into one's heart; one takes from it what
> one finds there.[62]

Existing only in the instant, the Marivaudian personage comes upon himself, so to speak, on the wing and by chance. He catches himself by the same motion that makes him live. And if, as Marivaux claims, "it is only feeling that can give us relatively sure intelligence of ourselves," it is because we are made by our feeling, and because between being and knowing there is no difference when it is a question of a being who is simply his own passions, and a thought that is not different from the movements of the heart. Consequently this instinctive thought, immediate and fortuitous, triumphantly completes the actuality of the Marivaudian being. My thought prolongs my being and my feeling. It accompanies them on their instantaneous flight. It never breaks away from them:

> I should reproach myself for evading the situation of mind in which I find myself; I deliver myself up to the feeling it gives me . . .[63]

VII

At the extremity of the instant there is then the rapid consciousness of the motion which makes the instant. But this consciousness, precisely because it is the consciousness of a motion, is the consciousness of a passage. Just as in the case of Montaigne, in Marivaux a person apprehends himself only in a sort of creative flight that simultaneously makes him, and makes him become other. The very intensity with which he feels transforms his delightful feeling of coming to life into an inverse feeling, that of a prolongation, a continuation, a kind of duration: "My love then seemed to me not so much being born as continuing." [64] —"It is like the movement one has given to anything; it does not stop all at once." [65] It does not stop being motion, flight, metamorphosis. Thus in the very instant when, in the play of our emotions, we confusedly feel ourselves to be such as we are, we also foreshadow ourselves, confusedly, as we shall be:

If you asked me, did I have any design of loving her, I had no determined design; it was solely that I was charmed to find myself in the amiable good graces of a great lady; *I was sparkling with this prospect,* without knowing where it would end, without thinking of the behavior I ought to adopt.[66]

. . . Hearts such as yours *sigh often in advance,* pending the moment when they will know why.[67]

Marivaudian presentiment is thus not foresight. It is less a *fore-seeing* than a *fore-living,* a *fore-feeling;* the feeling of being on the threshold of a future instant and a new mode of being. The passage from the present to the future is so prompt, the allurement so irresistible that one lives as it were simultaneously both the one and the other. While one is still what one is, one is already what one will be. Thence, with the Marivaudian being, a new occasion of losing oneself and finding oneself again in the moving feeling of one's being:

Someone led me and I followed. What will all this *turn into?* What will *come to pass!* thus I spoke to myself in an amazement that left me helpless to think.[68]

Here the Marivaudian being is amazed not solely at *being;* he is astonished at *becoming.* The *What am I?* and the *What shall I be?* overlap one another, so to speak. One vacillates between two instants which are only one. Or rather one finds oneself thrown into a present so transitory that it vanishes, and out of a past still so warm that one falls into an unknown, imminent future already almost actual:

—Where am I! and when will this end? [69]

—To what will this bring us?
—As yet I know nothing about it . . .[70]

—What shall I do? I know not where I am.[71]

—If you continue always to speak to me in the same way, I shall very soon no longer know of what sort my feelings for you will be: of a truth, I dare not examine myself on that subject.[72]

There was an infinity of them who, in traversing those precincts, were working on them and touching them up; for they
could only come and go, only pass, only quickly succeed one
another, without allowing the time for anyone to perceive
them clearly; they were there; but hardly had one caught
sight of them when they were there no longer and one saw
others in their place who passed in their turn to make room
for still others.[80]

Carried along in a perpetual metamorphosis, the Marivaudian
being thus perseveres in being, only by means of a continual
substitution of what he is to be for what he is. His temporal existence is no more than an incessant inconstancy:

—Ah, well! I guess I no longer love her.
—That is not so great a misfortune.
—If it were a misfortune, what could I do about it? When I
loved her, it was a love that had come to me; now I love her
no longer; it is a love that has left me; it came to me without
warning, it has departed in the same fashion; I hardly think
myself blamable.[81]

In a world in which everything is reduced to being only what
one feels, and for only just as long as one feels it, there is no
true permanence: no fidelity is possible to oneself or to others:

—This heart that goes back on its word when it has given
it a thousand times, does its job; when it has been false a thousand times, it does it still; it goes wherever its motions lead
it, and would not know how to do otherwise. So far from infidelity's being a crime, I pretend that one should not hesitate
a moment to be fickle when one is tempted, unless one wishes
to be untruthful.[82]

And in this perpetual mutation of the affective duration, it
is vain to hope to draw some fixity from the fact that one continues to love the same person, for as one can never love for
two successive instants in the same fashion, one never ceases to
be inconstant even in fidelity:

—I sometimes love more, sometimes less, sometimes not at
all; it depends: when I have not seen him for a long time, I
find him very lovable; when I see him every day, he bores
me a little: if there were a little more movement in my heart,
that would do no harm, surely.

—But is there not a bit of inconstancy in you?

—Very likely; but one puts nothing in her heart; one takes what one finds there.[83]

When I wished to have a knavish air, I had a bearing and an attire that accomplished my aim. The next day one found me full of tender graces, on the following I was a modest beauty, serious, nonchalant. I kept the most fickle man steady; I tricked his inconstancy, because every day I renewed his mistress for him; and it was as if he had taken another one.[84]

Hence the existence of the Marivaudian character always seems a little like the story narrated in the *Voiture embourbée:* it is an "impromptu novel" [85] narrated in turn by different characters much less interested in what the past narrators have said than in what they themselves are going to say. The Marivaudian being is always so passionately occupied in becoming his future that he always quits his past with the same facility that an awakened sleeper quits his dreams:

. . . It is a man who awakes and who sees disappear at once all the illusions he dreamed in his love. He knows not where those so tender feelings have gone.[86]

They have gone into the past, that is to say into the kingdom of the feelings one no longer feels. The Marivaudian being, like the Proustian being, continually loses himself along the way. Behind him lies all the *time that is lost*—and, as with Marivaux, there is no memory, lost time is irrevocably lost.

But in the Marivaudian world no one seems to regret that loss; neither the author, nor the characters, nor even the reader or the spectator. If everything seems in effect to be continually dissolved behind, like the wake of a ship, everything appears at the same time to be continually refashioned ahead. And that without rest, without respite, without any pause, so that one never sees things and beings except in the confused and multiple image they offer in passing. Everything has the same plurality of aspect as the character of Nature in the tale of the *Miroir:*

. . . That person, or that Divinity, who in the main seemed to me to have a youthful and yet an antique air, was in a

perpetual and at the same time so rapid a motion that it was
impossible for me *to look her in the face.*

What is certain is that in the motion which agitated her,
I saw her under so many aspects that I thought I saw pass
successively all the physiognomies of the world, *without being
able to seize hers,* which seemed to contain them all. [87]

In this uninterrupted movement it becomes impossible, then,
to look anything in the face. Human beings cannot acquire or
keep the permanent characteristics they would have if they were
viewed in repose and at a distance. They lack what one could
call with Joubert a temporal *perspective.* Condemned to having
no past because, without even noticing it, they incessantly betray it; condemned to having no future because with them the
future is something so close to them that they confound it with
the present, they have to offer us only that infinite series of moments which are substituted one for another before we have had
time to distinguish them, and what the author of the sixth part
of the *Paysan parvenu* calls a "succession rapidly varied." But
this radical dissimilarity of all the points of time lightly touched
upon each in its turn by the temporal motion does not, however,
carry with it an equivalent discontinuity. In the world of Marivaux a human being differs from himself every moment, but
there is no hiatus whatever between these different moments. It is
like a continuous slope the whole length of which sensations,
feelings, and thoughts follow each other and pass away:

> *No vacuum;* I am like nature, I abhor it.[88]

> It is not at all a question here of a piece of work *regularly pur-
> sued;* nor is it a matter of *detached thoughts* . . . Each one (of
> these reflections) *has insensibly brought to birth another.....*[89]

Reflections, feelings, and moments thus incessantly issue forth
without interruption, by a continuous generation. In contrast to
Cartesian time, therefore, Marivaudian time is not composed
of independent entities. Rather, in the manner of Bergson, it is
made of a continuous flow which in new moments incessantly
prolongs its inventive duration. A passion is composed of an in-

finity of modulations which engender one another; and without
interstices, without *interior space,* by a sort of indecomposable
gliding. It is, like the life of Marianne, "a *tissue* of events," [90]
a moving tapestry. A tapestry of points so serrated that one ends
by renouncing any desire to count them. Nonetheless, are not
these points all the particular instants whose significance had
seemed to us so great? And by a singular turn, does not the
writer who had seemed to us pre-eminently the writer of the
instantaneous, now appear to us the least "instantaneous" that
could be, the one all of whose work consists only in the drawing
of a temporal line in which the point of the instant disappears?
But Marivaux is precisely both this and that: the point and the
line; a point that extends out, and prolongs itself, and is transformed into a line; an instant which exceeds and lengthens itself, and which is transformed into time.

A time which runs the risk of remaining perpetually that of
pure successiveness, for, between the events which occur within it,
no link is discovered, and one is lost then in an indefinite motion
in which, in the final analysis, nothing survives except a sort of
vaporous memory of all that has happened. And it is that sort of
time along the length of which the novels of Marivaux end by
evaporating. But there is also that other sort of time which holds
its unity by means of a particular passion. The duration of love is
necessarily for Marivaux something so brief and so precarious
that it could not support an action unless that action were reduced to its extreme minimum of duration: which is precisely
the case with theatrical action. Actually, no author accepts more
cheerfully than Marivaux the restrictions of the French theatre.
They have saved his plays from the fate of his novels; they have
preserved them from "dissoluteness of thought" [91] and from the
inevitable disaggregation of the duration which perpetually
menaces the Marivaudian creation. The characters of the plays
arrive aptly at being characters because they have precisely the
time to play their role, that of love. The plays do well as plays,

because what one sees in them one "sees over and over again in a thousand other momentary little situations which spring from the dialogue of the characters [in such a way that] you are stirred with an interest so lively and *so sustained,* and which is moreover so unfailing, that outside of extremely pointed passages, *you no longer distinguish the instants* during which it seizes you, nor the springs which hold them." [92]

Thus the whole of Marivaux's art consists in passing from a sort of instantaneous plurality to a continuous plurality, and that becomes more than a problem of action, it becomes a problem of expression. But how can one find in language something equivalent to this multiple, interior "wheeling about" which is the lived moment, and to this vertiginous gliding which is lived time? How else except by inventing a language artless enough to express every transport, supple enough to espouse each change, a language which would be susceptible of detecting the briefest cries and the most modulated transitions? A language which by its spontaneity *would actually be* all the variations of the heart:

> Here it is the bare heart that speaks to me: as feelings come, it intimates them to me.[93]
>
> I express myself as I feel.[94]
>
> I say what occurs to me.[95]

From feeling to thinking, and from thinking to speaking, with neither translation nor interval. Nothing but the same birth and the same motion. Just as the Marivaudian being seemed continually to be born of its feelings, so the Marivaudian style seems continually to spring forth from that being. Perfect marriage of being and word, flung into the same adventure! But is not that also what the Mallarmean poem will seek to realize? Both the one and the other by the sole virtue of language seek to mime all the variations of being. The play of time and of chance becomes a marvelous "play of words."

Chapter II Vauvenargues

I

You know that you are alive; no insect is unaware of its own existence.[1]

In the lowest form of life as in the highest, there is found the consciousness of the activity which constitutes its essence. From top to bottom in the chain of being a life-current flows and, in flowing, forms both being and consciousness. We are activity and the consciousness of that activity. We are lives that know that they live. For Vauvenargues the *Cogito* implies the consciousness of a positive force in which one recognizes oneself, and in which one recognizes oneself conforming to the laws that govern universal existence:

> Fire, air, spirit, light, all live by action; thence the communication and alliance of all beings; thence unity and harmony in the universe. Yet this so fecund law of nature we find to be a flaw in man; and, because he is obliged to obey it, being unable to subsist in repose, we conclude that he is out of place.[2]

> One cannot condemn activity without indicting the order of nature.[3]

The sense of being is experienced in action, through action. It is one of the forms of that very action. To think is to act and to feel oneself acting. It is to discover oneself the possessor not

simply of the possibility of action, but of an acting force. If in
Vauvenargues's eyes "it cannot be a fault in men *to feel their
strength,*" [4] if indeed it is a virtue, that is because there is nothing
which is more profoundly natural and by means of which man
can more perfectly attain the essence of his being and the essence
of being:

> The laws of creation are not all foreign to us; they constitute
> our being, they form our essence, they are entirely our own;
> and we can boldly assert that we act of ourselves when we act
> simply in accordance with them.[5]

Thus man is no different from his feelings, his desires, and his
actions. He is this positive thing, marvelously apprehensible in
his very actuality, which is his strength in action. To act is to be,
to live; and "the more we act the more we live." [6] In this ap-
prehension of our being as activity, there is something intoxicating not only for the senses, but also and especially for the
consciousness itself:

> There is in the passion for physical exercise a pleasure for
> the senses and a pleasure for the mind. The senses are pleased
> to act, to ride a horse at a gallop, to hear the sound of a hunt
> in the forest; the mind enjoys the aptness of its senses, the
> force and dexterity of its body, etc.[7]

Since the realization of our existence is the realization of our
strength, it is both a love and a joy; a love of this being which
is ourself, because it is a power, and the joy of being this power.
The more one acts, the more one feels oneself to be, and the
more one feels oneself to be, the more one loves oneself, the hap-
pier one is:

> Pleasure naturally attaches to being.[8]

> Man . . . can revel only in action, and loves only that.[9]

> One enjoys only in so far as one acts; and our soul finally and
> truly possesses itself when it fully exerts itself.[10]

But this self-possession is true possession only because it is
actual. Doubtless in a sense this force is perceived, so to speak, in

its potentiality, in the trajectory and duration through which it passes from potency to act. It is brought about, it happens, it becomes, and this becoming is made into a duration. It pervades, it dilates, it expands, and this expansion is accomplished in a certain space. In itself, however, in so far as it is possessed by the mind, it is neither a space nor a duration. What is perceived right from the start in the first experience of being as force is something which, even in a figurative sense, has no extension or temporality. It is, it lives, it is ourself. It is active, powerful, real. It is given and perceived as having actuality and magnitude. The actuality of the being-force which perceives itself as such is so total only because it transcends or precedes all consciousness of time; only because it transcends or anticipates all consciousness of space. Being and the feeling of being are pure presence and pure present.

The present which is found thus revealed and possessed is still unattached to either a past or a future. It belongs only to itself, to us. "Action makes the present perceptible." [11] A present which is the immediate possession of the being by the being in the being; a pure actuality, with man as with God.

A present which is also a presence, a power, and a magnitude:

> We draw from the experience of our being an idea of magnitude, of pleasure, of power which we should always like to increase.[12]

What I feel and what pleases me is the very force that fills and constitutes me; it is wholly an interiority at every point of which I find myself, I bestir and extend myself. It is both myself and the field this self occupies. A field, moreover, that is unlimited, in which the being that I am "devotes the total activity of his mind to a limitless career." [13] Neither limit nor division; neither aspects nor appearances; neither without nor within; but the feeling of a vast expansion of the mind itself. It is all there is, and there is nothing beyond this fullness in which it recognizes itself and delights in itself. "Filled with its own magnitude, it reposes thereon, content to possess itself . . ." [14] At this point activity and repose coincide as in the *energeia akinesis* of Aristotle. And if it is inexact to say that this fullness is spatial, it is none the less true that it is the fullness of a being which apprehends itself as something great and vast. This is more than a metaphor drawn from exterior space. It is the intoxicating feeling of unquestionably being both a force and the very spot, the interior place where that force freely and instantaneously develops its own activity:

> There are moments of power, moments of elevation, of passion and of enthusiasm, in which the soul suffices itself and disdains all assistance, drunk with its own greatness.[15]

II

If it were granted to us always to live in these "moments of greatness, elevation, and enthusiasm," or if our life were constituted only by a single one of these moments, the feeling of being would confer upon the creature who experiences it something of the divine immensity and eternity. It would be sufficient unto itself, as God is. But it is Vauvenargues's originality to postulate simultaneously in the human mind, alongside the feeling of being, a no less fundamental but contrary feeling: the feeling of its imperfection. No doubt the same opposition can be found in Pascal between man's sense of greatness and his feelings of misery. But with Pascal it results from the radical and mysterious contradiction which is introduced into one's being by the supernatural presence of sin. For Vauvenargues, on the contrary, the duality and deficiency of being are purely natural and must be considered as immediate data implied by the very gift of consciousness. In the very instant that I perceive myself as the free energy constituting my being, I experience the feeling that this energy is, so to speak, exhausted before having attained its end and its perfection. I perceive myself as a being that lacks being. I begin to see besides myself the absence of something that ought to be part of myself. In the midst of the joy I experience at sensing my greatness, strength, and life, I suddenly discover my weakness, my smallness, my misery:

> . . . And then, my dear Saint-Vincennes, man experiences anguish; he recognizes the power of it and finds beyond himself only that dreadful void which you have experienced.[16]

> I do not want to give you to understand that I am sufficient unto myself and that, invariably, the present fills the emptiness of my heart.[17]

This emptiness of heart, this "dreadful void," is indeed localized in the "heart," in the very core of the being, but it appears there precisely to form there the consciousness of exterior things. When in the pure feeling of being, everything appeared as an interior fullness from which nothing was excluded, then in the feeling of the emptiness of being there is discovered a double limit: that of a force which does not succeed in accomplishing its whole task, and that of a being which does not arrive at completion. There is outside of the self a zone of which one can as yet say nothing, since it is not yet occupied; there is within oneself a force which has not as yet exerted itself throughout its whole field of action. On the one side as on the other, appears a vast unknown region reaching far beyond us. All one knows of it is that it is not us, that it is not ours, that it is *outside.* That region is space.

It is also time. For "the feeling of our emptiness and our imperfection" is also, and very exactly, the feeling of a temporal insufficiency. It is the feeling of an imperfect and abortive force, of a force that has not succeeded in actualizing itself as it should. The moment which it produces does not satisfy our exigencies. And, in that tedium which "comes from the feeling of our emptiness," [18] we apprehend that "the present does not fill the emptiness of our heart." On this side and that, of the actual, we discover irremediably separated from us by its nonbeing something that one can call, indifferently, either duration or the possible. Time, like space, is of the nonactual, the unaccomplished. It is what is indefinitely denied us, what is indefinitely held out in front of us by our powerlessness to be entirely actual. Disquietude, tedium, disgust, all man's painful feelings are formed simply of the consciousness of a time and space exterior and negative which deny man the right to a full existence: ". . . The feeling of his imperfection constitutes his eternal torment." [19]

Such is the tragic see-saw by which in Vauvenargues as in Pascal one moves from the intoxication with human grandeur to the feeling of a dreadful void.

But unlike Pascal, Vauvenargues never pauses for a moment in this kind of hell of the consciousness. Pascal cannot do otherwise than remain sunk there indefinitely until a supernatural intervention brings to an end a situation that is itself supernatural. Redemptive grace alone can counterbalance original sin. But for Vauvenargues, being and the imperfection of being are two natural data which, far from neutralizing each other, immediately engender a new cycle of activities. All our passions spring from that. Our passions are simply the result of a force transformed: "Activity is born of a restless force." [20] Being and nonbeing, force and agitation, at once wrest the imperfectly active being from its half-nothingness. They attract it and hurl it beyond its limited place into space. They tear it away from its imperfect present in order to fling it into duration. Since being is action and since being is never achieved, there remains for it only to continue, to prolong its action, to fulfill its task, to fill up with being and action the double hollowness of duration and space.

Who can hope to pass an hour without boredom, if he does not take care to fill up this short space to his liking? [21]

But man, precisely because he is man, because he is active and conscious force, cannot do otherwise than strive to fill up this space, all spaces:

It is so completely impossible for man to subsist without action that, if he wishes to refrain from acting, he can only do so by an act still more laborious than the one against which he sets himself.[22]

The natural act of man is to go outside himself, beyond his present, beyond the place he occupies, to seek to make himself a greater, more actual self, by means of which he will finally be able, without tedium or disgust, to know himself, to love himself, and to enjoy himself.

Thus arises the passion of love, which is simply an *extension* of the love we bear ourselves. The person we love is the enlarged part of our own self which we discover and project outside of ourselves:

. . . One can seek his happiness outside of himself; one can *love himself outside of himself* more than inside his own existence . . .[23]

Love is nothing else than an exteriorization of being, an effort to possess oneself, outside of oneself, in space.

It is thus one of the thousand forms our tireless activity can adopt in order to take flight and spread in the double extent of time and space. It is this indefatigable activity which, despite ourselves and often unknown to ourselves, sweeps us off to the indeterminate regions of diversity and successiveness:

. . . There is a distraction, very similar to dreams in sleep, that occurs when our thoughts float about and follow each other of themselves, without force and without direction.[24]

I have always been obsessed with my thoughts and my passions; this is not, as you think, a dissipation, but a continual distraction and a very lively occupation, although almost always disquieting and useless.[25]

But besides the "precipitate flight of our thoughts," [26] besides the unquiet dreams conceived by a being that stamps his hooves and champs at the bit, besides all these feints and false starts, there is the sure movement, invading time and space, that with the help of all our other passions is engendered by the essential feeling of human hope. For to lack hope is to lack being. It is to abandon oneself to the sole feeling of our imperfection; just as being enthusiastic is to give oneself up to the sole feeling of being. It is necessary to hope against very despair. Having arrived at one of the darkest moments of his life, "weary of serving without hope," did not Vauvenargues dare to invoke an extraordinary aid, and, addressing himself scandalously to the king, exact from him, as later Kierkegaard or Lequier would exact from God, the realization of a hope that was really despair? But still at that moment the cry for help which he utters is directed less toward another than toward himself. His plea for grace is not so much an act of prayer or of confidence in another as an effort to summon back to life and action the hope he places in himself:

> I am ashamed, Sire, to let you see how presumptive I am; but I have often noticed that the most ridiculous and audacious hopes have almost always been the cause of extraordinary successes.[27]

Despair is then "the greatest of our mistakes." [28] It is also the greatest of our faults. It is against nature. Conversely, hope is a positive good, a virtue, and almost the only joy we can have in the presence and in despite of the feeling of our fundamental imperfection. We can redeem ourselves, enlarge ourselves, triumphantly recover ourselves, in the voids of time and space. We can make of these two voids one fullness.

Of all hopes the purest, because it is the most active and the most rich with promise, is the hope of glory:

> The glow of dawn is never so sweet as the first glances bestowed upon us by glory.[29]

> . . . Glory, that strong and noble passion, that ancient and fecund source of human virtues . . . ; the hope of glory, that powerful motive . . .[30]

For Vauvenargues, then, as for Vigny, the thought of glory is—in the present—the sharp consciousness of the future: "The

love of glory attracts and reorders the future." [31] The future
is no longer that indifferent or despairing thing, the region of
nonbeing and the nonactual. It is a thing already ours, already
touched by the anticipative antennas of our thought, already
actually lived by the very act which we perform in order to attain
or merit it. "To labor for glory" [32] is to triumph over time, to
transcend the present, to spread one's energies in the future.

But it is also to spread one's energies outside of oneself. For
the movement toward the future, born "of the feeling of our
emptiness and our imperfection," is a movement "to form a new
being out of ourselves." The passion for glory thus tends to "enlarge us beyond ourselves," [33] in space, just as it tends to enlarge
us beyond the present, in time.

Thus our anxious and imperfect actuality overflows its spatial
and temporal limits. Far from being an *energeia akinesis,* that
immobile activity which would be ours, had we within us only
the feeling of being, we are, by reason of the very deficiency we
experience in being, a mobile activity that, resuming each time
its flight, goes forth to conquer and to annex times and spaces,
those two nonbeings:

> Remove their hope of glory, and what force will sustain
> them? . . . What will move the spirit to those noble efforts in
> which virtue, superior to oneself, shears away the mortal limits
> of its brief flight, and with a strong and buoyant wing escapes
> its bonds? [34]

III

> Give greater scope to your soul, and have no fear for what
> follows.[35]

> We must leave our accustomed ways and advance to a less
> limited field . . . . Dare to make a higher flight . . .[36]

There is no flight without a sort of uprooting, no enlarging
of self without a stripping of self. Making each time a new start,
the soul thus each time quits both its narrow sphere and itself.

Each instant it abandons being and thought to regain them,
perhaps enlarge them, in every succeeding instant. And thus in
one of its aspects such a course, made up of flights renewed, is
composed also of successive deaths:

> The present escapes us of itself and is annihilated in spite
> of us. All our thoughts are mortal, we do not know how to
> retain them.[37]

> Our thoughts die the moment their effects are made known;
> when action begins the principle has vanished.[38]

The very activity which urges us on toward the future leaves
our present thoughts behind us. They die, and we die with them,
since they were we, and we they. They and we, we become that
extinct thing, the past. In Vauvenargues's eyes the past is a thing
so totally past that it is impossible to find in his writings even
the slightest trace of that sort of inferior or remote life which,
in the limbo of memory, the past continues to have, for the
romantics for example. There is no one less retrospective than
Vauvenargues; no one who has less need of encouraging himself
to put off the old man. The prospective flight is for him a libera-
tion always as spontaneous as total. One would call his a soul
which, without regret but not without hardness, detaches itself,
like successive cadavers, from the carcass of his dead thoughts.
And it is doubtless for this reason that his genius finds a particular
fitness in the detached form of maxims. Vauvenargues's mind is
fond of pauses and breaks. It finds its fulfillment in provisorily
shattering the sally of a reflection:

> The mind attains greatness only by sallies.[39]

> What one finds obscure at certain moments, one easily
> understands another day, or at another hour; and sometimes
> one suddenly ceases to understand what one had understood
> completely. Penetration, invention, vivacity, prudence are not
> the same once and for all.[40]

But if the thought is broken off, it recovers; if the activity
seems for an instant exhausted, it very soon goes into action

again. The dead past is dead indeed, but death lays hold on life, and being once more becomes being. In the repeated flight of Vauvenargues there is to be sure a continual passing from life to death, but also from death to life. And such must be in effect the contrary characteristics of a being always imperfectly active, but always active. Its existence is made of a surging up of self beyond self, of a series of failures and recoveries.

It is true that,

> if our soul were not succored by that indefatigable activity which restores the perpetual flow of our mind, we should last only a moment; such are the laws of our being.[41]

But it is no less true, by reason of these same laws, that this instantaneously exhausted duration is also, through the exercise of the same essential force, instantaneously recommenced:

> The activity that destroys the present, restores it, reproduces it . . .[42]

No passage expresses more vigorously than the following lines the perpetual triumph of the being-force over its own imperfection and insufficiency:

> My passions and my thoughts die, but only to be reborn; I myself die upon my bed every night, but only to recover with a new strength and a new freshness . . . The active force of my mind restores to life its dead thoughts . . . I say in my wondering heart: What have you done with the fickle objects which so much occupied your thought? Turn back in your own tracks, fugitive objects. I speak, and my mind awakens; those mortal objects hear me, and the shapes of things past obey me and appear before me.[43]

Passions, thoughts, and the past self, all are reborn and become once more myself at the sole insistence of an express order, issued by my present will. After my death I regain my life.

The movement of being and thought in Vauvenargues is thus none other than a continued creation.

A creation which, for Vauvenargues as for Leibniz, must undoubtedly be attributed to the action of a preserving God. For how can we conceive that the creature is stirred at any instant by an incitation different from that of the Creator? [44]

On the one hand, then, all energy never ceases actually to emanate from that supreme source of creative energy which Leibniz described as a fulguration. But on the other hand, for Vauvenargues as well as for Leibniz, what God in each instant creates is precisely a being which, itself also, is energy, and which, because it is energy, unceasingly renews itself. The idea of time thus becomes for Vauvenargues the idea of a spontaneous activity which, by reason of its very nature, is saved every moment from nothingness and continuously draws forth its being from the depths of its nonbeing. My existence is formed by a series of pulsatory efforts, of acts of thought by which each of my lived moments is made, is exhausted, and is replaced, each one having for its substance only the leap by which it hurls itself beyond itself, beyond its death, toward the future of the following moment:

> We can retain the present only by an action which goes beyond the present.[45]
>
> The state of human affairs is that of not being able to subsist except by a continuous generation.[46]

Time, conquest of the mind, is thus a possession always contested and reaffirmed. There is no such thing as time given once and for all. There is only a duration that is always new, an existence that is always momentary:

> Each action is a new being which begins and was not.[47]

However, as our being is action, it is we who recommence being and who recommence not having been. Thus the temporal flight is, for Vauvenargues, like the lived duration and *élan vital* of Bergson, something essentially active, without however having the supple continuity of the Bergsonian duration. One would call it a stiffening and then a leap, the effort one makes to jump close-legged over a chasm. In this duration being and nonbeing never cease to alternate, in such a way that the moments remain profoundly isolated one from another, as in Cartesian time. But that is by no means to say that for Vauvenargues as for Descartes, moments would have only an independent and detached existence. On the contrary, for Vauvenargues each moment has for its mission and its end the fomenting of the moment which will follow. It is indeed a *generation* in the precise meaning of the term: the perpetual act of transmitting life.

IV

But if time is no more than a succession of moments that engender one another, is not the atomism of this duration going to carry with it the irremediable fragmentation of the being that lives it? Will not his existence be decomposed in an infinity of momentary acts? This is not Vauvenargues's idea. With the being-force, what is unceasingly outstripped, destroyed, or transcended is never anything more than an imperfect and insufficient version of being; what always refashions itself intact in the mind is a self-image of an inexhaustible perfection. The man of passionate desire never ceases to transmit to his future the thought which absorbed his past:

> The passions of men of profound mind are more stubborn and more invincible, for they are not obliged to be diverted from them like the rest of men by an exhaustion of thoughts; their reflections, on the contrary, are a constant upkeeping of their desires, which excites them; and that explains also why those who think little or who could not think for any length of time on the same subject, have only inconstancy as their lot.[48]

> What ordinarily constitutes a virile soul is that it may be dominated by some lofty and courageous passion, to which all others, no matter how lively, are subordinated; but I do not wish to conclude by saying that divided minds must always be weak; one can only presume that they are less constant than others.[49]

True time, human time is therefore basically constancy, and constancy consists in the tenacity with which we pursue the fulfillment of our being and our passion. Thenceforth it becomes possible for us not only to exist momently, but to have a duration; a true duration, since it is coherent, persistent, and continuous; a duration which is also truly ours, since it is established by a design that is conceived and executed by us. It is "folly not to apply ourselves completely to the ordering of our life . . . We believe in the future, and we abandon it to chance." [50]

If our future is ourself, then it is up to ourself to make our future. The repudiation of chance has for Vauvenargues as its complement the affirmation of human continuity. Not only can man order all the moments of his life, but he can order his whole life, he can decide what his destiny and his authentic existence shall be. And if, shortly before his death, in an interval of exhaustion, Vauvenargues, conscious of the ruin of his plans, will say sadly speaking of himself: "He believed that we make our own destinies . . . He always over-reached himself," he knew very well on the other hand that this constant reaching toward the heights, agent of his defeat, had also been the agent in a success which transcends all defeats, since it had made of all the moments of his life, despite defeat and approaching death, one single effort to confer upon himself one self-same destiny.

For life is judged as life, and not by what ends it:

> . . . They say: If death is the end of everything, why give ourselves so much trouble? We are fools indeed to be so anxious over the future, as much as to say: We are fools indeed to commit our destinies to chance, and to provide for the interval that lies between us and death.[51]

Or again the famous maxim: "The thought of death betrays us, for it makes us forget to live." [52]

To live is then to make one's future, all one's future; but it is also to remain constantly faithful to the passions and resolutions which now constitute our past.

So then the whole of time is found gathered up in the moment of action, provided that man in this moment of action be constant and inflexible. Man then recognizes himself as he has been and as he will be: possessor of a time that is no longer empty and exterior, but which, before him and behind him, is made replete by the persistence of one self-same thought. As in the case of Vigny, the eye of Vauvenargues can take in the whole field of existence. In these supreme moments, time seems extended, transformed, in a temporal space which the mental sight freely embraces:

> A great mind never loses sight of anything; the past, the present and the future are immobile before its eyes; it turns its gaze far and wide; it embraces this enormous distance . . .[53]

—enormous distance which is now no longer temporal, no longer exterior, for it is the very field in which thought is fully exercised and allies itself to everything, holds to everything. Source of activity, the human being recognizes itself in all the activities that constitute the world:

> Nothing is strange to him; neither the infinite difference in customs, nor that of conditions, nor of countries, nor the distance of times hinders him from reconciling all human things, from joining all of them together in a common concern.[54]

Thus Vauvenargues ends with an identification of action and knowledge. Our loftiest action is the most vast, and the most vast is that which binds the totality of life together through thought. Thought is identified with the universe, and exterior space becomes an interior space:

> A mind well-outspread contemplates human beings in their mutual relationships; at a glance it apprehends all the ramifications of things; it reunites them with their source and in a common center; it brings them under the same point of view; finally it diffuses light upon great objects and over a vast surface.[55]

> A mind well-outspread diminishes objects in appearance in confounding them within a whole which reduces them to their just measure; but it really enlarges them in developing their

relationships, and in forming out of all the irregular parts one single and magnificent picture.[56]

—a picture that is so great and so vast only because it is a picture of a space that has become interior, and because he who contemplates it is no longer an external spectator who can never see things except one by one, and in a single aspect. Intellectual space is not, like external space, the place of isolated points of view. It is, on the contrary, the place where thought can see simultaneously "the different relationships and the different aspects." [57] When the "true scope of genius lays hold of objects and their relationships, embraces them altogether and reunites them," [58] it "embraces at the same time all aspects of each subject," [59] it "brings together things one thought were incompatible." [60] The space of the mind is not constituted by a multiplicity of heterogeneous places. It is not composed of reciprocal exclusions. It is not built out of contradictions: "There are no contradictions in nature." [61] There are none either in a thought, which in extending itself to embrace all the aspects of nature, would succeed in containing and comprehending them. Thenceforth the supreme effort of the mind must be an effort of comprehension, of conciliation, of union: "It seizes in no time the secret place where one can reconcile extreme opinions . . ." [62] —"It is for lack of penetration that we reconcile so few things." [63] As with Leibniz, and as with Proust, the progress of thought in Vauvenargues culminates in a sort of transcendence of time and space, conceived first as exteriorities and places of reciprocal exclusions. It all ends in a moment of consciousness in which the human being, surmounting his ontological imperfection, without stages, without ratiocination, by an act of instantaneous thought, transforms the world into his own being, and simultaneously touches all the points of the universe:

> One would have said that in all his considerations he never went by the stages and the inferences that beguile other men; but that truth, without transition, was revealed completely and immediately to his heart and to his mind.[64]

Chapter III Chamfort and Laclos

Chamfort is to be considered only from the time he became
the author of the *Maximes et Pensées* and the *Caractères et Anec-
dotes.* Before that there had undoubtedly been other versions
of Chamfort: an ambitious hack, a dandy, a passionate lover.
But these personages who had in their turn been Chamfort remain mysterious and fragmentary. They seem to us the blackened
remains left after a fire in a place since then empty. And nothing
would be more mistaken than to want at all costs to link them
up again to the true, the only Chamfort, in order to give him a
background and an historical continuity. The essential thing
about Chamfort is precisely that he is linked up to nothing and
to no one, not even to his own antecedence. He is, in the full
meaning of the word, a creature who is not continued, who
wishes that nothing be continued, for it is only if everything is
interrupted and commences again that it can have a chance of
being acceptable to man and to the world. So, at the *hôtel de
Polignac* as in the Clubs, Chamfort is always the perfect revolutionary, one who demands of himself and of the world a total
revolution: "It is necessary to begin human society over again,
just as Bacon said it was necessary to begin human understanding

45

over again." [1] There is no question of rectifying, progressing, ameliorating. Everything is so degenerate that nothing is any longer perfectible. What therefore matters is to invent a new world and a new man, to have start off on a new stage a brand new performance brought forth from the workshops óf reason.

Indeed, at the time, this exigence of novelty was not at all exceptional. We see it manifested throughout the entire eighteenth century. What philosopher had then not conceived a machine-man, an animated statue, a virginal being in the first moment of its existence? Already that utopia was shaping up for Chamfort at the time when he was not yet Chamfort, when he was still one among the crowd of minor writers in the eighteenth century:

> Genius, he writes in 1767, is a phenomenon which neither education, climate, nor government can explain . . . . It is not men who make the great men. These do not belong to any family, any century, any nation; they have neither ancestors nor posterity. It is God who, in His compassion, sends them forth to the world fully formed in order that they may *renew man and his degenerate reason:* like those stars that draw close to our sphere after a long revolution of centuries; who, revealing to view the place from which they have come, reanimate, so to speak, the vigor of worlds and rejuvenate nature.[2]

Thus at the age of twenty-six, Chamfort dreams of an absolute recommencement for man and for humanity. Such is the mission the man of genius must fulfill. Springing up in his epoch like an epochless being, removed from time and the degeneration that affects people living in time, the man of genius is the only one who can reanimate the world to vigor and restore man to his state of Heir of the Sun. From then on, with the contempt the young Chamfort feels for a humanity which, historically, by degrees, got bogged down in the temporal morass, there is associated a hope of high intensity: that of seeing man, by the power of genius, remake himself as he was before his degradation, rediscover "the profound and energizing feeling he experienced when, awakened out of nothingness by the voice of the Creator, he stood up alone in the midst of the world." [3]

Now, and this is the essential point, in this dream of the young man there is nothing which cannot be found again, unadulterated, in the Chamfort of maturity. However, everything is changed to the point of being unrecognizable; the dream of the youth can only appear to the eyes of the grown man as a grotesquely naïve desire, worthy of the worst sarcasm. Here we have one of those invisible and nevertheless absolute transformations which occasionally occur with regard to the whole outlook of a man, and which, leaving intact the objective meaning of his ideas, impress upon them a totally different subjective significance. This is the reason why it is so difficult to understand what Chamfort was before he appeared as a sort of mortal enemy of the man he had been. Between the being he was and the being he has become, a whole personal history unrolls which can only be called the history of his own degradation. The man of genius, instead of coming to regenerate humanity, has let himself degenerate with it. He knows now, he knows, thanks to the experience of his adult life, how absurd it is to hope that any man can preserve himself from temporal debasement. All humans without exception, by the very fact that they are born and that they live in time, are contaminated by time. How could one hope of them, or even of a single one among them that he might miraculously be preserved from this universal decomposition? It is laughable to think that one might, across the sloughs of history, get back to an original moment of vigor, integrity, and innocence. It is too late! The return to the golden age has forever become a myth.

One could thus imagine Chamfort as a sort of Rimbaud, disillusioned with everything, even Abyssinia, or like a Lorenzaccio who discovers himself a prisoner of his own degradation. But this would be to forget that the Chamfort of maturity has not at all reduced his exigencies. Not for an instant does he cease to crave the renewal of his being and the world. But to renew no longer means now to go back across the course of history to the beginning of humanity. One must renounce, once and for all, everything that lies behind, to make a clean break with all the pasts, those of humanity, the self, and myth. To begin over again now means one thing only: without troubling oneself over a first beginning, now lost forever, to find a second beginning, a new point of departure which would also be for one an authentic commencement, that is to say setting itself against a background of nothingness.

Thus any recommencement implies a preliminary annihilation. Every revolution implies first the demolition of the old Bastilles. There is true recommencement for the self and for the world only by an explicit and concrete act which can only be a breaking and a break. And such an act must be of extreme violence: "The earth is more fertile after the eruptings of volcanoes." [4] Such is not only the conviction but the intensely lived experience of the Chamfort of maturity, and it makes of him a being as different from what he had been in his youth, as revolutionary France from the France of the old regime. In effect, Chamfort inaugurates the social revolution by a private and inner revolution. It is he who, before welcoming the Terror in political life, established it as a permanent state in his own conscience.

But in what does this inner revolution consist, this Terror which, with its pikes and its guillotine, Chamfort one day installed in the depths of his mind? To this question there is no plainer answer than that given by Chamfort himself throughout his Maxims. For the human being Chamfort constantly executes in the Maxims (in the sense in which one executes a person who has been condemned to death) is indeed Chamfort himself. With a rigid mercilessness, born of a hatred of the lukewarm, Chamfort ceaselessly pursues, arrests, and suppresses a criminal in whose countenance he perpetually recognizes his own: a sort of *ex*-Chamfort, a personage of the past, a symbol of all the

compromise and all the human cowardice which, by a violent effort, it is necessary to abolish in order to prevent forever the
commencing over again of what one has been. Between himself
and himself Chamfort always thrusts a denial as sharp as the
guillotine's knife: "I no longer know what passion is." [5]—"I have
destroyed my passions in somewhat the same way that a violent
man kills his horse, not being able to control it." [6] And then this
extraordinary statement which more than any other reveals to
us what a will to destruction Chamfort brought to the work
which he accomplished upon himself: "A philosopher must start
by experiencing the happiness of the dead." [7]

Here one could compare Chamfort to Descartes. There was
in fact something already revolutionary and even terroristic in
the decision one day taken by the author of the *Discours* to destroy
all his habits of thought in order to ground it in the certainty
furnished by a moment independent of all those that preceded
it. But there is nothing hypothetical about the destructive act
of Chamfort. What he wants to do is not only to deny to his
past any demonstrative value, it is verily to extirpate it, as one
might pull up a plant that clings tenaciously to the soil into
which it has thrust down its roots. The undertaking to which
he devotes himself is indeed that of which Benjamin Constant
will a little later understand the atrocious vanity. It consists
in no longer tolerating within oneself the slightest trace of sensibility, the least attachment of feeling to ancestral, traditional,
habitual values; it consists in suppressing the passions, not by
limiting or directing them, but by killing them, as one might
kill a runaway horse with a pistol shot.

This destruction of the past is thus a detestation and a dis-
owning. It is the hate one has for a victim once dear:

> The moment of losing one's illusions and the passions of
> youth often leaves its regrets; but sometimes we loathe the
> delusion that has deceived us. Armide sets on fire and destroys
> the palace in which she was enchanted.[8]

Behind him, Chamfort leaves now only an empty place. He cuts himself off from his past as a fox to free himself gnaws off his leg caught in a trap.

Sometimes this mutilation which he performs on himself gives him an astonishing lucidity that is made up of negative knowledge, of the consciousness of being situated in a place in the mind from which certain inner truths are forever excluded. The person who stifles his sensibility by this very fact prevents himself from ever again understanding what he was at the time he had feelings. Thus Swann is astonished on being cured of the frenzy into which he was thrown by his love for Odette. "Love," says Chamfort, "has not permitted its secret to be revealed; man knows it only on the condition of not being able to divulge it, and he loses the memory of it the moment his passion ceases, for that secret is nothing other than love itself." [9]

But at bottom there is nothing in these words that is basically Proustian. Nothing is more opposed to nostalgia over lost time than Chamfort's mind. For him, if time is lost, it is well lost. One must apply oneself not to repair, but to complete its loss. One must *forget oneself,* just as one erases from the blackboard incorrect mathematical calculations:

> Every day I enlarge the list of the things of which I speak no longer.[10]

> Let someone lead me to the River of Oblivion, and I shall find the Fountain of Youth.[11]

> When one has been much tormented and is deeply fatigued by his own sensibility, one finds out that it is necessary to live from day to day, to forget a great deal, finally *to sponge life off* as it passes.[12]

"To sponge life off as it passes." An astonishing saying which Chamfort lets fall just at the end of the great intellectual and moral adventure of the eighteenth century, as if to show to what a nothingness it had come.

For the whole effort of the epoch that precedes Chamfort had consisted in attempting to endow the moment of feeling with an intensity of absolute life. Life *is* in the instant, in the sensation that constitutes the instant. Nothing is more precious than that ever instantaneous efflorescence of being in the act of feeling. It is necessary to place one's all in the moment and to hold fast to the moment, for there is nothing on either side of the moment. Was it not the young Chamfort who said:

> To fix, to eternalize each instant of one's being,
> Is it a fate more sweet, a pleasure more affecting? [13]

Next comes a Chamfort so disgusted with feeling that the present moment appears a futile and contemptible object which he must get rid of on the spot. The act of violence and interior destruction Chamfort commits against himself no longer affects simply the past, all that depth of past lived and disavowed; it is now leveled against actual existence as well.

To live is to become conscious of an actuality that is not worth the trouble of being lived; and to live well, to think right, is to disillusion oneself of the present as much as one disillusioned himself of the past.

But it is also, therefore, to disillusion ourselves of all that surrounds us. Actuality is not simply a moment of life, it is an ambient space, a social milieu with which one finds he has the closest and most intimate relations. But Chamfort thinks all these relationships factitious and corrupting. To live *in* the world one would have to be invulnerable:

> One would have to be an Achilles *without a heel,* and that would seem to be impossible.[14]

> The more one judges of things, the less one loves.[15]

> I do not conceive of a wisdom without mistrust. The Bible says that the fear of God is the beginning of wisdom; as for myself, I think it is the fear of men.[16]

> Steer clear of any intense and deep feeling . . . Never give anyone any claim upon you . . . Politely keep everyone at a great distance.[17]

In the midst of the world, a jeering and cold Chamfort plays a part more cunning and more solitary than that of Alceste. He has no need of escaping to the country to put "a great distance" between himself and other men. It suffices him to retire within himself, to take refuge behind the vitreous carapace of his scorn. Someone once accused him of being a misanthrope: "No, I am not one," he replied, "but I have seriously considered being one; indeed I have earnestly tried to see to it."—"What has prevented you"—"I chose to be lonely." [18]

"Preserve, if you can, the interests that attach you to society, but cultivate the feelings that separate you from it." [19] Detached from the past, cut off from the present and from the world, Chamfort, in an ever narrowing circle, cultivates a chilling thought that is made of denial, distance, and voluntary separation. In his determination to clear on all sides an empty space as with the sweep of a scythe, there still remained to him the resource of *hoping* to make that vacant place the one upon which the future would rebuild a new world and a new human understanding. But in its turn and like all the others, the faculty of hoping perishes under the blows of the knife-blade:

> I believe in friendship, I believe in love; that idea is neces-sary to my happiness: but I believe still more firmly that wis-dom enjoins *the renunciation of the hope* of finding a mistress and a friend capable of replenishing my heart. I know that what I tell you makes you shudder: but such is human de-pravity, such are the reasons I have for mistrusting men, that I believe I am wholly excusable.[20]

> Hope is only a charlatan that deceives us without ceasing. And, for me, happiness began only when I lost it. I would willingly write over the gate of paradise the line that Dante inscribed over the gate of hell: *Lasciate ogni speranza, voi ch'entrate.*[21]

Weird happiness, strange paradise, that which consists in "dis-pensing with the future," [22] not through contentment or mod-eration, but by a sort of inhuman detachment that reduces desires and needs to insignificance:

My real state is thus that of a man who, coldly and humorlessly awaits an event that is announced to him as imminent; who does not believe in it for having been too often deceived, and from whom painful memories have removed every kind of desire, even those which accompany hope.[23]

Someone says we must ceaselessly strive to curtail our needs. It is above all to the needs of self-love that this maxim must be applied: they are the most tyrannical, and what one ought most to combat.[24]

I beg you to believe that I have no need of anything which I lack.[25]

Thus a curve is drawn that returns upon itself:

The man of the world, the friend of fortune, even the lover of glory, all draw before themselves a direct line that conducts them to an unknown terminus. The wise man, the friend of himself, follows a circular line, whose extremity brings him back to himself.[26]

The point to which Chamfort finds himself brought back is Chamfort. Nothing of him survives except that point in which a consciousness burns without depth as without extent, without past as without future, absolutely separated from all objects, reduced to its own single flame:

I have contracted my whole life within myself.[27]

I have reduced myself to finding all my pleasures in me, that is to say in the sole exercise of my intelligence.[28]

By an extraordinary movement of withdrawal, Chamfort has reduced himself to a completely solitary consciousness of self: a consciousness without shadow of either regret or hope, emptied of all feeling and all warmth, a sort of impersonal thought which, indifferent to times and persons, strangely resembles that consciousness of consciousness to which, in the twentieth century, there will also be deliberately reduced another Chamfort, M. Teste.

And, in one aspect, this arid and narrow possession does indeed engender still another and final feeling, a feeling of sufficiency:

I know how to suffice myself, and if the occasion come I shall know very well how to dispense with myself.[29]

I study only what pleases me, I occupy my mind only with the ideas that interest me.[30]

Such an absolutely *separate* thought, the ironic reflection of all the interior and exterior events of existence, can no longer be susceptible to alteration by existence. It is out of play: "I have only to hold my tongue." [31] It is always disposable and always detachable. It would thus not know how to be taken unawares. Withdrawn from the vicissitudes of time, it considers them with the same calculated indifference:

Time will bring about or will not bring about the circumstances which will make me make profitable use of my attainments. In any case, I shall have had the inestimable advantage of not having vexed myself but of having been obedient to my thought and my character.[32]

Thus there chooses to be sheltered from all actuality, in the nontemporality of the possible, a thought intensely conscious of remaining pure thought, pure reflection, no matter what comes:

One has found the *me* pronounced by Medea sublime; but one who cannot say the same in all the accidents of life is not much of anything, or rather is nothing.[33]

In the face of a time made up of exterior and successive accidents, Chamfort has thus now only to order his thought as a reflective power, always the same, always remote, isolated in a curious permanence, and yet always mobile, by reason of ceaselessly reflecting a comedy of endlessly changing peripateias. So that, in one sense, in abolishing all memory and all hope, in living without passion, in forbidding himself intimate participation in the temporal movement of existence, Chamfort becomes an exile from time and condemns himself to exist outside of all that is carried in its flow, even his own existence; and yet, in another sense, this immobilized and exiled thought is discovered to have no other end than that of perpetually following with close attention this temporal movement from which it is excluded: "I am immutable when things do not change, but I am mobile when they do." [34] On the one hand then, Chamfort's thought is that of a person who asserts himself "to be master of his own actions exclusively;" [35] on the other, it is thought passively delivered up to the most insignificant or grotesque variations of an existence it never ceases to consider absurd. In such a case the absence of all feeling, the atony of being, the lassitude one experiences with respect to all that one continues to observe, because there is nothing else to observe, all of that delivers the mind up to a sort of final inertia which is no longer concealed by irony and cynicism: ". . . Without being apathetic or indifferent, I have become as if immobile, and my actual position seems always to me to be best, because what is good in it results from its immobility and increases with it." [36] This mental stillness is not despair; for despair is a feeling, and here all feeling has become impossible. It is rather the hollowed-out place, the interior emptiness left in the mind when it has been deserted even by the last possible kind of feeling:

> It is a fine allegory in the Bible, that of the tree of the knowledge of good and evil which bears death. That emblem means that, when one has penetrated to the bottom of things, *the loss of illusions brings about the death of the soul;* that is to say, a complete disinterestedness toward all that touches and occupies other men.[37]

It is fitting that Chamfort's life ends in the frantic tumult of the Revolution and the Terror. He brought to it, not his passion—he no longer had any, not the life of his soul—that was "dead," but a disinterested energy that took joyless satisfaction in the exterior collapse of a world that he had already a thousand times foresworn and destroyed within himself. To wipe the slate clean, it was now only a question of putting the finishing touch to that general enterprise of destruction which he had made his life's objective. One last blow, and the emptiness was finally complete.

II

Laclos is the author of a single book. The rest of his work is entirely negligible. One can be surprised at it. There is no reason to regret it. No author ever expressed himself more completely in one book. No doubt one can imagine a Laclos greatly different in his life from what he is in his novel. But the thought that presided over the creation of the *Liaisons dangereuses* succeeded in presenting so adequately in it the different successive aspects of its own development that the circle was made perfect; there was nothing more to say.

In order to understand the single work of Laclos, it is enough to retrace step by step the path taken by the thought which is conceived, developed, experienced, and achieved therein.

Now that thought begins by being pure thought, that is to say by being, in a certain mind, the presence of a certain idea, which is as yet only idea, which is not yet realized, but which is realizable, and which, tending to realize itself, constitutes, outside of time but relative to time, what we call a *project*.

Thus it is necessary to take up Laclos where we laid Chamfort down. For Chamfort was a person who, having done everything to prepare himself for action, became in the end resigned to inaction. But Laclos and his heroes belong to a subsequent epoch in which men already prepared for action already outline the movement which is going to transform their intention into action.

The project is already then a commencement of action. It is an anticipatory movement that is projected from the present toward the future in order to impose on it the desired shape; or again, it is the will to substitute for an undetermined future that is the work of chance, another future, predetermined, which is the work of the will. The project implies the recreation of time by voluntary thought.

Valmont presents us with a perfect type of that voluntary thought. He is essentially (like his feminine rival, the Marquise

of Merteuil) a man of projects. He is a calculating thought fixed
on the future in order to impose upon it the precise form that
thought sets for itself as an end.

As soon as Valmont appears in the novel, one observes him
write: "I am going to confide in you the greatest project I have
ever formed . . . This is the goal I intend to attain." [38] Or
again: "This project is sublime." [39] Constantly the words *project,
plan, designs, principles* reoccur. And a witness who judges him
harshly, but very exactly, says this of him:

> . . . Never, since his earliest youth, has he taken a step or
> said a word *without having a project,* and never has he had a
> project which was not dishonest or criminal . . . *His conduct
> is the result of his principles.* He knows how to calculate every
> horror a man can permit himself without compromising him-
> self.[40]

"His conduct is the result of his principles." There is perhaps
no more significant sentence in the entire novel. For one now
begins to discern the real subject of the *Liaisons dangereuses.* It
is a novel written to discover whether the course of behavior one
follows always coincides with the course one had planned to follow, and whether the actual present proves to be the result of
the past in which one had decided upon it, and identical to the
idea of it one had then conceived.

Thus Laclos' novel presents absolutely original features which
give it simultaneously the double aspect of a conquest of time
and of an inquiry into time. It consists in a verification, by experience, of the accuracy of the calculation man makes when he decides that his future conduct will be the result of his principles
and his anterior projects.

"When," Mme. de Merteuil will say proudly, "have you ever
seen me swerve from the rules I have prescribed for myself, and
betray my principles? . . . They are the fruit of my deep reflections; I created them, and I may say that *I am my own work.*" [41]

In other words, I verify and accept myself as the present fruit
of my past thought. Hence the cold and purely intellectual in-

toxication that such a novel exudes resides in the sharp consciousness of that domination of time by the human will; so much so that, superior to time, consciousness here seems to take the part of Providence and the transcendent government of existence by thought. Thus, assuming a superior position to Valmont, overseeing him, controlling him, criticizing him, Mme. de Merteuil, appears as a sort of superconsciousness of Valmont, which, high and removed, will always be there to judge whether the work accomplished corresponds to the work projected.

But the project is not only directed toward the future. It is also oriented toward the exterior. It consists in a movement toward the outside; it strives to realize itself in the tangible world of beings and things; it wishes to impose itself upon the real. A project is almost always a project of conquest. Now the atmosphere of the period was favorable to conquests: the conquest of Silesia by Frederick the Great, the conquest of power by the Jacobins, soon enough the conquest of Europe by Bonaparte. The subject of the *Liaisons* is also a conquest: that of a human being by another human being. "I will have that woman," [42] schemes Valmont.

Thus Valmont is the type of person who schemes to make a conquest of others, and whose will is projected upon another in order to conquer her.

But if the project is the exterior projection of the will upon another will, and if it has for its goal the possession by the will of that other will, the result is that the essence of the scheme is found to be extremely complex. For that alien will exists, not only in the manner of an exterior object, situated in a space that is easily invadable; it exists interiorly, it has its own secret destiny, its own time. The scheme of the seducer consists then in his wanting to impose upon that being a new temporal existence, a new manner of living in time, a different destiny which will have for its creator and ruler the seducing will. This is precisely the enterprise Valmont proposes to himself with regard to the lady presi-

dent of Tourvel. He wants to become in her eyes "the God she
shall have chosen." [43] The sovereignty he wishes to exercise over
her is a temporal and providential sovereignty which will be af-
firmed, not in one single moment, but in the totality of existence. ". . . I shall have no successor . . . She shall have existed
only with regard to me . . ." [44]—"When I give attention to it,
the impression I leave is ineffaceable." [45] That definitive possession of the being by the being will really be accomplished only
when the one possessed shall surrender, not only her body, nor
one simple minute of existence, but her independence, her right
to continue to live her own life and to choose her own fate.
Thus the whole project of seduction strains toward a moment
of absolute triumph and of absolute defeat, which the consent
will perpetuate indefinitely:

> That I may be truly happy, she must give herself to me. [46]

> It is not enough for me to possess her. I want her to surrender
> herself up to me. But for that to happen not only must I pene-
> trate to her heart, but I must arrive there with her expressed
> recognition . . . [47]

> My project . . . is that she should feel, and that she should
> feel deeply the worth and extent of each of the sacrifices she
> will make for me; not to lead her so quickly that remorse could
> not follow; to make her virtue expire in a slow agony; cease-
> lessly to fix her attention on that distressing spectacle; and to
> grant her only the happiness of having me in her arms, after I
> have forced her no longer to dissimulate her longing for me. [48]

From then on, it would seem, Laclos' novel is found to be entirely formed and entirely determined in advance. It must consist
in the progressive realization of an idea that already wholly
contains it. Like the novels of Balzac later, Laclos' novel seems
to imply a total elimination of chance: "I dare leave nothing to
chance." [49] "I wish to owe nothing to occasion." [50] Thus it will
be the verification of a calculation, the realization of a program,
or again, as in Aristotelian thought, the regular and progressive
passage of potentiality into act. We shall see in it, as in *l'Attaque*

et la Défense des places by Vauban, that "purity of method" [51]
which assures the success of military sieges and even allows one
"to calculate their duration with a certainty sufficient for ulterior
projects." [52]

Nothing could be more different from the duration that forms
the basis of the novels of the eighteenth century. One thinks of
the titles of Crébillon's novels: *le Hasard du coin du feu, la Nuit
et le moment.* There is nothing in Crébillon's novels except
chance and moments, a disconnected series of successive instants,
of occasions happy or unhappy, but always fortuitous, *always
momentary.* An example of this in the *Liaisons* is the story of
the insignificant and ephemeral conquest of little Volanges: "I
was very glad *for once,*" says Valmont, "to observe the force of
the occasion, of the occasion alone." [53] But the general time of the
Liaisons is the very reverse of this instantaneousness. It is mean-
ingful. It is significant. It has homogeneity, cohesion, coherence.
It is the operative field of the project. It measures the shrinking
distance that separates the seducer from the goal he has set himself.
It is a visible progresssion toward an end conceived and designed
from the very first. Finally it is the realizing milieu in which the
seducer takes formal cognizance of his efficacy; for each foreseen
event, in being brought to pass, furnishes him with a piercing
and delightful confirmation; he apprehends himself as both a
thinking and an acting potency, in the forced testimonials to it
which his victim constantly gives him. Thus in entirely concentrating his thought upon another person, the seducer aspires to
receive from this person one sole assurance: that he does not de-
pend in any fashion upon the slave that serves him, and that he
possesses "in himself alone the fullness of his happiness." [54]

Now the seducer tastes this profoundly egoistic happiness in
small draughts, so to speak. The seducer knows very well, he
knows very exactly in advance "the length of time this adventure
is going to take." [55] And the infinitely renewed attraction he finds
in it, "all the nuances of feeling," [56] which he savors in each ap-

parently indivisible moment, incline him not to hasten the course of the adventure but to slacken its pace, in order the better to enjoy one by one its sudden and gratifying turns. It is necessary that the victim surrender, but above all it is necessary to keep her from yielding too soon:

> Ah! allow me at least the time to observe those touching struggles between love and virtue . . . Such are the delicious pleasures this heavenly woman offers me every day; and you reproach me for savoring these sweets! Ah! the time will come only too soon, when, degraded by her fall, she will no longer be for me anything more than an ordinary woman.[57]

But as sequel we already feel in that insidious desire to dally along the way an almost impalpable change that little by little transforms, not the design, but the behavior of the seducer, and as a consequence also the allure of the novel and the nature of its duration. For it is now no longer a matter of a time that was the simple progressive realization of a previous scheme. The seducer is no longer following his timetable. More than that, between what he anticipated and what he is actually experiencing, there is no longer perfect coincidence, so greatly does the enjoyment of the reality surpass the anticipation.

> . . . If first affections, Valmont writes almost dreamily, seem more honest and one might say more pure; if at least they are slower in their course . . . it is because the heart, surprised by an unknown feeling, stops, so to speak at every step, to enjoy the enchantment it feels; it is that this charm is so potent to a young heart that it fills it to the point of making it forget every other pleasure. That is so true that an enamored libertine, if a libertine can be enamored, becomes from that moment less hurried in his enjoyment.[58]

Thus in a novel of the premeditated conquest of a victim by a seducer there is surreptitiously introduced another novel, unexpected, unforeseeable, the novel of the unpremeditated conquest of the seducer by the victim.

And during the course of the *Liaisons dangereuses* these two hostile novels will never cease to interpenetrate and combat each other. Subtle duel, which is not solely that of two persons but of two different species of destiny. For as the seducer approaches his triumph, he also approaches his defeat. And if his triumph was predetermined, his defeat on the contrary is entirely accidental. *Les Liaisons dangereuses* is so admirable a novel only because Laclos knew how, in counteraction to a most rigid theme, to bring to bear as countercurrent a theme exactly the inverse, the most fortuitous, the most "eighteenth century," that of the agile and flexible reapparition of chance amidst the precise calculations of thought:

> I admit it, I yielded to the impulse of a young man and kissed that Letter with a transport of which I did not believe I was any longer susceptible.[59]

Slender graceful phrase, very Louis XVI, but one can appreciate its charm only in finding it among the cynicism and aridity of a thousand others.

And yet at every moment in the novel one meets again with the unexpected springing forth of that responsive fountain:

> . . . I had surrendered to such a point that I wept too; and clasping her hands again, I bathed them in tears . . . Besides I gained also by it the chance to gaze on that charming face, enhanced by the powerful attraction of tears. My forehead became feverish, and I was *so little master of myself* that I was tempted to avail myself of this moment.
> What is this weakness of ours? What is this *empire of circumstance,* if I, *forgetting my projects,* risked losing by a premature triumph the charm of long struggles and the details of a painful defeat?[60]

Is this indeed Valmont, this being that avows himself *so little master of himself?* Is this still the *Liaisons,* this novel which is no longer that of a project accomplished, but a novel of a project *which one forgets?* And this duration which threatens to become *the empire of circumstance,* how much does it not differ from that other duration in which one aimed at establishing the empire of the will?

As the novel progresses, the hero who wanted to be master of himself, master of time and of destiny, more and more confirms himself as the intermittent slave of circumstance. Time reassumes its character of capricious and fatal vicissitude:

> But I forget in speaking to you about her, that I did not want to speak to you about her. I don't know what power it is that impels me to keep coming back to the subject . . .[61]

> But what fatality binds me to this woman? [62]

> Shall I then, at my age, be mastered like a schoolboy by an involuntary and completely alien feeling? [63]

With all his strength, the voluntary Valmont stiffens himself against the involuntary:

> Let us dismiss this dangerous idea; that I may become myself again . . .[64]

But in reality, Valmont will never become himself again. If he resumes his designs with increased eagerness, if with a more feverish energy he pursues the accomplishment of his project, the very tension of that will proves that it is no longer a question of project, of design, of a campaign carried on according to "true principles" with a grand "purity of method." Nothing is more impure, nothing is more turbid, on the contrary, than the impetuous ardor that hurls him now toward the president of Tourvel; as if he were no longer bound to her by intentions or calculations, but by a feeling of hateful passion, which sweeps him along, which maddens him, and which basically is the most obscure and most imperious image of a destiny to which he is delivered up forever: "For me there is no longer either happiness or repose, except in the possession of that woman whom I hate and whom I love with equal fury. I can *endure my fate* only from the moment in which I shall have hers at my service." [65] But even when he shall have that coveted fate at his service, his own fate will not be any the less insupportable. For it will be a *fate,* that is to say an existence that has escaped the control of the will, a duration no longer calculated but continually incalculable. A human being who wanted to direct his existence *from afar,* as Vauban claimed to order *at a distance* the assault upon a place, suddenly finds himself hemmed in, assailed, forced to improvise, thrown into the heart of the fray. The *Liaisons dangereuses* is indeed the history of a project, but of a project that turns out badly. The man who projects a mastery of time is mastered by time.

Thus the two attempts made at the begining of the Revolution to establish a sort of dictatorship over time both end in a defeat. One ends in paralysis, the other in frenzy.

Chapter IV Joubert

To Gabriel Marcel
and to the memory of Charles Du Bos

I

I wish, I tell you, to be perfect. It is the only thing that suits me and can make me happy.[1]

Man's happiness lies in his full and absolute existence.[2]

To be happy and to be perfect are the same thing. All his life Joubert pursued the same superhuman quest. But precisely in Joubert's case the object of this quest does not seem superhuman. Between man and what he searches for, there is no insuperable distance. The ideal is within reach. A natural affinity exists between man, happiness, and perfection.

But how can one become happy, perfect? In 1779, Joubert, a follower of Diderot, thinks he knows the answer. It is evident that happiness is not an object. One would not know how to conceive it as some exterior thing; one cannot acquire it as one acquires riches. A completely interior thing, it is a certain way of existing and possessing our existence. But on the other hand happiness is possible only if our existence embraces all that which is exterior to it, in such a way that, nothing being excluded, it may be all and enjoy all. There is happiness only in an existence which would be at the same time the most concentrated, since everything would be contained within it in the instant of enjoyment, and the farthest extended, since nothing would be missing within it, nothing would be left out. A "complete and absolute" existence, a perfect existence.

But how, Joubert asks himself, can we make of our existence something that is absolute and complete. Our existence is temporal and spatial. Now when we say a temporal existence we are speaking of an existence which one can enjoy only moment by moment, and part by part. Far from being complete, it is always partial; far from being simultaneous, it is always successive. And when we speak of a spatial existence, we mean an existence that is always separated from what it wishes to enjoy, by distances and limits. Far from being absolute, it is always relative; far from being all-inclusive, it exists outside of almost everything. Only the divine *Totum Simul* realizes the two conditions of happiness. A simultaneous possessor of an infinite existence, God concentrates a totally interior immensity in a single eternal moment. But man is a prey to the successiveness of that which is Within, and to the externality of that which is Without. How can he come to enjoy the perfection of a human *Totum Simul*?

An immense task, but it is one which, in Joubert's eyes in 1779, does not appear to be absolutely impossible. For on the one hand, if the human moment is not eternal, at least as long as it lasts it is certainly the interior milieu in which things become ours and form part of our own existence. And, on the other hand, if space with all it contains is exterior to us, it is no less true that its limits are extended when our being enlarges, and that by the action of our feelings we are able to widen our sphere so that we enjoy within ourselves what once was situated outside ourselves. Such is the action of the "feeling of universal good-will":

> Good-will links to our faculties and our pleasures the pleasures and the faculties of all the objects it embraces. Man is so

to speak an *immense being,* that may exist incompletely, and his existence is the more delightful as it becomes *fuller* and *more complete.*[3]

The starting point of Joubert's thought is therefore, as with Diderot, a movement of expansion and communion: "All pleasures are born out of some sort of communion." [4] Thanks to the feeling of good-will, objects outside us cease to be outside, and cease to be objects. Their faculties become ours. We can feel as they feel, exist as they exist, enjoy their pleasures. Thus we attain to an immediate intimacy with the universality of beings: "Beings are made one for another, by the same necessity that causes them to exist." [5] The dream of Joubert is thus the same as that of Novalis and the Renaissance thinkers. It consists in the will to restore to the sensible moment that spontaneous associative power that bound all beings together before the Fall. Happiness really exists only in the moments that are passionately enlarged by feelings of universal sympathy:

> In order to write *perfectly,* one would need to write and think as a man perfectly constituted would write and think *in the moment* in which all his faculties were perfectly ordered within him. Such a situation would be possible in that state of mind in which *all his passions were developed to their full force and extent* and combined in a perfect equilibrium.[6]

II

> My mind inhabits a place through which the passions have passed, and they are all familiar to me.[7]
>
> . . . The human passions always make themselves heard in the human heart, where, as it were, their echoes reverberate.[8]

There had been a period, then, when Joubert was given over to the passions and when he heard reverberate within him the immediate echo which their passage awakens in the heart. That sonorous dilatation, prolonging itself in the interior spaces and filling them with a confused sound, had been able to appear to him for a moment as the fullness of which he dreamed, the spreading of an "immense being." But almost at once Joubert had to undergo the inverse experience and to discover in the very instant in which he was abandoning himself to the movement of the passions the astonishing narrowness of the spatial and temporal field which is theirs. For the human being who is a prey to passion is at once and almost totally the slave of his actual sensations:

> Passion or emotion gives man only the nature of a moment.[9]
>
> Passion hinders progress.[10]
>
> His individual boundaries, his own self, reach neither beyond the place he occupies nor beyond the instant in which he occupies it.[11]

Without memory, without imagination, without intelligence, filled up but blocked off by brute sensation, man now has only "a numerical and mathematical present which is susceptible neither of addition nor division." [12] His sensibility is "reduced to the moment in which he exists." [13] He is confined "to the existence of the moment, to sensations; he is aware of neither the past nor the future; he is only aware of the present." [14]

The person who feels intensely, feels nothing beyond what he feels. The more lively his emotion, the more limited it is.

And also the more obscure it is. Not only does one who feels see nothing beyond what he feels, but he does not even see what he feels. He can only feel it. Blinded by that huge carnal presence that sticks to him, seizes his very fibers, and blocks his escape, he can neither distinguish himself from it, nor distinguish what the motion is that carries him along. It is a fluid motion, a sort of outflowing by virtue of which strength is continually changed into weakness and the being into another being. Like the surface of the sea, the ground of sensations is an indescribable entity, "a moving ground" [15] in which every form swells and subsides of itself, invades and withdraws, giving place to some other instantaneous wave. Thus nothing is fixed; there is no moment which is not superseded by other moments; each is an immediate that is always immediately changed into something different from itself. And that without pause, without rest, without interval, in a continuity which is the continuity of uniformity and formlessness, in a spatial and temporal density, similar to the viscosity of Sartre, in which it becomes impossible to get unglued, to tear oneself loose from the sticky paste of what one experiences, and to be elsewhere than in the place where one is and in the moment when one feels:

> Forces always at work, an activity without rest, motion without intervals, agitations without calm, passions without melancholy, pleasures without tranquility! It is to live without ever sitting down, to grow old standing up, to banish sleep from life and to die without ever having slept.[16]

> We have . . . the look of galley-slaves chained to their oars.[17]

> What a glue entraps us to earth . . .[18]

Thus there is revealed to the eyes of Joubert the paralyzing and harassing tragedy of a time made up of sensations: a time constituted of a concatenation of moments which always follow each other without ever being linked one to another, which pass before the attention without ever being able to rest there, which replace one another in feverish haste; the time of minds who, like their master, Voltaire, "never take their rest"; [19] the time of the eighteenth century:

> These times in which events have no known connection, no real extent, but are rapid, sudden, and cross each other like streaks of lightning, and chase each other like waves . . .[20]

All this, by its ceaseless flux, forms, if one may say so, a kind of continuity, but a monotonous continuity, composed of radically dissimilar elements: "desires without possession and voracities without prey," [21] "torments without respite and a perpetual frenzy." [22] Long before Bergsonism, Joubert had foreseen what is inhuman, literally intolerable, in a continuous duration com-

posed of heterogeneous elements. For there is neither renewal
nor variety where there is only an uninterrupted replacement of
perceptible occurrences. Their very differences annul one another; and out of the extreme diversity of succession is formed a
time in which all diversity is abolished, in which nothing can be
distinguished or detached from anything else, in which the succession of moments is no more than a succession of heads of
cattle in a nondescript herd:

> The uniformity of seasons, days, hours, with regard to the
> turmoil of the passions . . . The mind that is in turmoil dif-
> ferentiates nothing. Everything round about it is uniform be-
> cause its mutation and perturbation are always the same.[23]

The formless identity of a time made up of undifferentiated
feelings finally enwraps all lived moments in the same colorless
veil. Human existence no longer seems then to be that of an
immense being, coinciding with all spiritual extent, but a general agitation of a thousand little temporal particles pressed one
against another and communicating to one another the perceptible shock that made them tremble. Hence comes Joubert's horror at that false plenitude which is only the fullness of being
filled up:

> I found nothing reverberating there, nothing that rolled
> along easily and freely in a space greater than itself.[24]

> We are deceived by the fullness and the false solidities.[25]

> They construct a plenum without space; their ship cannot
> move along.[26]

Thence the following condemnation of the Cartesian *fullness:*

> Thought can gain for itself therein neither light nor place.
> One is always tempted to cry out, as in a packed audience:
> Air, air! Space! One suffocates, one is ground to death.[27]

In this universe in which everything is in contact with everything else, and yet nothing adheres to anything, space and time
are no more than a conglomeration of points and moments whose
very bulk weighs down the mind. The latter is reduced to the

span of an instant, a *locus* without depth, through which whirls
constantly the same confused eddy. Far from being extended into
the universal, one feels compressed on all sides by a gigantic force
of atmospheric pressure. Just as in Poe's story, the sensitive man
is a prisoner who watches the walls of his dungeon coming in
closer and closer upon him. A tremendous feeling of claustration,
suffocation, and exhaustion is the end of man's effort once and
for all to master the reaches of space. There is neither happiness
nor perfection in a plenum made up of feelings. One is engulfed
in it. One perishes in it for lack of air and space: "Without space,
there can be no light." [28]

Without space, there can be no plenitude. "Too much proximity is obnoxious." [29] "One thinks oneself in possession of the
full light of day when one is blind . . . We crawl blindly along
the ground, we are lost in the undergrowth, we are swallowed up
in the mines, our labyrinths are those of the mire." [30]

Turning away from these labyrinths of mire, Joubert's thought
is going to orient itself toward what Gabriel Marcel so profoundly calls "a seizure, not immediate but *at a distance*, of the
conditions of plenitude . . ." [31]

A seizure of space.

III

Metaphysics. At least the mind finds space there. Elsewhere
it finds only a plenum.
The mind demands a phantasmagoric world in which it may
move and wander. And it takes pleasure there not so much because of the objects as because of the space it finds there. —For
the soul and for the body, space is a great good, a surpassing
beauty.
—And as children love the sand and the water and whatever
is fluid and flexible because they can mold it to their will . . .[32]

This metaphysical world in which one takes refuge from the
oppression of the feelings and the engulfment in the flood of
things is fantastic precisely because, beyond sensations and emo-

tions, it constitutes a milieu which nothing can ever completely fill up, a place in which one touches nothing, in which one "feels" nothing. Such is, long before Mallarmé, the great discovery of Joubert. Beside, above, perhaps all about, certainly and by its very essence *beyond* the filled-up world, which is that in which one finds oneself in a sort of body-to-body relationship with reality, there is another world of which one can as yet say nothing, because one can feel nothing of it, a world that is perhaps nothing, or nothing more than a sort of distance or a veil that one puts between oneself and the rest, a world that is surely spiritual since this distance is the very distance the spirit establishes between itself and all the rest, a world, finally, which one could risk calling *imaginary,* on the condition of exploring at length the meaning of that epithet. A world eminently Platonic and ideal, if one means by that not necessarily a world of essences and images, but rather the inner realm in which ideas and images can manage *to find a place,* situating themselves elsewhere than in the sphere of sensory experiences "where nothing delineates them and gives them their true value, where they are, so to speak, superfluous." [33] Let us say then that a human being is a being who, on the one hand, finds himself inextricably buried in the mass, and who, on the other hand, finds himself mysteriously capable of producing in the interior of himself an open space. Hence, each time he feels himself pressed upon by sensory experience, enclosed within all the simultaneous determinations and the successive enchainments of the actual, it becomes possible, doubtless not as Mallarmé will attempt it later, to abolish all that, to deny the reality and presence of it, but to deaden the shocks of it, to extend its frontiers, to establish between all that and oneself a buffer zone, a "reserved" zone, in which there is nothing, literally nothing, except the infinite possibility of molding that nothingness to his will, of mentally ordering it in any way whatsoever. Space is precisely that: an hiatus, a cleft or gap that widens between reality and consciousness, the virtual place

in which the mind discovers the power to evolve, where, without
risk of running afoul of matter and being trapped in the actual,
it can "travel the open spaces." [34] Space is freedom of mind.

Freedom of a mind "that plays in waves of light, where it perceives nothing, but where it is penetrated with joy and splendor." [35]

Thus besides the sensory experience there now appears an experience of a significance and a nature that are entirely different,
which one can call spiritual. In the one experience, we perceive
ourselves making one body with a confused reality, so close to
us that we are blinded by it. In the other, we apprehend ourselves in the transparence of an invisible sphere, "rolling on
easily and *freely* in a space greater than oneself." Man is a being
who simultaneously finds himself engulfed in the fluid fullness
of sensory experiences, and swimming or flying in a spiritual ether
that is propitious for all evolutions. If on the one hand I am the
slave of all determinations, on the other I am the master of all
indeterminations. There are then in Joubert as it were two simultaneous *Cogitos,* by one of which man apprehends himself in the
capacity of feeling, and by the second of which he discovers himself in open spaces flooded with light. Is it so astonishing if to
the desire of making one body with a universe that is everywhere
perceived and everywhere sensible, there succeeds the desire to
float forever in the interior of an immensity where "one perceives nothing," nothing, except the infinite *opening* of the invisible constantly making room for the free flight of the spirit?

> Therefore I call space all that which is not I, and which is
> in no way determined. [36]

All that is beautiful is undetermined. [37]

Ineffable experience, undergone in a supreme detachment from
the palpable. There is somewhere, within us, around us, a realm
of clarity and light, where nothing is felt, nothing is seen, but
where everything can be situated, and which the soul freely traverses and inhabits. In it we are, we move, we find our being

again, each time we succeed in attaining our deliverance from the actual. Place of splendor and beauty, place that consequently brings about our completion and contentment. Full contentment is not in the plenum but in the void. If one wishes to be happy, perfect, he must "give himself space to spread his wings." [38]

Joubert, or the anti-Pascalian: the experience of space is a joy, not a terror.[39]

IV

Spaces, I shall almost say, *imaginary* . . .[40]

One cannot *imagine* any form for the whole, for each form is only the visible and palpable difference of the object which is clothed with it.[41]

If space is *imaginary*, it none the less remains unimaginable. Thus despite the ineffable joy it brings with it, the intuition of spiritual extension is still for Joubert that ultimate thing that the mind cannot conceive without disappearing within it, just as the soul is swallowed up in the presence of divinity:

The earth is a point in space, and space is a point in the spirit. I mean here by spirit the elemental, the fifth element of the world, the space of the all, the bond of all things, for all things are in it, live in it, move in it, die in it, are born in it.—The spirit . . . supreme limit of the world.[42]

Supreme limit, too, of human thought:

In that operation (of imagining God), the first means is the human form; the final term is light. And in the light the splendor. I do not believe that the imagination can go farther. But here the mind continues . . . Extension . . . finally infinity . . .[43]

Skies of the skies, heaven of heaven . . .[44]

In this prolongation of thought which, upwards beyond space, still finds infinitely more space, Joubert believed he saw opening within him, before him, a vast transparent and invisible reality in which we live and in which we move:

Beyond bodies, beyond worlds, beyond all,—beyond and about bodies, beyond and about worlds, beyond and about all, there is the light and there is the spirit.[45]

. I used to ask myself, if at the border of the material world one extended one's arm, where would it be? In God! Ah! We are there. *In ipso vivimus, movemur (moremur!) et sumus.*[46]

A human arm extended at the apex of the physical world, a human thought that reels at the highest peak of the mind, a soul half disencumbered of its body and all ready to start venturing in that pure spiritual extension which is "the road of souls separated from their bodies," [47] that is Joubert in those unique instants when, by means of the intuition of space, he believed not that he could touch or imagine, but simply that he could conceive the enveloping reality of the divine. God is an immanent immensity which can appear to us only as a nonappearance. He is that Plenitude of which we can gain some idea only in casting our gaze upon empty space. Space and God are identical; or, at least, space would be the absolutely faithful image of God, if space were an image:

In pure logic or mathematics, God is intelligible extension without end, without limits.[48]

These are the very words of Malebranche. Elsewhere Joubert translates them, marvelously, into his own language:

Space is really God, whose face, so to speak, we do not see. Newton calls it his *sensorium,* not daring to call it his body. It is properly speaking his stature.[49]

But if space is God's stature, that ultimate reality which is invisibly discovered after and beyond all thought, it is also that primal and original reality which must invisibly be situated before and prior to all thought, precisely in order that a thought may be born and be:

Space is the common place in which all places and all bodies are contained. Therefore space had to be: space exists because it was necessary; necessary to motions, to existences, to placements and displacements.[50]

And first of all he created place, or the capacity of containing what he was going to produce next.[51]

Passages that are decisive, because in them we see the means by
which Joubert is finally going to emerge from that Mallarmean
paralysis in which he was kept by the double presence of sensory
reality and spiritual immensity. Up until now we have seen him
given over entirely either to the consciousness of the plenum,
or to the consciousness of the void. In the plenum, no thought
can be shaped, because everything there is compressed and restrained by the thick presence of sensation: "What can you put
in a mind already filled up?" [52] Inversely, in the void, no thought
can be figured, because no figure can express the unimaginable
reality of the invisible. Silence alone is permitted: "Having
found nothing worth more than emptiness, he leaves space vacant." [53]

On the one hand, there is silence by suffocation, on the other
by impotence. In the former instance there is room for nothing;
in the latter there is infinite room which can be filled by nothing.

But if, instead of enclosing oneself by turn in the consciousness of one or the other of these two worlds, man tries to bring
them together; if, instead of denying the existence of the one
through the agency of the other (as Mallarmé will do), we strive
to place the one within the other, then everything changes, everything becomes easy, everything is saved. Saved as if by grace!
There is no human activity possible except it proceed forth from
a *given* space in which that activity is born, develops, and takes
form. For the thoughts of man, as for the works of God, there is
only one way of arriving at existence: it is to find, ready to
receive them, a vacant interior milieu, a spiritual space: "If you
wish to think well, speak well, write well and act well, first of
all create places . . ." [54]

This is the prime task of man. It no longer consists in feeling,
nor in striving to transform his sensation into sympathy or
thought. A purely sensible being, we have seen, is a being that

can go only from sensation to sensation by an uninterrupted movement as harassing as it is vain. On the contrary, what man must do is break the sensuous enchantment and enchainment, turn aside from the actual, establish between what he has felt and what he is going to think, an *interior distance,* a zone of calm, of reserve, and of silence, in which the seed of thought will find the ground and the time necessary, over a long period, in which to take shape. He must "space his words, his sentences, his thoughts." [55] "First of all one must create an open space, a place, a spot . . ." [56]

This open space, one must first create it within the sphere of one's own existence. Now human existence is a temporal existence. The establishment of the place of ideas, of the ground in which they must germinate, will therefore be above all for Joubert the establishment of a new time, essentially different from that of successive duration. Instead of the crowded and rapid flux of sensations, it is rather a question of husbanding a duration in which events are made remote, their colors are blurred, their resonances are progressively weaker; a time in which rests alternate with motions and take a greater and greater place. Instead of a crowded time, it is a time in which there is ease, play, patience, and slowness:

All perfection is slow.[57]

Like Dedalus, I fabricate wings for myself. I fashion them little by little, affixing one feather a day.[58]

A time of labor but also a time of vacation and vacancy, of labor in vacancy:

There is established between our senses and all our perceptions, between the impacts of all things and all their commotions, between all the shakings and our determinations, a distance, an interval, a time, a void, an extent where all becomes calm, all becomes temperate, diminishes, becomes silent, slackens its pace.[59]

Modesty, the secret virtue which Joubert has unforgettably sung, is the founder within us of that spacious time which precedes and prepares our creations.

v

Silence.—The delights of silence.—Thoughts must be born of the soul, and words out of silence.—An attentive silence.[60]

This time-space, made of waiting and of calm, is so to speak formed within us of itself and without effort:

Note that in all true meditation a pause naturally succeeds each motion.[61]

If we were not always precipitated from sensation to sensation by our frantic agitation, we would easily perceive within ourselves that spontaneous creation of repose which is accomplished, almost without our suspecting it, by the silent gliding of the present into the past. Every lived moment is like a being that strays away and quietly enters into solitude, and if with our eyes we follow his withdrawal, we see stretching between him and us a retrospective extent which grows ever larger. Nothing is more different from actual and successive time than the almost negative duration of which we take cognizance when, disregarding all intermediate events, we seek in ourselves a certain moment of the past. After a time it appears to us, not as it looked when it burst upon us in the brief explosion of its occurrence, nor as lost in the midst of the chain of other moments that encompassed it, but floating in the serenity of the distance, infinitely far, not of ourselves, but of our sole actuality. Such for Joubert is the primary and most important signification of memory. If memory, as the eighteenth-century philosophers maintained, was only weakened sensation, that was already a boon and a gain, because, in losing its vivacity, actuality would become less harassing, and because, in becoming the past, the present would be more bearable. But the past is not solely a kind of weakened present. It is something that is reborn beyond its very absence. It is a recollection, and a recollection surrounded by forgetfulness. It encompasses itself "with empty spaces which give it a kind of vista." [62] If, as Joubert enjoins, "one must provide oneself with distance, create for oneself perspective," [63] it is not at all in order to contemplate the curve of one's destiny or the plenitude of one's accomplishment; it is in order to disengage from its gangue of actuality each particular moment and, having thus set it apart from every other moment, in a solitary region of thought, to render it finally visible and expressible:

> One should write down what one feels only after a long period of quietude. One must not express oneself as one feels, but as one remembers.[64]

But to remember is also to render visible and expressible—thanks to the perspective of memory—a temporal depth which is analogous to the spatial depth. Like Baudelaire, Joubert studied the effects of perspective in all of the arts:

> All things must have their own sky. Let us put some sky everywhere.
> The sky or perspective is what makes poetry. The echo is what makes music. Chiaroscuro in painting. The dream or the depth of the mind in all things. Finally the soul or the spirit and the spiritual world, etc. Space.[65]

Memory is a magical transfiguration of ourselves and of the world, which is effected *in* and *through* space:

> Perspective or remoteness is necessary for events, in order for us to be affected (or touched) by them poetically, and in order for us to give them poetic *treatment*.[66]

Now this treatment that the poet applies to the past is less a reviviscence than a recreation.

Already, and solely by means of its passage through time, the lived moment is found transformed by a mysterious process of elaboration and purification. What we feel, at the instant we feel it, is not yet ours. It becomes such only in the course of time in being completed within ourselves, by ourselves, slowly. The penumbra in which it recedes and by which it is veiled becomes the secret place of its formation. Anything superfluous in it evaporates; anything violent or impure "quiets down and deposits its own excess." [67] Thus even the noblest grief ought not to be lived in the actual. If we lose a loved one, we should not give in to the sharp pang of that loss: "Heart and memory, judgment and feeling come into collision with each other, in that *first moment*. Time will purify our recollections . . ." [68] In another place Joubert writes: "I have crossed the river of oblivion . . ." [69] On the other side of that river, we come to ourselves once more and find the most harrowing moments of our life marvelously tranquilized and purified, and finally worthy not only of being felt, but of being thought and lived. At bottom, the past is very simply a present which we are permitted to recover, a new chance which is given us to enter once more upon the existence of our lived moments, but, this time, at a distance, at an interval remote enough to allow us to rectify them. Our life is lived twice: in actuality, when we haven't the time to do anything well, and in inactuality, when we have time enough to perfect the substance of it. We first of all live at the wrong moment, and then we are able to take this moment again and shape it at leisure in time:

Memory delights only in that which is excellent. [70]

My memory preserves now only the essence of what I read, of what I see, and even of what I think. [71]

There are griefs which fastidious souls ought to defer . . . in order to experience them as more complete, more *perfect,* more *absolute.* Do not give yourself up to yours at the wrong moment. [72]

Pure griefs are equivalent to joy . . . [73]

The imperceptible purification of all our most violent feelings entails, therefore, not only an intrinsic perfection, but something more, something which Joubert calls here an *absolute,* and calls in several other passages a *rounding-off* of lived experience. In being "turned over in my mind for a long time," [74] my former experience ends by losing its sharp edges. It is no longer a fragment detached from my sensory history. Reduced to its essence, it is simply an image in the transparency of which there emerges an idea. At a distance, the lived moment has become a small world of its own, polished and gleaming, a thing that has "its rondure, its proper sphere, its limits, its *absolute totality*." [75] I contemplate it from afar as the perfect figure of a moment which once I imperfectly lived.

Does this moment which, outside myself, remote from myself, I have thus brought to perfection, still belong to me? Is it still a moment of my life? Its perfection isolates it as much as its distance does; its inactuality separates it not only from what I am now, but also from what it was lately. It no more belongs to my past than to my present; it belongs to space. It has become as nontemporal as that invisible permanence which envelops it and from which it distinguishes itself only by the frame of its finite perfection. It is one small bit of circumscribed space surrounded by an indeterminate expanse. It is one small visible idea which has taken shape in the invisible. It is no longer a moment which belongs to me, which I live and which I feel in the turbid closeness of the actual. It is a moment of which I think; it is that imperceptible germ of thought which my emotion once smothered and which now my mind delineates and colors. For all that we feel teems with ideas, but we never distinguish them in actuality because of their transparency and our absorption in sensation. Let however these moments which we have already lived become once again manifest to us in the depths of memory, in those very depths which are the abiding place of all thought, and then thought, finding itself in the impalpable milieu which suits it, and yet always invested with a contour and tint of emotion which keep it from vanishing in its very purity, stands forth like a star or like an angel in the sky, a small island of perfection whose shores we ourselves draw on the map of space:

> Indeed stars are islands, surrounded as they are by air or ether; aerial or ethereal islands.[76]

> Picture to yourself our geographical maps. As the filled up parts are defined by the hollows of seas and lakes, just so, if I dare express myself thus, the finite is defined by the infinite, and motion by repose.[77]

> One cannot conceive them [the angels] without some kind of bodies, if not terrestrial, at least celestial or, if you wish, at all events mathematical, that is to say showing their bounds, their limits, their lack of infinity, of immensity, and by consequence giving themselves some kind of form.[78]

> . . . What is form if not bounded space? [79]

> It is always what bounds or limits a thing that gives it its character, precision, distinctness, perfection. It is what isolates it, encompasses it, separates it from the rest, encloses it within itself and leads it back to itself. Thereby it subsists, is distinct, is known; by that alone is it absolutely complete.[80]

Perfection does not reside, therefore, in the indeterminate vastnesses of pure thought any more than it is found in the confused profusions of brute sensation. It resides in a thought which in time one renders visible to himself by investing and coloring it at a distance with a little of himself, with his own imagination. It is something simultaneously intimate and remote, personal and general; it is something which is no longer myself, which never was myself, but which depends on myself, if not for its existence, at least for its incarnation:

> I call imagination the faculty of rendering perceptible everything that is intellectual, of embodying all that is mind, and in a word of bringing to the light of day anything whatsoever that is of itself invisible.[81]

> The imagination is pre-eminently the faculty of giving body and form to that which has neither.[82]

Form is indeed that which distinguishes one thing from all other things, that which separates the singular from the universal and makes it exist apart.[83]

Thanks to myself a lived moment has become afar the abode of a thought. A form detached from a confused temporality incarnates and expresses an idea detached from an inexpressible eternity. Small "luminous drop" [84] which I myself have formed, it now exists apart, at one and the same time within myself and remote from myself, in space and set against space: isolated in its own perfection.

VI

There must be, in our written language, sounds, soul, space, open air, there must be words that exist all alone, and carry their place with them.[85]

The most beautiful sounds, the most beautiful words are absolute and have between them natural intervals which it is necessary to observe in pronouncing them.[86]

Joubert's whole poetics is just a reflection and an echo of his cosmology. His recreation of words is a recreation of the universe. But the latter has now taken form. It consists in the deployment of a double spatial and temporal extent, an extent that in itself is unimaginable and invisible, in which the mind would be lost if it did not contrive to set at certain intervals within it clearly formed thoughts that find their place there. This extent is, if you will, the real world, which is neither inside nor outside human beings, but which is everywhere; or again it is the entirely interior extent of our mind: "There is a world within us. It is the Mind." [87] —"The mind," Joubert says in another place, "is a bit of intelligible space in which images, ideas, judgments, etc., can be formed and lodged and moved about and combined." [88] The mind is thus a hollow place, a pure capacity, which the forms of our thoughts can inhabit. But what is true of space is no less true of time. Joubert would willingly say that our thoughts ought to roll about in the vastness of an indeterminate duration. Thus again the mind is an indifferent continuity, a sort of temporal cavity in which moments come and go without experiencing any resistance. Mind and universe, time and space thus offer themselves to us as one same and boundless field in which our imagination can dispose ideas and forms just as we write words down on a blank page. All that we think or say best can then be spaciously arranged in our mind and in our works in such a way that we shall have simultaneously the consciousness of their isolated presences and the vast spiritual ensemble in which these presences are distributed. Thus, in the Joubertian universe, two kinds of existence are revealed: on the one hand, that of moments, places, sounds, forms, things slight, so to speak, in themselves; and, on the other hand, the essentially spatial and temporal existence of the limitless milieu in which they find themselves placed. One could call it an open archway, made of invisible immensity and eternity, through which, at long reaches from one another, the tiny distinct realities of moments, of points, and of words, sparkle in the distance.

Thus the fundamental continuity of a space and a time made up of indetermination and emptiness becomes apparent, and it is at the same time interrupted by the scattered presence of forms which in themselves have, so to speak, neither duration nor depth.

As a result, there arises for Joubert a new and very grave problem, on the solution of which hangs the fate of the fragile perfections he has created.

For if on the one hand these little islets of perfection find themselves encircled by time and space, on the other hand by their very nature they are detached from time and space; they no longer belong to time and space. In contrast to the Kantian world, the Joubertian world is a world in which things are not thought and felt *with* time, *with* space, but rather *against* time and space. They stand out in relief against a spatial and temporal background. Thus between these two modes of existence, that of things and that of the milieu which gives them place, there is opposition rather than rapport. The mind oscillates between the consciousness of the containing and the consciousness of the contained. Now it turns toward words, images, ideas, and then it risks beholding only shallow entities without depth. Now it turns toward those very depths, and then it risks discerning nothing of all that is enveloped and separately formed therein.

It is true that these depths are not only the place where forms are, but the place where they continue to move about. Any thought that issues from the mind never ceases to persevere there in a motion that is above all temporal:

> Time is motion in space, a ball on a billiard table.[89]

But this continuous motion appears as if discontinuous. Things do not always present themselves with the same distinctness; they do not always take the same affective tints. We cannot follow them continuously with our eyes; we must break off, and then return to them, and not only return to them, but reconstruct the invisible passage which they accomplished while they were not under our observation:

> It is necessary that this line unroll in our brain without any break, but our hand cannot trace it without interruption, and without restarting work again and again.[90]

> To choose to express ideas so subtle, is to choose to paint from nature an object that incessantly vanishes and reappears, displaying itself for only a moment. One must wait for it.[91]

This is the first discontinuity of which Joubert, more than anyone else, unless it be Maine de Biran, has had the painful consciousness: a consciousness of flights and failures, of enthusiasms and fatigues, of mental powers and bodily weaknesses. Joubert is a man who is perpetually obliged to interrupt his meditations and postpone till later the continuation of his dreams:

> . . . I know not what losses which can be repaired only by the immediate cessation of the operation which has worn

me out; hence a great irregularity and frequent discontinu-
ities in my intellectual communications . . . it is my flesh
and blood that are capricious, not I.[92]

To this first discontinuity there is added the discontinuity of
expression. For how can one express by a regular development
of the word what is revealed to the mind only intermittently and
in conformity with all the changing tints of the imagination?
Like Montaigne, Joubert confesses himself "unfit for continuous discourse": [93]

> A continuous style (or the didactic and uninterrupted suc-
> cession of phrases and expressions) is natural only to the man
> who depends on his pen and writes for others. In the mind,
> all is spurt and stop.[94]

It all consists with Joubert in detached phrases, isolated words,
unstrung pearls. If only "droplets of light" [95] ever fell from his
pen, it is doubtless first of all because he strove for that absolute
rondure of minute perfection, but it is also because the droplet
once fallen, the spirtle so to speak is cut off, and he must wait
for a new drop to form.

Flights followed by halts, movements encompassed by pauses,
that is precisely how Joubert's spiritual universe now appears to us.
But time is therein revealed as playing a much more important role
than we had first supposed. For this particular time is no longer
simply the permanence or the successive continuity of extension;
it is no longer that vague duration in which things come and go.
It is the very succession of these things and the kind of welter
they produce in appearing and disappearing in the continuous
and indeterminate. There is a time-rest, a time-space which is
"the distance that separates two motions," [96] but there is also
a time-motion that irregularly breaks the continuity of the time-
space. It is as if with Joubert discontinuity perpetually surged
up into continuity in order rapidly to delineate there a present
both absolute and ephemeral; as if an extent primarily spatial
in its essence were shot through with the brief flashes of temporal

events. From this point of view, "time and space correspond perfectly to movement and rest"; [97] and if it is accurate to say that "the movement is cut off by periods of rest," [98] it is still more exact to say, by reason of the priority of space, that space is the initial, neutral texture upon which the irregular movements of the mind perpetually produce "new cuttings." [99]

If therefore on the one hand time is a certain continuity, basically analogous to space, on the other hand it is everything that is successively registered in this continuity, that is to say the very contrary of space. In the midst of a repose which is both initial and final, which reappears through all the fissures of thought like an underlying woof, there is another time that consists of the discontinuous succession of thought in the mind.

A time that is comparable, no longer to space, but to the multiplicity of forms which can partially occupy it. Out of the "well-ordered intermixture of hollows and solids, of intervals and masses," [100] there is formed a discontinuous simultaneity that is supported by the pure continuity of initial space. "Everything is network, everything is fabric" in the universe.[101] The fullness itself "is only a great sponge. If one pressed it, if one forced the emptiness out of it, it would not fill up one's hand . . . A cloud, a meshwork is an image of the plenum." [102] But the cloud itself is made up of an infinite plurality of small isolated drops. Plenums succeed voids, and voids succeed plenums; everything is broken off in order to begin again after an interval; everything begins again in order to be broken off; to such an extent that the simultaneous discontinuity tends in the final analysis to be confounded with the successive discontinuity of Joubertian time.

A successivity which on the other hand must not be confused with pure sensory succession. The latter, as we have seen, was a continuous thing. Everything that was found therein was found to be boxed in between what preceded and what followed it. In Joubertian duration, on the contrary, everything is followed by an interval. Space reappears through all the gaps of time.

The ideal universe of Joubert and his mental life have exactly
the same appearance as the pages of his notebook and the work
he dreamed of writing:

> I should like to have thoughts succeed themselves in a book
> like the stars in the sky, in order, in harmony, but with elbow
> room and *at intervals, without touching each other,* without
> merging into one another . . . Yes, I should like them to roll
> along without fastening themselves and clinging to each other,
> so that each of them might subsist independently . . .[103]

> The sounds of the Aeolian harp (or lyre). They are not
> linked together, but they are ravishing.
> I am an Aeolian harp.[104]

> Poetry . . . like a *series of words,* luminous and variously
> colored . . .
> Verse. Poetry. Each word in it must hold the mind sus-
> pended . . .
> Each word should have so distinct a sound and sense that
> the attention dwells upon it with pleasure and relinquishes it
> with ease in order to pass on to the words that *follow,* in which
> another pleasure awaits.[105]

Successive time appears, then, as a perpetual renewal of
thought, as a rising of ideas that begin again from moment to
moment in the vacuum of the mind. Each moment seems to
"exist apart," [106] "to subsist independently," [107] to subsist uniquely
by reason of an act of the figurative and creative imagination.
Consequently this successive duration is also a sort of *continued
creation:*

> Duration is only a successive and continuous renewal of
> creation.[108]

But for Joubert this continued creation is clearly not at all
similar to that which one finds in Descartes or Locke. It is
continued, but it does not *continually* create something *continuous.* The successive moments which constitute it neither touch
nor adhere to each other. The creative influx, far from constantly
maintaining its action in order constantly to maintain its creature,
breaks off and takes up again, alternates pauses and motions,

suddenly abandons its inspiration and its universe to return to
and abandon them again. The Joubertian world is made of stars
whose scintillation is interrupted perhaps only because their
very existence is intermittent. Also, by very reason of the absolute
character of its minute particular perfections, the Joubertian
universe would be the play of an atomism infinitely more radical and more tragic than the Cartesian or sensualist atomism,
if, on the other hand, it were not, in its successive eclipses,
somehow replaced in the mind by the very presence of the place
it has vacated; and if this void were not basically the mind itself
restored to its own freedom, and savoring in repose the infinite
charm of its indetermination:

> The forgetting of earthly things, the turning toward heaven-
> ly things, the freedom from all violent passion and all dis-
> quietude, from all worry and care, from all trouble and
> striving, fullness of life without any least agitation. The de-
> lights of feeling without the strain of meditation. In a word,
> the felicity of pure spirituality right in the middle of the world
> and amid the tumult of the senses. *It is only the happiness
> of an hour, of a minute, of an instant.* But this instant, this
> minute of piety diffuses a sweetness throughout our months
> and our years.[109]

A continued but intermittent creation, an apparition by intervals of successive figures in a vague milieu or of this vague milieu
amidst the processions of its figures, it seems, however, that the
Joubertian universe is very loosely strung together, and that its
beads never form a necklace.

If the sounds "are not linked there together," [110] if one takes
leave of each word and each form at each instant "in order to
pass on to the words that follow, in which another pleasure
awaits," [111] in that case one can still recognize in Joubert the
existence of a continuous but absolutely indeterminate time,
the existence of a time that is successive but is composed of moments that never touch one another; but it would seem that one
can never find in Joubert any other time than this vague time

or this duration which cancels itself; and as a consequence the entire Joubertian universe threatens to scatter itself like "unstrung pearls," [112] or to evaporate in space, *into* space.

What is the work of Joubert? An infinite series of definitions of the undefinable.

It is the attempt each time "to circumscribe within a space which has no reality an object which has no body." [113]

It is an attempt forever made and forever defeated. Successive flights of soap bubbles.

VII

But is it not the same with music? Like the Joubertian world, the musical universe appears only in an indeterminate time enclosing small durations which annul one another. Sounds are succeeded by pauses, motions by rests and terminations. Through all the interstices of the sonorous, there is perceived a woof of silence, and the succession of sounds is a succession of distinct presences which as a consequence of their precision are found to be isolated one from another by the absolute interval of their qualitative differences. And yet the musical universe is never vaporized in either the spray of its sonorous elements or in the vague indetermination of its ensemble:

> . . . In music pleasure is born of the intermixture of sounds and silences; in the same way it is born in architecture of the well-ordered intermixture of voids and plenums, of intervals and masses.[114]

A temporal architecture issuing from the *well-ordered* intermixture of silence and noises, of permanence and successiveness, music constructs a composite time, a time of suitability and harmony.

It is the same with Joubertian thought. Issuing simultaneously from the vaguest consciousness of being and from the liveliest consciousness of the modifications which it undergoes, given over at one and the same time to the feeling of an indeterminate permanence that envelops the whole, and to a feeling of fugitive determinations that are figured forth in the whole, Joubert's thought can neither satisfy nor perfect itself until it has found a time which joins these times.

That is the particular express greatness of Joubert's thought. It consists in the search for a superior time which would make our existence something similar to music. It is therefore not at all a question here of discovering in the universal temporality some fundamental synthesis, hidden from our eyes by the apparent contradictions of the real. It is, on the contrary, a question of a syntheticization of the temporal existence, which would be the ultimate task of the mind. Of our mind and of our body, of all the perceptible events which the one experiences, of all the thoughts which the other perceives, it is possible to fashion for ourselves not a time that is given, not a time that is received, but a time that is conceived and composed, a time that is our own work.

But that is only possible if first the mind surmounts, without abolishing it, the double isolation of the moments taken by themselves, and the moments as they relate to ourselves. We shall, no doubt, never be able to contemplate the moments of our past except from a distance. But if these moments present themselves to us with the distinct and purified forms which precisely time gives them, they awaken in us an emotion which is none the less real for being directed toward them. Besides the cold memory, there is a warm memory, "almost corporeal," [115] which is that of our imagination: "The imagination is an *active* memory, a coloring, depicting memory." [116] "Memory takes hold of the mind only in so far as it becomes what we call imagination." [117] It is that present act, that act of our whole self, that "young feeling" thanks to which we, at a distance, give once again to our "old thoughts" [118] a perceptible existence. For "everything we think, we must think with our whole being, mind and body." [119] If we can never *be* our past, we can continually enter into the most intimate, even the most physical, relations with it.

On the other hand, the isolation of moments by themselves is not irremediable. The very example of music shows us that sounds move one toward another across the silence:

> In song, each note, though individual, is linked to another and makes continuity, by a kind of reverberation which serves as some sort of intermediary articulation. In the same way every point is joined to another point by a kind of swelling which serves as the means of contact and of identification between the two.[120]

It is the same with poetry. The sense reverberates in every phrase, in every word, and "always leaves behind it a large number of undulations." [121]

For if, isolated in their self-perfection, ideas can follow one another only at intervals, nevertheless there is always released from every one of them an indeterminate effusion of feelings which spreads through the intervals:

> Thoughts ought to *follow one another,* feeling alone ought to *flow.*[122]

These undulations, these effusions tend to be joined together again in space.

Let no one imagine that here Joubert falls once more into that philosophy of fullness which he rejected from the time of his youth. We are no longer in a universe where everything touches everything else, but in a world that remains eternally spacious and eternally populated by presences at a distance from each other. But in the exterior spaces Joubert divines the existence of "subtle emanations that keep up perpetual currents between the different beings." [123] In the same way, in our mind, despite the points or blanks that separate them, phrases, notes Joubert, "by a graceful linkage, a binding inter-phrase," [124] can establish communications between themselves, and a true coherence. Could we not then establish between all the moments of our life, between all the particular thoughts of our imagination, the same "well binding inter-phrasing"? The veritable human time would be, not a continuity in the plenum, but a continuity in and through the void; not a linkage but a network of relations:

> Thoughts must follow one another and be joined to one another like sounds in music, by their sole relationship,—harmony—and not like the links in a chain, or a string of pearls.[125]

This is not only the time of music but the time of poets:

> In their eyes, words have a shape, colors. One harmony *calls to another*. This separation between their words is between their thoughts. Their ideas are not linked in a chain, they *are placed in rapport with each other* like the stars in the sky.[126]

Then are revealed the infinite possibilities of a truly human duration. Such a duration, being made up, in large part, of space, is at the same time made up of indetermination. Freed from the law according to which the effect irrevocably follows the cause, it is freed at the same time from the law of irreversibility. The different moments which constitute it are not linked each to each, but seek and find each other in the spaces of existence. Every instant we can put ourselves in touch with every instant. Can we not then make a harmony of all our instants? Is it not possible for us, by regroupings and expungings, by the sorting out of qualitative similarities and dissimilarities, to redistribute all the moments of our life and all the forms of our thought, in such a way that instead of watching them file by in the uninterrupted concatenation of casual time, we discover them to be simultaneously very far from and very near to one another, echoing one another at a distance, resembling one another in their diversity, illumining one another with reciprocal fires, and forming, in any moment at all in which we would consider them, a vast "embroidered" expanse composed of time and space, of which our actual thought would be the center?

There is more to it than that. The call which is shouted by one to another during all the moments of a thought's existence is a call for help. With Joubert as with Proust, one would say that each lived moment imposes a task upon us. But in the case of Joubert the moments are neither irremediably lost nor irremediably enclosed within themselves as they are in the Proustian universe. And if, as with Mallarmé, distance is indeed for Joubert the means of uniting us again with our past or our thought, Joubertian distance does not at all have that character of vitreous transcendence which in Mallarmé lets rise up into view before the eyes of the dreamer only certain objects congealed in the cold. One would say that for Joubert all lived moments unceasingly maintain a resonance and a concern with their destiny. One would say that they ceaselessly ask to be completed, redeemed, compensated for; and that this appeal, which is the appeal of all music and all poetry, is made to the spaces of time because in them there resides a promise of perfection and redemption. Already in this life a *spiritual time* begins which "perfects all and destroys nothing,—which brings to completion"; [127]—which, completing or compensating for such a moment by another such moment, at a distance, brings it about that no moment is ever abandoned or lost, but that in our life there is always the possibility of its being *succored* by another. It is thus that we find established the solidarity, the harmony of all the moments of our duration. *Real* duration is made of measure, that is to say of moments that are bound together over the distance that separates them:

> And time alone (I am going to astonish you), yes, time alone seems to me to have a *reality*, because it is bound to the imperishable nature, to the intellectual and moral nature, for which, for example, there is repentance after error or forgetfulness after a good deed done.[128]

> God measures time as we do; though not by His successions, but by ours. Are the time of contrition and the time of error the same in His eyes? The time of our corruptions and that of our innocences? [129]

Thus there is "time even in eternity." [130] Against the background of divine space there perpetually appear "newly-cut figures." A temporal *reality* never ceases to form itself upon the
permanence of the immensity:

> All other motion is simple generation. But this is existence,
> essence, life.[131]

> It is a spiritual, incorruptible time . . . Its changes are
> ameliorations, developments. It is a time that consumes evil
> for the good and *replaces* the good by the best.[132]

Our terrestrial lives can already be an adumbration of this time
of the infinite perfecting:

> It is necessary to treat our lives as we treat our writings, to set
> in accord, in harmony, the middle, the end, and the beginning.
> With this in view, we need to make a great many *erasures*.[133]

Erasures which now no longer consist in the kind of forgetfulness by which we abolish in our memory the remembrance of our
old failings, but rather in the positive act by which we repair or
rectify them: "Repentance consumes the errors and the disposition which caused them." [134] We preserve within ourselves only
our good dispositions; we are now faithful only to the memory
of the moments which concur with them. Our whole being, then,
becomes a spontaneous rhythm, a "harmony of nature and pro-
priety." [135] It measures its activity according to a cadence that
echoes between body and mind:

> Of those who are *organized*, as to whom each point of their
> surface is a key, each fiber a chord, in harmony with their
> mind; each capacity a void, a reverberating space,—whose ac-
> tions and words are the notes of a music; whose life finally
> is a song . . .[136]

Thus little by little our being habituates and wins itself over
to becoming an "organized instrument." [137] All that it thinks, all
that it feels is "performed in a key that is determined." [138] It
knows "the rapport of the periods in the *harmonic succession of
its affections*." [139] It "possesses its mind and *feels all moments*

with their variations." [140] Its entire life is a "harmony in conformity to the eternal nomes." [141] It becomes "a perpetual con-
cert." [142] The "long contexture" [143] of our thoughts seems then
to undulate of itself over all its surface, like a fabric animated
by the wind. The mind traverses and moves about it,

> free of cares and given over to a thousand affections that *suc-*
> *ceed each other of themselves* . . . , a leisured intelligence
> that flies at random like the bee, that pauses on its way before
> a thousand objects without actually settling down upon any
> one of them, that caresses all the flowers and hums its pleas-
> ure.[144]

A spiritual time, which is made of free thought displaying itself upon the indetermination of space, and which prolongs itself
into eternity by "the perpetual change of peaceable dispositions
that takes place in the minds of the blessed." [145]

"Our life is woven of the wind," [146] says Joubert. Time—the
time of both our terrestrial and celestial lives is a stuff woven by
us upon space.

Chapter V Balzac

I

"So far he was at grips only with his desires . . ." [1] The moment in which the Balzacian being first discovers himself, the starting point of his conscious existence, is thus not a moment in which he would find himself in the plenitude of his present being, equal to what he is in the instant in which he is. Nothing is less Cartesian or less Cornelian than the Balzacian *Cogito,* which is that of a being immediately oriented toward what he is not, toward what he desires to be: "He had created for himself the most exigent and the most avidly insatiable life of all." [2]—"From his childhood he had shown the greatest ardor for everything. In his case desire became a paramount force and the motive power of all his being . . ." [3] To be, then, is to desire, that is to say to will to be. Like the God of Jacob Boehme, the Balzacian being at first discovers himself to be a sort of living void, a cry for life. Rather than having an existence, he is a need to exist: "I hunger, and nothing offers itself to my avidity!" [4]—"It is I who contain in my own breast this thirst, this hunger, this ardor of hell." [5]—"I thirst for the world, it lures and summons me." [6] Such a being can support his existence only by immediately linking it on all sides to the universe. Isolation would be insupportable for him:

"Man has a horror of solitude." [7] He has a horror of feeling himself limited solely to his consciousness of being, detached from the world and from time, enclosed within the circumference of the present. He must feel himself living in a moment that is immersed in time and surrounded by vastnesses of space. This is the moment that demands for itself, around and before itself, a world in which it can extend, unfold, and possess itself. It is like La Fosseuse, "her heart is *outside of herself*." [8] The being is beyond, outside, in the future and in space; it is the very thing one must think, desire, will, in order truly to be oneself. If then the whole *Comédie humaine* is going to become one gigantic theory (and practice) of the Will, that is because the Will, for Balzac, is at once the initial and the final point of the adventure of *being*. At first I am only my will. But my will consists in making every effort to be this or that, to be what I am not, to possess in myself the being of others: "I must relate my thoughts, my efforts, all my feelings to a being which is not myself . . ." [9]—"Other existences must co-operate with mine." [10]

But also, on the other hand, my being is the present act by which I link myself to all that is not myself. My being is not only without, in what I desire to be; it is within, in the act by which I desire. On the one hand, it is the immense field of my possibilities of being; on the other hand, it is the positive force with which I wish what I wish. Thus at one and the same time I discover myself in the infinite indetermination of my desires, and in the very real determination of my powers. I am a point, a center, from which I can set out to extend myself everywhere, exist everywhere, and become everything. The primitive being, who has not as yet spent any of his forces, "in whom consciousness has remained pure, and feeling strong," [11] is capable of instantaneously availing himself of a vast storehouse of energy. His will can, "by an entirely contractile movement of the interior being, collect itself," [12] concentrate itself on one point of life and strength, condense itself into a moment of pure creative energy. Like Louis

Lambert, every Balzacian being "possesses the gift of being able at certain moments to summon up extraordinary powers": [13] "Whenever thought remains in its totality, like a lump, and does not retail itself little by little . . . , it is likely to throw out flames of a prodigious intensity." [14] To throw out flames, to project its force. Thus the first real moment of Balzacian activity is a moment, without duration or breadth, starting out from which man projects himself into times and spaces; starting out from which, we might even say, he gives himself a time and a space in which to dispose all the possible objects of his desire. It is as if, in the first Balzac, the Balzac whom his "interior dissipation" has not yet worn out and who still possesses intact "the treasure of his glittering desires, the virgin gold of his longings," [15] there occurred at first, as in the God of the Cabala, a vast and instantaneous movement of withdrawal, a concentric mustering of the forces of his being, in order that within the void formed by "the contractile movement of the interior being," the amassed energy might flow anew, but this time spontaneously, triumphantly, to fill up the liberated expanses with his imaginings. Concentration and projection are the two complementary aspects of a thought that flexes itself in the instant in order to throw itself beyond the instant. Thus the Balzacian being begins his human adventure by darting forth into the infinite plains of the future. The future, "promised land upon which our eyes, brightened by celestial gleams, look down without encountering any horizon": [16]

> Almost all young men possess a compass with which they take delight in calculating the future; when their will is in accord with the boldness of the angle which they set, the world is theirs . . .
> I was measuring how long a thought needs in order to develop itself; and, compass in hand, standing upon a high crag, a hundred fathoms above the ocean, whose billows were sporting among the breakers, I was surveying my future, *furnishing it with works of art,* just as an engineer, upon an empty terrain, lays out fortresses and palaces. The sea was beautiful; I had just dressed after having swum . . . *To swim in the air*

after having swum in the sea! ah! who would not have *swum in the future*? Why was I thinking: how comes a misfortune? who knows? Ideas strike the heart or the head without consulting you. No courtesan had been more whimsical or more imperious than conception is for artists; one must seize it, like fortune, by the forelock, when it comes. Mounted upon my thought like Astolphe on his hippogriff, *I was riding across the world, disposing all in it to my liking.*[17]

Balzacian thought begins, then, by soaring in the sky or in the future, by "dashing itself into the future or into the sky," [18] by riding across a world whose expanses are as temporal as they are spatial; prodigious opening that man creates in the interior of himself, and which gapes and widens in order to become the field of the mind, the "milieu in which thought effects its evolutions." [19] To fly, to swim, to travel, to project, to rush forth, such are the analogous terms by which is expressed this first and a thousand times recommenced experience of creative thought. Like Louis Lambert, the Balzacian being "ceaselessly wings its way across the spaces of thought." [20] "His mind ceaselessly soars." [21]

And, at the very first, because these spaces are unconfined, the motion that traverses them is the happiest, the easiest, the speediest. "Oh! How beautiful is limitless space!" [22] If it is beautiful, that is because it has neither limits nor obstacles. Nothing impedes a thought that moves in itself, nothing slackens the speed of its flight. No bulkiness, no opacity, no resistance curbs its "velocity of mental vision." [23] To desire is to rush forth; and, by the same token, it is to offer to the multiple flight of its own thought, the interior field it discovers and traverses:

. . . Suddenly an idea bounds forth, leaps with the speed of lightning across the infinite spaces the perception of which is given us by our interior sight.[24]

The pleasure of swimming in a lake of pure water . . . would give the ignorant a feeble image of the happiness when my soul bathed itself in the gleams of I know not what light;

when I listened to the terrible and confused voices of inspiration, when from a source unknown the images streamed into my palpitating brain.[25]

Thus, like a streaming of images invading the "fields of thought," [26] there is accomplished for Balzac a primal possession of the world. It is not, as with Hugo, the feeling of being invaded by the anonymous flood of the forms of the imagination. It is rather the feeling of being at one and the same time the invader and the thing invaded, of being the act by which one projects and spreads out within oneself, in order to form out of the emptiness of one's thought an animated plenitude: ". . . life full, limpid and deep, like a tranquil and unknown lake in which millions of images are reflected . . ." [27] One is simultaneously a plenitude and a multitude, the space in which a world is reflected and also the movement by which this world spreads itself out. It is as if, as one and the same thing, we poured ourself into the outside world, and opened wide the sluice-gates of our brain in order to let the whole universe be engulfed therein. There is no longer any inwardness or outwardness. There is not here a subject that desires, and there an object external to this desire; there is instead an identification of the self and the world, which can as well be expressed under the form of an invasion of the world by the thought, as under that of an invasion of the thought by a world which, in pouring itself into the mind, rids itself of all exteriority:

> Marianine sank into a night deeper than that of the heavens, entered into the vast kingdom whose territory begins where that of the universe ends, that domain which no one penetrates except he be simultaneously *dead* and *living*, where man summons all nature to appear *outside of itself*, as if a mirror reflected its slightest secrets.[28]

> Have men the power to make the universe enter their brain, or is their brain a talisman with which they abolish the laws of time and space? [29]

"If the landscape," Lambert wonders, "did not come to me, which would be absurd to think, then I came to it." [30] If the world has not come to be reflected in me, then it is I who have invaded the world. In the movement of mind by which Balzac arrives instantaneously at making the inward and the outward coincide, there is, basically, nothing absurd in thinking that the outside becomes the inside or that the inside becomes the outside. I can as easily conceive myself as animated by a prodigious locomotive power, which allows me to join together immediately all the farthest points of the universe, as I can conceive myself invested with a reflective capacity which allows me to possess all the spaces of the universe in the extensionless point of my thought. I am always and everywhere where I wish to be. Everything is now simply an inner universe which my mind traverses in a flash. And this instantaneous possession of the universe by the human desire is no different from the desire of the angels in their celestial expanses. For the angelic spirit who, says Balzac, "commands motion and combines with everything by ubiquity," [31] all is "simultaneously sonorous, diaphanous, mobile; so that all things penetrate one another, space is without impediment and can be traversed by the Angels in the depths of the infinite." [32]

In these lines, already so purely Baudelairean in tone, as in the entire novel entitled *Séraphita,* Balzac has expressed his earliest experience, his experience of space. Space without obstacles and without distance, "upper abysses" [33] crossed and recrossed by desire in its pristine strength when it still retains its magical locomotive power. And this is no doubt what Balzac means, since he puts once again in Séraphita's mouth these words in which Swedenborgianism is combined with Claude de Saint-Martin's esoteric beliefs:

> In possessing the faculty of praying unweariedly, with love, with strength, with certitude, with intelligence, your spiritualized nature is soon invested with power. Like an impetuous

wind or like lightning, it traverses all and participates in the power of God. You have agility of spirit; in an instant you make yourself present in all the regions of earth, you are transported like the Word Itself from one end of the world to the other.[34]

To desire or to pray is no longer simply to collect or project oneself. To desire is to imagine, and to imagine is to possess. To the human being invested with such power or with such a locomotive faculty, space, time, forthwith are crossed over. One is where one is inclined to be, and then and there, without transition, without intermediary. To desire is immediately to be where one desires to be, instantaneously to be what one desires to be: "He desired as a poet imagines, as a scholar calculates, as a painter sketches, as a musician formulates his melodies . . . He hurled himself with an unprecedented violence, and by means of his thought, toward the thing wished for; he devoured time. In dreaming the accomplishment of his projects, he always suppressed the means of execution." [35]

II

If space exists, certain faculties bestow the power of crossing it with such swiftness that their effects are equivalent to its abolition. From thy bed to the confines of the world there are only two steps . . .[36]

. . . Man possesses the exorbitant faculty of annihilating, in relation to himself, space which exists only in relation to himself; of utterly isolating himself from the milieu in which he resides, and of crossing, by virtue of an almost infinite locomotive power, the enormous distances of physical nature; of extending his view over all Creation without meeting therein the obstacles by which he is stopped in his normal state . . .[37]

In the astonishing rapidity of his expansion, hardly has the Balzacian being discovered space than he forgets it: "His eye is unaware of space." [38] Bearing down upon its prey, overleaping in a flash the "enormous distances" which separate it from its object, the mind literally "leaves space behind it" [39] and has hardly any longer the time to see, between itself and what it desires, an expanse extending *ahead*. Space abolished is thus space transcended. Like light in the Newtonian universe, which, moving at infinite speed, takes no notice of the empty spaces it traverses and immediately reaches the object it illumines, Balzac's thought outdistances and denies the existence of that which separates it from what it thinks: "I leap over the intervals too rapidly; a thing perceived, I see the end of it; a reason advanced, I see the consequences of it . . ." [40] No interval then except an interval at once suppressed. Nothing could be more different from Mallarmean thought, which exists only in the feeling of the impassable transparency that separates it from the object dreamed of. Here, on the contrary, there is no window glass, no obstacle, no intermediate abyss. Or rather there is an abyss, but an abyss that is filling up, a penetrable, reducible space, which, instead of separating, brings together and unites: "For the man in such a state, distances or material objects do not exist, or are traversed by a life which is within us . . ." [41] There is no longer any space-distance, any space-obstacle; there is now only a transmitting milieu across which thought freely, instantaneously overtakes its object.

Besides, precisely by reason of the rapidity, the instantaneity of this conjunction, there is not simply abolition of the spatial distance, but also volatilization of the temporal distance: "The *energetic* or interior being perceives neither the time nor the space which impedes the exterior being . . ." [42] We have already seen with what facility this energetic being joined a future to his present. But it is not solely the future which he possesses and surveys. He as easily rejoins and peruses his past, all the pasts:

> He possessed all memories: those of places, of names, of words, of things and of faces. He not only recalled objects at will; he rebeheld them within himself, situated, lighted up, colored as they were in the moment he had perceived them. [43]

Balzacian memory is thus essentially voluntary and imaginative. Like anticipation, it permits free voyages in time; or, in the abolition of all intermediate duration, the instantaneous repossession of a far-off moment of life. Nothing is less Proustian than this possession of all times by an "energetic" being whose *action* is as easily directed toward the past as toward the future. It is "just as easily that things formerly perceived are faithfully reborn within him, beautiful or terrible with the primitive feelings of grace or horror which had seized him." [44] His power is even extended well beyond the personal past; it has a command of the historical past. Like Lambert, the Balzacian being can relive in spirit all the incidents of the battle of Austerlitz; like Vendramin, bring to life again the pageantry of ancient Venice; or, like Rubempré, at the moment of suicide, contemplate the walls of the palace of Saint Louis, reconstituted "in their original state." Like Melmoth he can say: "I read hearts, I see the future, I know the past. I am here and I have the power to be elsewhere! I am dependent upon neither time, nor space, nor distance. The world is my servant." [45]

A time upon which one is no longer dependent, a space from which one is set free, such is the interior distance that separates the dreamer from the object of his dreams. With Balzac there is never, as with Hugo or Proust, the feeling of restless sadness which man experiences at the idea of a "time" buried in the "dark coils" or in the "basements" of the past. One never finds him experiencing, as Gautier or Flaubert did, the nostalgia for the irrevocable; nor, with Baudelaire, the inverse feeling of the irreparable. Balzac is never obsessed or made ashamed by the idea of a time from which he should feel excluded. And if, in contrast to Walter Scott and in spite of numerous attempts, Balzac in the end renounces the writing of historical novels, it is not because the past seems inaccessible to him, but on the contrary because, like all the times, it appears to him to be at hand, and in full view, a sort of past without distance, without obscurity and without any secret, which, as a consequence, hardly differs from the present and so loses a good part of its power of fascination. But if he

is unaware of historical perspectives, if he is incapable of that
retrospective regard which searches in the depths for an object eternally veiled by distance, Balzac nonetheless possesses, and
to the very highest degree, the feeling for the past; a past not dissimilar from the future moreover, since he can transport himself
backward as instantaneously as he can project himself forward
into the future:

> There is only one single thing that gives me hours which are
> almost happy, that is to relive in thought certain past days
> which return with a surprising fidelity of impression and clar-
> ity of memory. Upon closing my eyes, I am there.[46]

Thus on every hand there opens up for Balzac a time that is
undifferentiated, reversible, without characteristic or exclusive-
ness, a time that can always be crossed. And occasionally the intoxication of voyaging through it and of swimming within it
finds with him accents similar to those of De Quincey:

> Did you ever launch yourself into the immensity of space and
> time while reading the geological works of Cuvier? Carried
> away by his genius, have you hovered over the boundless abyss
> of the past, as if upheld by the hand of an enchanter? [47]

The mind that "voyages over the vast fields of thought," [48] that
gives itself up "to the immense pleasure of moving without being
trammeled by the cords of time or by the shackles of space," [49]
thus espouses a time indifferently prospective and retrospective,
a time without obstacle or distance, and in no way different from
space. And in one sense Balzac's universe *is* this space-time, this
immensity forever traversed; but in another sense it is also the
movement which traverses it, and which in traversing it abolishes
it. Movement, no doubt, "cannot be conceived at all without
space," [50] yet it also suppresses space. In the whole work of Balzac nothing recurs so frequently as the proclamation of the annihilation of space-time by an act of mind:

> I already had in my power the most immense faith, that
> faith of which Christ spoke, that boundless will with which

one moves mountains, that great might by the help of which
we can abolish the laws of space and time . . .[51]

(Our inner nature) is an invisible creature so actively and
reactively sensitive, and endowed with faculties so extensive, so
perfectible by usage, or so powerful under the sway of certain
occult conditions, that [it can] by means of a phenomenon of
vision or locomotion, abolish space in its two modes of Time
and Distance, of which the one is intellectual space and the
other physical space.[52]

But look, the specialists of space and time, what will they say
with their categories? When in a dream the mind *in its little
space* or in its emptiness figures forth spaces that are immense,
does space then exist, where are its laws? When one flies in the
twinkling of an eye through terrifying distances, without the
body's having budged, without the laws of time being observed,
what becomes of the arguments founded on such and such a
property of time? What, the greatest is contained in the least?
and spaces, times disappear and are mutually swallowed up in
an infinite stronger than they.[53]

One would say then that for Balzac the disappearance of space-
time is accomplished by a kind of absorption. If the immense
spaces without become the little space within, in the last analysis
they no longer effect even the *appearance* of space, reabsorbed
as they are in the consciousness of the movement which traverses
them, of the interiority which is filled with them. All time, all
space are there, but reduced by intussusception to an internal
existence, condensed into the actuality of a thought which encloses them. All time, all space are there; *there,* that is to say in
the moment in which one thinks, in the place where one is in
process of thinking.

Time is devoured by the moment; space is absorbed by the
point.

Thus, "undergoing the effects of a mysterious optics which
enlarges, shrinks, exalts creation," [54] Balzacian thought, "so fluid,
so expansible, so contractile," [55] having first passed from concentration to dilatation, passes then from dilatation to concentration; for the mind "has the strange power to expand as well as

to contract space." [56] If then the point of departure is indeed
a point, that is to say a temporal and spatial center from which
the mind starts projecting itself eccentrically toward that which
it desires, then as soon as it has traversed these spaces, the mind
contracts and re-encloses itself in whatever it seeks. Then the
distance is suppressed and there is only an instantaneous possession of the object by the will.

The will nullifies distance and obtains everything in one moment of prodigious density.

To desire is to possess:

> In fact, does not desire constitute a kind of intuitive pos-
> session? [57]

> "A desire," he said, "is a fact entirely accomplished in our
> Will before existing exteriorly." [58]

Instantaneous fulfillment of an infinite desire, the Balzacian will
attains to a magical actuality, of a strength, a brightness, a lux-
uriance unheard of:

> Imagine a sublime creation in which the visible marvels of
> creation are reproduced with a grandioseness, a lightness, a
> rapidity, an extensiveness that are incommensurable, in which
> sensations are infinite . . .[59]

> Instead of flowing a long while between two monotonous
> banks, in the backwaters of a counting-house or a lawyer's
> chambers, existence boils up and flies like a torrent.[60]

> . . . Sublime paroxysm of the aroused intelligence, during
> which to the agonies of childbirth there succeed the pleasures
> of cerebral overexcitement.[61]

> . . . Interior view whose swift perceptions bring one by one
> into the mind, as upon a canvas, the most contrasting land-
> scapes of the globe . . .[62]

Under the pressure of creative desire, Balzacian thought becomes a gushing forth of a plurality of images that are crowded
together in the narrow stratum of the brain and overlap each
other:

. . . I think of a thousand different things that fly on the wings of the imagination with so swift a confusion that I am unable to stop.[63]

. . . Inspiration unrolls for the poet transfigurations without number and similar to the magic phantasmagoria of our dreams.[64]

Stunning multiplicity which, in the fever of inspiration as under the action of stimulants, makes of the mind a sort of atom of space and of time in the interior of which durations crowd together, great expanses spread out, universes whirl round:

These immense savannas, where monuments were pressed together like men in a mob, overcrowded their narrow brains where empires, cities, revolutions unrolled and passed away within a few hours! [65]

How many events are pressed into the space of a second! . . .[66]

. . . I who make a hundred years of existence fit into a single night . . .[67]

. . . In a small space the appalling accumulation of a whole world of thoughts.[68]

One makes of a second an eternity . . .[69]

Thus Balzacian thought, born of a universal desire, tends to realize itself in a kind of simultaneous creation of all its objects. "The problem of life is not its duration, but the quality, the diversity, the number of its sensations." [70] To be is to live ecstatically in the instantaneous multiplicity of one's imaginings.

III

He took leave of real life, ascended by degrees toward an ideal world, arrived at the enchanted palaces of Ecstasy where the universe appeared to him piecemeal and as it were in strokes of fire, as once the future passed flaming before the eyes of Saint John on Patmos.

A multitude of pain-wracked faces, gracious and terrible, obscure and lucid, remote and near at hand, rose up by masses, by myriads, by generations.[71]

The "factitious universe" which thought creates for itself, "just as youthful fancy creates a mistress for itself," [72] thus deploys itself fantastically in the instant, only to transform immediately the instant's pleasure into pain. Ecstasy is excess, and excess is disorder and suffering. One suddenly feels "sick of all these human thoughts"; [73] and the actual moment, inordinately strained, bending down under the weight of all times and places, heavily encumbered by all the forms of life, finds itself overwhelmed by the very profusion of its own imaginings, "impeded by forms springing up, which, like the monsters produced by the footsteps of some evil genie, endlessly give the mind battle." [74]

One would say that with Balzac (as with De Quincey, whom he imitates) the imaginative power in a way exceeds its object, all its objects, and that in a kind of hideous drunkenness the mind in its turn finds itself overrun and swallowed up by the very universe it once devoured. Balzac's desire no longer takes possession of the world; it is the world that takes possession of him and carries him off: "I was prey to a throng of reflections . . . My thinking faculty turns like the carriage wheel which bears me along; it mounts to I know not what fantastic region, leaping over all the frontiers of common sense." [75] Beyond the frontiers of the imaginable, even beyond all conceivable forms, the mind discerns with horror spaces more vast and durations even more profound. If it "suffocates under the debris of fifty vanished centuries," [76] if it "conceives the past of the universe as a sort of retrograde Apocalypse," [77] on the other hand it "sees by anticipation the bones of twenty worlds." [78] Pasts and futures are heaped up together, in disorder, in ruin, in "bits and scraps and spurts of fire," in a depth of confusion which in the final analysis "obliterates itself within its own darkness." [79]

> Thus I envelop the world with my thought, I mold it, I fashion it, I penetrate it, I comprehend it or think I comprehend it; but suddenly I wake up alone and find myself in the midst of the depths of a dark night . . .[80]

At the farthest limit of the "creation in the void," [81] there is thus again the presence of the void. Mind, conqueror of space, is reconquered by space. Thought, left to itself, is a "force without equilibrium," [82] a power of projection which, not being stopped by anything, traverses everything, and finally loses itself in an imageless night. Desire, "that king of creation," [83] annihilates all creation: "Extreme heat, extreme misery, complete unhappiness, all the absolute principles reign over spaces stripped of all produce; these absolutes wish to be alone; everything that is not themselves they choke to death." [84]

Thus the creation of the world by human desire ends in a destruction of the world, in a frantic creation of a void. It is "work and execution destroyed by a too great abundance of the creative principle . . ." [85] It is "the suicide of art." [86]

But it is also the suicide of life. If the man of desire sees his factitious world vanish into nothingness, he also feels "his own life diminish by very reason of the strength of his desires or the lavish dissipation of his ideas." [87] All desire is "a prodigious loss of fluid." [88]—"I feel myself losing my forces and faculties which, inordinately strained, collapse." [89] —"I feel that life is abandoning me, that the vital fluid is failing me." [90]—"Can one live very long if he eats away his own life every hour?" [91] Such is the anguished cry that rises to the lips of the Balzacian being when he sees his own life flowing away like water from "an emptied pitcher," [92] like "the water from a vase that has been knocked over." [93] Sometimes it is the consciousness of a "successive diminution of strength which is like unto death"; and sometimes the dizziness of a "sudden thunderbolt." [94] But in any case it is always the feeling of an existence that is shrinking, of a duration that is drying up, of a narrowing and a constricting of strength which is already the pang of death. No one more than Balzac has actually lived in the instant; no one more than he, tasted the intoxication there is in pouring all the energies of being into the instant; but neither did anyone see more clearly than he the folly of exchanging his share of human duration for the mess of pottage of a single moment of power ecstatically complete. A moment that blazes up and is consumed by a sort of "instantaneous combustion." [95]

> . . . There is such a combination of thought as in less than a minute makes of a healthy man a corpse.[96]

> Our heart is a treasure, empty it at one stroke, you are ruined.[97]

Ruined, worn down, the Balzacian character survives the instant's destruction only to sink into a moral apathy. In such a case desire is nothing more than a feeling without efficacy, in which, "eaten away by a consuming demon," [98] one sorrowfully rediscovers that absolute distance which separates him from that which he desires:

> Who could depict this purely corporeal languor into which the abuse of dreamed-of pleasures plunges us, and which leaves still within the soul its eternal desire, and in the mind its pure faculties. But I am weary of this torment which makes me understand that of Tantalus.[99]

There is nothing more tragic than this rediscovery of space, no longer under the appearance of a conveying medium in which one soars or swims, but under the aspect of an impassable gulf, beyond which one can only glance covetously and in vain. Thus, for instance, the miser who robbed himself in his sleep, searches through the void, as through the Mallarmean window, for the treasure which he buried in a place of which he has lost all memory:

> He often remained standing for entire hours, casting his eyes on everything at once, plunging them into the void. Soliciting the miracles of ecstasy and the power of sorcerers, he tried to see his riches across spaces and obstacles. He was constantly lost in an insupportable thought, devoured by a desire that consumed his entrails . . . He possessed and did not possess his treasures; entirely new, entirely strange torture, but continuously terrible.[100]

Finally, then, the miser differs in no way from the prodigal
and incurs the same punishment as he. Because, having desired,
he has dissipated. He also finds himself empty-handed. Every
squanderer of energy experiences the same "enraged awakening:
impotence attends his bed." [101] An impotence, a powerlessness
which is always revealed by the same metamorphosis of fullness
into emptiness, of life strength into attrition of body and soul:

> "This battle with men and with things," said Savarus, "to
> which I have incessantly turned my strength and my energy,
> for which I have so completely used up the springs of desire,
> has, so to speak, undermined me interiorly. Though keeping
> the appearance of strength, of health, I feel myself ruined.
> Each day tears away another shred of my inmost life." [102]

The sense of time is thus as grievously altered as that of space.
It is no longer a time which opens up and through which one
soars; it is instead a time which closes down and through which
one staggers along towards death. In its furious ardor, the Balzacian existence has passed without transition, so to speak, from
adolescence to senility. Thus the existence of Lambert,

> centenarian of twenty-five years, already old with thoughts,
> used up by centuries of reflections, lost through the moral en-
> joyment of all the human pleasures perceived without the
> body's being an accomplice in them, otherwise than being
> ruined by the abuse of thought.[103]

In face of the void, in face of death, seized by apathy, separated from a world it possessed only to lose, the being now finds
itself again alone with its desire. It thirsts, but "thirsts in the
midst of the desert." [104]

IV

> Then one day when I had need of restoring my brain in-
> jured by too great a wastage of thoughts, I went out . . . .[105]

Adventure most common, sentence most ordinary, but one
which all the same we could inscribe at the beginning of every
Balzacian novel, for the Balzacian novel exists only from the mo-

ment when the hero, deciding to leave home, goes forth "to wander, to seek, to become living drama, to risk his life." [106]

Adventure most important then, and the very pivot of the
whole of *La Comédie humaine.* As we have seen, in the adven-
tures of interior thought, a Louis Lambert, a Victor Morillon,
a Raphaël de Valentin clasp, in the final analysis, only the ghost
of a world, and their desire goes astray and exhausts itself in aim-
less solitudes. But when one comes out of one's home and out of
oneself, when one quits the prodigious and factitious mental universe of one's own room, one finds oneself on a street with pav-
ing-stones, trees, and passers-by. All that one meets there has now
the particularity of having a body, made of a certain matter, not
easily penetrable, occupying, at a greater or lesser distance, a
place in a space that has its own laws, exterior space. As a consequence, the being who ventures into broad daylight, into the
real, passes into a world in which all the conditions of existence
have changed. He is always a being of desire, but he grapples
now with something more than his desires. Everything is still
offered to his avidity, but everything also refuses to yield to
his avidity. He is in a world of resisting objects, opaque, and
separated from him and from each other by measurable distances, by veils of matter. His thought is no longer an inner
vision, the mirror in which a universe is reflected; it is no longer
all that his mind thinks or desires; it is only now thought of
what is seen, desire of that which is perceived. The being who
leaves home and takes his desire for a stroll into the real, will
no longer now encounter a total desire, but the precise object
which, met on his way, arresting his gaze, will determine his
action.

> In the burning desert of its infinite and objectless desires,
> does not youth train all its forces upon the first woman who
> presents herself? [107]

The first adventure, then, that one encounters in the sphere
of reality is the adventure of passion. But in itself passion is no

different from interior desire. Because it is also essentially voluntary, passion, like interior desire, is a concentration and a projection of the forces of the spirit. However, from the moment the object and the final aim of desire are found to be situated outside, everything changes its nature; and the center toward which the powers of being converge, being no longer situated within, is no longer a point of departure from which man spreads and disperses himself eccentrically in a void, but the tangible and certain center toward which, outside himself, he is going to direct his action. Instead of "generously scattering his life and his feelings among the sham images of a plastic and empty nature," [108] he now "does not scatter the forces of his mind; he concentrates them on a sole idea"; [109] and that idea is a concrete idea, an outward object he covets and to which he aspires: "It is *thou* whom I desire." [110] Who does not sense in the brutality of this brief phrase a new tone, one not to be compared to that of the frenzies to which the desires of the imagination give themselves over? There is in it an express knowledge of the being desired as *other*, a being exterior to oneself, coveted and desired by oneself; a being which one must treat as a personal enemy because, by reason of its very otherness, it affirms its independence, it refuses and resists: "It seems to me a proved fact, therefore, that under the sway of passion, which is the will gathered to one point . . . , man can bring to bear his entire vitality, whether for attack or for resistance." [111] All passion is a duel that implies a double attack and a double resistance. For the being whom one desires and whom one attacks is also the one who attacks you in inspiring in you this desire, and in order to resist there is no other means than to triumph over his resistance. Hence, in passion, there is no longer simply an isolated subject that triumphs illusorily over factitious objects. There are two beings engaged in a hand-to-hand fight which makes each of them experience the reality of the enemy against whom the desire runs counter:

The Movement, by reason of the resistance, produces a combination which is life.[112]

Every passion is then not only concentration upon a being, but violent projection towards and against a being, in order to attain, in order to penetrate, in order to possess it:

> With what violence my desires mounted toward her! How many times I asked myself, as a madman repeats his refrain:— Shall I have her? If during the preceding days the universe had become vaster for me, in a single night it had a center. My wishes and my ambitions attached themselves to her.[113]

> Let us examine your state; you are young, your faculties are great and beautiful, their strength is incalculable, you have directed them all toward one selfsame goal, toward one point, increased and made strong one by another they form an amalgam of violent desires . . . What is the remedy? Is it in you? No . . . Then the remedy lies outside of you . . . It is therefore unquestionable that the possession of Sténie is the sole means of preserving you.[114]

> I felt that strong will to possess, that imperious need of the mind and the senses . . . It was in this lapse of time that I had interiorly sworn that I would not die without being satisfied! Call it a crime, an attempt at crime, tell me that I am no longer virtuous, everything disappears before my invincible desire, it is no longer love, it is a fierce rage; I love as Sylla had to love . . .[115]

> . . . I hold out my arms to you, I desire you! Immense gulfs separate us! . . . No matter, I leap to seize and savor you as prey! [116]

But in order to seize his prey, man who is in external space must first overtake it. Before conquering and possessing the enemy, he must first conquer and possess those "immense gulfs" which separate us from it.

In his impassioned invasion of the outside, the Balzacian being discovers the gap. The desired object is situated, across the distances, in its own particular place, which must be reached. Then under the effect of concentrated passion, the man of desire is forced to fill up that interval, to extend his being to that very

object. It is no longer an easy dreamlike gliding over the length
of "an ideal road." It is a real projection, outward, of energies
which ordinarily spread and are expended within. And this first
manifests itself by an exterior radiation, the apparition of a sort
of aura which, exhaled by the body seems to dilate it in percep-
tibly extending its effectual force. Many a time Balzacian characters assist in the electric discharge of this vapor of ideas:

> Whence comes that flame that shines about a woman in love
> and singles her out from all the rest? . . . Is it the soul es-
> caped? [117]

> The smoke of the fire that ravaged her seemed to ripple out
> of crevices ripped open by a volcanic eruption.[118]

> The man whose mind acts with force is like a poor glow-
> worm which, without knowing it, lets light escape from all its
> pores. He moves in a brilliant sphere where each effort brings
> about a flash of the gleaming light and delineates his move-
> ments by long tracks of fire.[119]

> Often the most stupid human being manages, under the
> effort of passion, to arrive at the highest eloquence in the idea,
> whether or not in the language, and seems to move in a lumi-
> nous sphere.[120]

Beyond his being, beyond his body, by glance, by voice, by
gesture, by all the means of physical or occult transmission, the
man of desire, hurling forth his will, "produces a veritable atmosphere about himself." [121] It is as if exterior space were filled up,
or rather as if it were composed, as in the theories of Herschel,
of a plenum made up of an "ethereal substance, without weight,
diffused everywhere," [122] across which, by undulations, the feelings propagate themselves:

> In fact, if, as the finest analytical genius has said, the
> geometrician who has hearkened most to God at the gates of
> the sanctuary, the bullet of a pistol fired on the shore of the
> Mediterranean causes a motion that is felt as far as the coasts
> of China, is it not probable that, if we project outside of our-
> selves an extravagance of force, we must either change the con-
> ditions of the atmosphere about us, or necessarily influence,

by the effects of that live force which seeks its place, the beings and the things with which we are surrounded? [123]

Space is then invadable. Like sound and light, desires and thoughts propagate and propel themselves by waves, and therein subsist with a perceptible life:

> Feeling imprints itself on all things and traverses all space.[124]

Thus, just as bodies really project themselves in the atmosphere, leaving to subsist there that specter seized by the daguerreotype which arrests it in passage; in the same way ideas, real and active creations, impress themselves upon what must be called the atmosphere of the spiritual world, produce effects within it, live there *spectrally* . . .[125]

There is nothing more striking in Balzac than this luminous invasion of the surrounding milieu by the magnetic fluid of desire:

> . . . Never had rendezvous more highly excited his senses, brought to light bolder sensual pleasures, or better occasioned the bursting forth of love from his center to be diffused as an atmosphere all around.[126]

> . . . And the indefinable empire of which the stranger was, unknown to himself perhaps, the principle and the effect, diffused itself about him with the progressive rapidity of an inundation. A torrent of thoughts flowed from his brow . . .[127]

> What incantation seized hold of me? The most subtle substances in my being were set in motion; an emanation lovely as the arc of a rainbow flowed from Sténie and surrounded me; is there then not a phenomenon between us two? [128]

But of all the passages in which Balzac described the translation of desire, there is none more astonishing than that in which the painter Sarrasine, without budging, solely by the projected force of his will across the whole length of a playhouse, draws near to the point of touching the object of his passion:

> Sarrasine wanted to rush upon the stage and possess himself of this woman. His strength, multiplied a hundredfold by a moral depression impossible to explain, since these phenomena occur in a sphere inaccessible to human observation, tended to project itself with a painful violence . . . He was

so completely drunk that he no longer saw the room, the spectators, or the actors, no longer heard the music. Much more, *no distance existed* between him and the Zambinella, he possessed her, his eyes fastened upon her and mastered her. An almost diabolical power allowed him to feel the breath of that voice, to smell the scented powder with which her hair was sprinkled, to see the planes of that face, to count there the blue veins that shaded that skin as soft as velvet.[129]

"No distance existed . . ." But who couldn't help noticing that here abolition of distance is no longer the instantaneous annihilation of an unreal space by the free decree of the imagination, but rather the progressive reduction to nothingness of a rigorously actual space by, as it were, a physical operation of the will. One sees literally accomplished that suppression of distances, this unprecedented drawing close to the object by the enlarging power of a vision that is magnified a hundredfold. Desire becomes a magic opera glass, by the help of which, despite distance, the gaze and its object have succeeded in pressing themselves close one to another, like bodies.

Thus the will is a telescope. It is also a microphone. It conquers distance by the prodigious development of hearing. It is thus, thanks to "the power with which an impassioned creature often knows how to abolish space in order to be united with its other self," [130] that Claës's wife hears far away the sound of her husband's footsteps. Or again, it is less an abolition of space than of the objects which encumber or obstruct it; for one sees, despite people chattering four-deep, and in the general buzz and hum of a gambling hall, Raphaël de Valentin, "by a privilege accorded the passions which gives them the power of annihilating space and time," [131] become capable of distinctly hearing the words of the players, and of knowing which of the two turns up the king.

Passion is thus a sort of infinite multiplier of the sensorial power. And it even goes beyond that, by occult sympathies, by telepathic transmissions of thought. One dies in Normandy the

moment one's son is shot down in the Morbihan. One feels pain
in his own limb when his loved one "suffers injury there." [132]
Like Vautrin, one *knows* at a distance, "in spite of distances," [133]
that Lucien is in danger. The whole of *La Comédie humaine* is
filled with "phenomena of moral paternity," [134] with "sympathies
which do not recognize the laws of space." [135] The Balzacian
world, like the terrestrial universe, is enwrapped in a perceptible
atmosphere which transmits intersecting influences. Sometimes
space is therein revealed under the form of a milieu in which
mutually hostile desires cross each other; and it is then, like a
double flash of lightning, the engagement, at a distance, of two
wills, endowed both the one and the other with a mysterious
thrust, with a "forth and back flexibility" [136] comparable to that
of two duelists whose swords seek each other out and interlock.
And then again, as in the beams of searchlights aiming from
all sides at one spot besieged by enemy forces, there is discovered
a space that is riddled with convergent desires, at the center of
which a victim finds himself caught. Everywhere in Balzac there
are to be distinguished "certain forces that tend one toward
another by a generating movement"; [137] and everywhere "the
life of worlds is drawn toward certain centers by starved aspira-
tions." [138]

But in the Balzacian universe there is not solely the spectacle
of the motion by which desire moves towards its objects. The
translation of desire is the translation of an influence. To the
effusion of desire outside of itself into space, there corresponds
the infusion in the being from whom one is separated. "Ideas
are projected as a direct result of the force by which they are
conceived and they strike wherever the brain sends them by a
mathematical law comparable to that which directs the firing
of shells from their mortars." [139] It is thus that, "illumined by
the fires of his paternal passion," [140] Goriot succeeds in strangely
agitating the being of Rastignac. It is thus that the music into
which Ursule Mirouet "pours the feelings which disturb her"

speaks to the soul of her fiancé and "envelops him as in a cloud with ideas that are almost visible." [141] And it is indeed in the very same way that the "powerfully projected" will of a soldier isolated in the desert with a panther "succeeds in modifying the character of his female companion." [142] There is not one of the great strong-willed characters in the Balzacian novel who does not compel us to witness a hundred times this imposition from a distance of his magnetic will:

> It seems then that there is sent forth from the brain and carried by the word an invincible influence, that each gesture injects the will of the man into others.[143]

> This flash of intelligence and of will was like lightning and sounded like thunder.[144]

Unremittingly in the Balzacian novel there is the visible exercise of a "communicative power." [145] Thanks to a sort of "contagion of feelings," [146] it transmits from one person to another, overleaping physical space, the suggestions of the will. There is no finer example of this than in that scene in *Albert Savarus:*

> Rodolphe, leaning against the door frame, watched the Princess with a fixed, persistent and piercing glance, attractive and charged with all the human will concentrated in that feeling called *desire,* but which in such a case takes on the character of a violent commandment. Did the flame of that look reach Francesca? Did Francesca expect any moment to see Rodolphe? After a few minutes she glanced at the door, as if drawn by that current of love, and her eyes, without faltering, plunged themselves into the eyes of Rodolphe. A slight shudder agitated that magnificent face and that beautiful body; the shock of the mind was reacting! [147]

A marvelously Balzacian passage, first of all because therein one can seize upon, without the slightest metaphorical nuance, and consequently under the most naive and pure form, the translating action which, reaching across the physical world, realizes what one could call the mystery of Balzacian intersubjectivity; and, in the second place, because this action is essentially and entirely dramatic; we are present in it, we follow it on its journey, we feel the distances traversed, we perceive the shock it produces, the flame which it kindles when it meets its object. No one as well as Balzac has known how to render so physically perceptible the action, at a distance, of human beings empassioned by one another.

V

> The approach of an extraordinary event is foreseen; it announces itself and lays hold upon one before it occurs.
> . . . The mind of man experiences indefinable motions when it is about to receive strong impressions; it *feels from afar*.[148]

> Has moral nature, then, like physical nature, its electric communications and its rapid changes of temperature? My heart palpitated at the approach of secret events which must change it forever, just as animals perk up at the prospect of fine weather.[149]

Thus under the action of impassioned desire there is a metamorphosis of time analogous to that of extent. For, in *La Comédie humaine,* what appears to be the lived time of impassioned beings is neither the totality of existence which the anticipatory imagination instantaneously embraced, nor the narrow actuality, ignorant of the future, forgetful of the past which is the time of beings without passion as without imagination. Here, on the contrary, is an alert, impatient present which goes forward to meet the instant that is going to replace it. Rushing toward his destiny, the Balzacian character sees his destiny rushing toward him. It is like a gap that is filling up, a temporal distance which ceaselessly diminishes. One would call it the coursing of a planet and a sun to a meeting with one another, avid of producing, in a sort of *end of time,* a triumphal conflagration. And so present and future no longer appear as two radically different entities, of which one comprises all that is, and the other all that which is to come. The present wills itself future; the future wills itself present. There is a double effort which seems to set out from the farthest regions of duration, from the anteriority of the efficient cause, and from the posteriority of the final cause, in order to suppress the temporal interval which exists between what man is and what he wishes to be, in order to confound the time of desire and the time of assuagement in a moment of consuming actuality. Human duration becomes the contracting distance that separates the projectile from its object. On the horizon of the great Balzacian personages there looms unceasingly larger an ardent and obsessive image, in whose flame they shall end by losing themselves, the image of their joy and of their death.

As a consequence, somewhat in the fashion of the *Liaisons dangereuses,* the Balzacian novel often appears as a project and projection toward the future. It is the act of a thought that loves to "suck up its honey in advance," [150] and that *sees* less what is happening than it *foresees* what is to be. Everywhere in *La Comédie humaine* one finds these magic moments in which a certain future, big with promise or menace, appears at the end of a straight line, the length of which the human being travels without hesitation:

> Strange power of an idea or of a desire! Nothing seemed impossible to these two beings. In those magical moments when pleasure cast its reflections into the future, the mind could foresee only happiness.[151]

But it involves also other "magical moments," during which what surges up in the consciousness of the being, to whom passion gives "sudden revelations of our destiny," [152] is a premonition of the unhappiness to which it is destined and dedicated:

> In the aspect of the young man, Michu sensed a prophetic prostration of this kind. He was seized by a mortal presentiment; he confusedly caught a glimpse of the scaffold.[153]

But in the Balzacian world it is the women especially who have these "presentiments the precision of which is so marvelous." [154] It is they who have the "sudden warnings, the unquiet hallucinations of the mothers," [155] all the "effects of second sight which true passion confers." [156] Thus, when she is near d'Arthez, Madame de Maufrigneuse becomes capable of "reading his future in a simple gesture." [157] Thus—a more striking example because therein one sees rise up from the depths of a completely temporal horizon the vision of the future—Marguerite Claës after her quarrel with her father:

> When he had disappeared, Marguerite remained in a stupor which had the effect of isolating her from the earth, she was no longer in the parlor, she no longer had a sense of her body, she had wings and flew through the moral spaces of the world where all is immense, where thought draws together distances and times, where some divine hand lifts the vast veil of the future. It seemed to her that entire days elapsed between each of the steps of her father as he climbed the stairs; then she had a shudder of horror the moment she heard him enter his room. Impelled by a presentiment which flashed through her mind with the poignant clarity of a stroke of lightning, she leapt noiselessly up the dark stairs with the speed of an arrow, and beheld her father, who was aiming a pistol at his forehead.[158]

"Poetry of prophecy," [159] which brusquely illumines with a fatal light the feminine minds of the Balzacian world, for "passion summons up the nervous forces of woman to that ecstatic state in which presentiment is tantamount to the *vision of the Seers*." [160]—Or again, to the *vision of the dying*. It is indeed significant that Balzac calls the "poetry of prophecy" the "gift of clear sight, *before* or *behind*," which is given "to the dying, whose flesh only is destroyed." [161] Death, like passion, is one of those moments in which, in the condensation of its nervous forces, the human being can attain, like Madame de Mortsauf, Pons, or Goriot, to a superior and, as it were, supratemporal knowledge of its whole life. For the dying one comprehends himself in his past as the being of desire hurtles himself forward into his future. In Balzac's mind, therefore, the human being is by no means split or dissociated into three distinct knowledges, of the past, of the present, and of the future. Essentially composed of desire, if he tends to one end, if he gives himself over to his future, it is because this desire pre-existed in germ in the roots and in the anteriority of his will:

> In yielding himself up to the Marquise, Charles was being obedient to one of those pre-existing texts of which our experience and the conquests of our mind are only, later, the perceptible developments.[162]

The existence of the Balzacian personage is an obedience, a fidelity of the future to the past, and of desire to itself; desire which is behind being in order to press it forward, and ahead of it in order to draw it forward.

And so the duration of the Balzacian personage has something of the Aristotelian duration. It is a *becoming,* which goes from the past to the future, continually drawing together potency and actualization; while above this becoming there reigns, like a sort of nontemporal permanence, the constant, substantial form of the *fixed idea.* A passion, always similar to itself, presides on high over its accomplishments.

But despite its premonitions or its returns upon itself, it is rare that the Balzacian being perceives the whole "harsh fixity" [163] of the destiny that directs and awaits it. Living continuously "under the power of an idea," [164] reduced thereby to "a horrible vassalage," [165] it does but seldom possess consciousness of its state. It is not aware how much its life and its duration are constituted by the "constant triumph of the unique thought." [166] There are therefore two Balzacian durations. There is, on the one hand, for the reader of *La Comédie humaine,* as for the spectator at the tragedies of Racine, the feeling of an inflexible continuity, of a destiny already entirely accomplished in idea before being accomplished in act; on the other hand, there is in the mind of the character a sort of turbid actuality in whose eddies the idea of the future becomes many a time confounded with that of the past in which that future pre-existed, if only obscurely.

This explains, for example, the explosion of desire in Nucingen at the sight of Esther:

> He allowed himself to be led like a child . . . This sudden breaking forth of childhood in the heart of an old shark, is one of the social phenomena that physiology can more easily explain. Compressed under the weight of affairs, stifled by continual calculations, by the perpetual preoccupations of the chase after millions, adolescence with its sublime illusions reappears, and bursts forth, like a causal principle, like a forgotten seed, whose effects, whose splendid blossoms are obedient to chance, to a sun that breaks through and shines tardily.[167]

More often still, the moment of passion becomes completely impregnated at one and the same time with the future and the past, with memory and with hope. "Hope," a Balzacian character says with profundity, "is a memory that desires." [168] And the culminating instants of passion are those in which the actual emotion is charged and swollen with a double weight of memories and hopes. Then "one triples present felicity with aspiration for the future and recollections of the past." [169]

> What surprises me more every day, is the activity love gives to life. What interest hours, actions, the smallest things take on! and what admirable confusion of the past, of the future, in the present! One lives in the three tenses of the verb.[170]

And especially that page on which Balzac is perhaps inspired by a famous passage from *Adolphe*:

> In love, as in everything perhaps, there are certain facts which are insignificant in themselves but the result of a thousand little anterior circumstances, and whose import becomes immense in recapitulating the past, in tying in with the future. One has felt a thousand times the value of the person loved. But some nothing, the perfect contact of souls united in a stroll by a word, by an unexpected proof of love, carries the feeling to its highest degree. Finally, in order to express this moral fact by an image which, since the world's first age, has had the most undeniable success: there are, in a long chain, certain necessary *connecting points* in which the cohesion is more profound than in the mere concatenation of links. That recognition between Rodolphe and Francesca, during that

evening, before the world, was one of those *supreme points* which bind the future to the past . . .[171]

Admirable passage, and in truth one of those supreme points toward which almost everywhere in the work of Balzac, as in a symphony of Beethoven, or in the brain of César Birotteau, one sees that "all the powerful musical tones have converged." [172] For desire incessantly tends to transform itself into ecstasy, and if, on the other hand, ecstasy is an essential connecting point in the long ringed chain of existence, on the other hand it is also an extreme point, in which feeling, suddenly carried to the highest degree, seems to detach itself from all the other points of duration in order to live for itself alone in a blazing and purely instantaneous life. This apparent contradiction between the continuity of a passion, of which the moment of ecstasy is only the most condensed expression, and the discontinuity of the impassioned *tempo*, in which the rhythm, by a sudden *fortissimo*, passes to a maximum of intensity and celerity, is one of the phenomena one meets most frequently in the Balzacian novel. It produces a sort of sudden leap in the rigorously linear development of destiny, as if the character, under the pressure of events, decided all at once, not to change existence, but to live more swiftly, more intensely, and to plunge itself more deeply into the course of destiny. One would say that the mind collects all its strength in order the faster to project itself towards its end:

> In an instant cousin Bette had become herself again. In an instant, that character of the Corsican and the Savage, having broken the feeble bonds that curbed it, had resumed its menacing level, as a tree escapes from the hands of the child who has pulled it down to him in order to steal its raw fruits.[173]

> With the convict and with the duchess it was the same phenomenon. This woman, beaten, dying . . . , suddenly recovered the strength of a lioness at bay and the presence of mind of a general under fire.[174]

> The human will returned with its electrical torrents and vivified that body from which it had been absent so long.[175]

The will returns, as from its source water that had disappeared; it infuses itself through the structure prepared for the play of its constitutive, unknown substance; and then the cadaver becomes man, and the man, filled with strength, hurls himself into the supreme struggle.[176]

In unhappiness, in danger, in ecstasy, the impassioned person *finds himself once again* in the present such as he promised to *become* in the past. It seems that he rejoins himself at a bound. Or rather, it is as if, beyond a slow duration in which the being lingers and lets himself be outrun by his desire, he hurls himself into a mobile moment, extraordinarily rapid, in which the speed of the man and the speed of the passion coincide, in which the being finally adheres totally to the passion in order the better to rush toward his future.

In such a case this moment appears as a generative point, from which being and passion spread throughout time:

> Both of them, during this swift instant, experienced one of those lively commotions whose effects on the mind can be compared to those produced by a stone thrown into the depths of a lake. The most pleasant reflections arise and succeed one another, undefinable, multiplied, purposeless, agitating the heart like the circular ripples that disturb the water a long time after leaving the point where the stone fell.[177]

From this point of view, there is no more extraordinary passage than that in which Madame de Langeais sees Montriveau again. It must be cited in its entirety:

> The general marched past nearly beneath her in all the splendor of that military costume the effect of which on the feminine imagination is confessed by even the most prudish of persons. For a woman deeply in love, who had not seen her lover for two months, must not that swift moment have resembled that phase of our dreams when, fugitively, our view embraces a nature without horizon? Only women or young men can imagine the stupid and delirious avidity which the eyes of the duchess expressed. As for grown men, if, during their youth, they experienced, in the paroxysm of their first passions, these phenomena of the nervous force, later they for-

get them so completely that they come to deny those luxuriant ecstasies, the only name possible for such magnificent intuitions. Religious ecstasy is the madness of thought disengaged from its corporal bands; while in amorous ecstasy, the forces of both our natures confound, unite and embrace themselves. When a woman is prey to the furious tyrannies to which Madame de Langeais submitted, definitive resolutions succeed themselves so rapidly it is impossible to take account of them. Then thoughts arise one from another and careen through the mind like clouds carried away by the wind over a greyish depth that veils the sun.[178]

A marvelous passage, perhaps the finest in all the work of Balzac, which commands unreserved love, even in the comical sentences of its beginning. As in the Leibnitzian monadism, everything is disposed under the aspect of a point of force, of a condensation of the entire existence in a unique moment, which *replaces* duration, since pure actuality abolishes all virtuality; a unique moment, so charged, however, with generative power, that, starting from it, with a sort of profusion, time itself recommences, but like a torrent that flows away, as the water behind a dam drains out when the dikes are broken and a free space suddenly opens to receive the crumbling effusion. And this new time, which seems to be fulgurated by the moment of ecstasy, is on the one hand the successiveness of thoughts which "arise one from another"; but it is also the field they invade, the immensity of a "nature without horizon." A temporal, prospective field, identical to space, an unlimited expanse which the impassioned being discovers with astonishment before him, when grown impatient of advancing through life at the ordinary pace, he decides to reject every other interest save that of his own passion, to make of himself and of the world a sort of *tabula rasa* for passion. Then every scruple, every adventitious preoccupation, disappears. Space and time are no more than a naked depth which a sole thought inhabits or tumultuously traverses:

What am I going to do? Far, far away, reason, rules, the limits of the arts; I begin to see an immense space lighted

with a new fire . . . My friend, I cannot cope with the violence
of the torrent.[179]

> . . . She was reaching that degree of desire in which every-
> thing becomes indifferent; she was arriving at that moment
> so lofty that one is aware of neither laws, nor times, nor the
> earth; that moment, finally, when one is alone with him whom
> one loves, when all has disappeared except herself and him.[180]

In the abolition of all that is not desire, earth and times
and laws, all the concrete presences of material reality disappear
like the vapors of a dream:

> In feeling the sting of a higher voluptuousness, he was car-
> ried away *beyond the limits* within which he had until then
> imprisoned passion.[181]

No doubt these borders crossed are the laws of the real world,
laws which constitute or guarantee its solidity, its density, its
capacity for resisting the forces of the spirit. In the excess of his
passion, the monomaniac breaks out of the real as one breaks
through a paper hoop. Beyond those limits there is no longer
either time or space; unless it be the emptiness of "imaginary
spaces": [182]

> I tell you, Pauline, I have remained for whole hours in a
> stupor caused by the violence of my passionate wishes, re-
> mained lost in the feeling of a caress as in a bottomless abyss.
> In those moments, my entire life, my thoughts, my forces are
> dissolved, are united in what I call a desire, for lack of words
> to express a nameless delirium.[183]

The delirium of passion reunites thus with the delirium of the
imagination. For, finally, that which one desires has neither
name nor body, and no longer tolerates the presence of any
reality in the vicinity of itself. It is like a kind of whirlwind
continuously making a void. The possession of the world by passion ends, therefore, in the same catastrophe as the possession
of the world by dream. And "the minds that direct all their
forces toward one single feeling" [184] consume their world, their

time, and their being, just as others disperse themselves in a
universal desire.

VI

"All exorbitant motion is a sublime prodigality of existence."
This sentence, taken from the *Théorie de la Démarche,* served
as epigraph for *La Fille aux yeux d'or.* But it could serve as
epigraph for the whole comedy of human existence. For it applies as well to the social life as to the intimate life of men, to
the folly of interests as well as to the folly of dreams and of
passions.

All of society is "a vast field incessantly shaken by a tempest
of interests." [185] Into this whirlwind, unforgettably described by
Balzac at the beginning of *La Fille aux yeux d'or,* all human
beings find themselves snatched up. Willy-nilly, they have to
"exceed their forces," [186] "abuse their senses," [187] and find themselves the prey of a contagious agitation which is simultaneously
a way to life and a way to death: "In order to obey this universal
master, pleasure or gold, it is necessary to devour time, to hasten
time, to find more than twenty-four hours in the day and
night . . ." [188] Human existences are "torrential existences." [189]
Solicited by all the desires, worn out by all the needs of producing or of enjoying, thrown in all directions by the gusts of the
flesh and the spirit, men "toboggan over the things of life," [190]
and whirl about the streets of their cities like the dead leaves
of an early autumn. In Balzac's eyes, social existence could only
appear as a general orgy of movement and life, perpetually fed
by the destruction of durations and the shortening of individual
existences.

And the same experience is met with again in the depths of
interior being. In 1847, three years before his death, Balzac
wrote to Madame Hanska: "Nothing nourishes me; I devour my
thoughts. I don't wish to paint my moral state for you, it is

frightful." In the interior, as in the exterior, it is always the same
spectacle, the same experience. Existence is a combustion, a consumption. Everywhere and always there occurs the same shrinking of vital space and time to live, symbolized by the talisman
of Raphaël de Valentin. Throughout his life, Balzac never ceased
to regard with horror this progressive diminution of existence,
which was for him a worse torment than Ugolino's. One cannot
understand the profound significance of a work such as *La Peau
de Chagrin* without recalling that Valentin is not simply a being
condemned to die, but condemned to provide from moment
to moment for the continuation of his own existence by acts that
imply a corresponding diminution of that existence. The drama
of time is therefore of a very special kind for Balzac, a drama
more unbearable perhaps than for another mind, since it is the
drama of a being condemned to feed himself with his own substance, forced, in order to *endure,* to *consume his own duration*
as the Catoblépas ate its own flesh.

From his very childhood, and under the influence, moreover,
of his father's famous obsessions, Balzac had a frantic "desire
for longevity," [191] that is to say the need of escaping at any cost
from the torment of a time that one shortens and a vital space
one narrows down. This dream is embodied in a curious novel
of his youth, *Le Centenaire,* which is the story of a vampire
capable of indefinitely prolonging its life in repairing the attrition of its own duration with thefts from the duration of others.
Or it is also the renewal of the dream of the alchemists, the
elixir of life, which, after senile exhaustion, restores a new
youthfulness: "I have found a means of resuscitation." [192] And
in the words of old Ruggieri, it is always the anguished desire
of Balzac that expresses itself:

> . . . All that is the actual *ego* perishes! But I want the actual
> *ego* to continue beyond the term assigned to its life; it is the
> present transformation for which I wish to procure a longer
> duration . . . We have already extended our senses, we sur-

vey the stars. We ought to be able to *extend our life*! Before power, I put life . . . A thinking man ought to have no other occupation than to search, not to see if there is another life, but for the secret in which his actual form is grounded, in order *to continue it at his will*! That is the desire that turns my hair white.[193]

"I am subject to neither death nor time, I have conquered them," said the mythical hero of the *Centenaire*. The Balzacian being, on the contrary, lucid victim of his desire, declares with consternation what "human longevity has lost . . ." [194]

To exist is to desire, and to desire is to surrender oneself to time and death.

It seems then that that leaves only one solution. In order to "extend life," it is necessary to refrain from living, it is necessary to live a life without life, a life without thought and without desire.

As later for Baudelaire, there is a great temptation for Balzac. It is the temptation of sleep, torpor, imbecility.

To reduce existence to a duration without events and without thought, a brute duration. Rather *last* than *live*. Just as the hero of the *Ecce Homo* has to become a centenarian by following the existence of a cretin.

Such is the sort of backward progression one finds in the story of Raphaël de Valentin:

He thought vaguely of the mechanical desireless existence of a peasant of Brittany . . .[195]

Almost cheerful at becoming a sort of automaton, he was abdicating life in order to live.[196]

He had shrouded himself in a profound silence, in a negation of movement and of intelligence.[197]

Balzac dreams of attaining to longevity by "inertia of thought." [198]

But the automatism of which he dreams, however, is never quite the same as the total negation of thought that characterizes a personage such as Poiret. If, like Louis Lambert, Balzac would willingly resign himself to "abdicating the empire of the intellectual world," [199] to stifling within himself any germ of idea-desire, it would be in order to reside provisionally "under a form almost vegetable." [200] Still to live, but to live the obscure, indefinitely prolonged life which is that of plants. And under the fascination which the vegetative existence exerts upon him now and then and in a surprising way, Balzac's nature approaches that of a Flaubert or a Guérin:

> He tried to associate himself with the intimate motion of that nature and to identify himself completely enough with its passive obedience, as to fall under the despotic and conservative law which rules instinctive existences.[201]

This is a quietism with a strongly naturalistic trend. In this form of existence, as in all the others, Balzac has been able for an instant to incarnate his thought, but his thought was unable to settle down in it, precisely because it was thought, that is to say desire, will, activity.

There then remained that very clear dilemma which Blondet poses to Valentin and Balzac to Balzac: "In a word, to kill feelings in order to live to an old age, or to die young in choosing to become martyr of the passions." [202]

One of two things: either a life without duration, or a duration without life. It is necessary to choose.

But our life, which is thought and desire, chooses for us itself. It chooses activity.

How can one prevent this activity from being mortal, since in the interior as in the exterior, without as within, a human being discovers only incitements to desire, a desire over and over to live to excess, that is, and to die?

Such, one can say, is the decisive point in the dialectic of the Will for Balzac. Is there possible for man a position such as, on the one hand, permits him to be man, that is to say, to exert his will upon the world in time, without, on the other hand delivering it over to the world, that is to say to an unbridling of incendiary images which consume it almost instantaneously?

VII

> *To wish to* burns us and *To be able to* destroys us; but *To know* leaves our feeble organization in a perpetual state of calm . . . In a word, I have placed my life, not in the heart which breaks, not in the senses which become deadened, but in the brain which does not wear out and survives all.[203]

A celebrated passage, and one in which Balzac has doubtlessly described less the "perpetual state" in which he would have succeeded in situating forever, in the shelter of time, his own true existence, than the "perpetual state" to which he wished that the highest part of his thought and his work might attain, when the temporal whirlwind of the world and of being finds itself transcended and translated into the serenity of knowing.

For if the human being must always desire, and by consequence always destroy his existence, if there is for him no real longevity, there is at least an almost absolute longevity which is promised his intellectual action. Man dies, exhausted by the ideas he creates, but the ideas, far from participating in the death as in the life of their creator, become independent beings, susceptible of an infinite duration:

> Yes, gentlemen, ideas are beings . . .[204]

> Yes, everything, within us and outside, attests the life of those ravishing creations which I compare to flowers . . .[205]

> Have not ideas a life more durable than that of bodies? [206]

> I tell him that our ideas were organized, complete beings that lived in an invisible world . . .[207]

> He had recognized the possibility of the existence of a spiritual world, of a world of ideas.[208]

Moreover Balzac claims no longer now to attain to a human existence which would be equal to, which would be identical with, this invisible world of independent ideas, to which his imagination gives him access; no more than he claims now to equal or identify with that other visible world, made up of real existences, into which passion enters. These two attempts end in catastrophes. What he means to do now is to identify his life, the impersonal life of the author, with a thought that is free of attrition and desire, in which the universe of real existences would be exactly represented by the equivalent and imperishable world of the creations of the mind.

Thus there would be established, in place of the frenetic expenditure of energy which all imagination and all passion demand, an equilibrium which would be a *mental* equilibrium. Provided they be identical one to another, reality and ideality come into mutual counterpoise. In this fashion the unique problem of resistance and movement is resolved. All the dangerous influences emanating from reality are moderated by the transposition of the reality into the corresponding representative ideal; and the infinite activity of the mental life finds its limits precisely in the very act of transposition:

> What remains of a material possession? An idea. Think then how beautiful must be the life of a man who, able to impress all realities into his thought, transports to his soul the sources of happiness . . . What men call griefs, loves, ambitions, misfortune, sorrow, are for me ideas which I change into reveries; instead of feeling them, I express them, I translate them; instead of letting them devour my life, I dramatize them, I develop them, I amuse myself with them as with novels which I would read by means of an interior vision.[209]

A passage that brings to mind two others no less famous:

> . . . All the human passions augmented by the play of your social interests come to display themselves before me, who remain dispassionate. Then your scientific curiosity, a kind of battle in which man is always worsted, is superseded in my case by the penetration of all the motives that actuate Humanity. In a word, I possess the world effortlessly, and the world hasn't the slightest hold upon me.[210]

Abjure love . . . Ah! if you could know with what magic force a man is endowed, what treasures of intellectual power he has and what longevity of body he finds within himself, when, detaching himself from every kind of human passion, he employs his energy to the profit of his soul! [211]

Instead of yielding oneself to their influences, participating, by means of a passionate identification, in the contagious frenzies of human beings, it is now a question of abjuring every passion, except that for knowledge, and of establishing between other human beings and oneself a zone of calm, of detachment, in order that, reduced by distance to being no more than representative types of dramatic ideas, they may become the pawns of a superior move, the characters of a simple *comedy*.

But if Balzac's thought, like Joubert's, now intends no longer to be an immediately subjective participation in the universal life, if it intends to *detach itself* from the world in order *to possess it from a distance,* how will it succeed in attaining its object? For in the domain of knowledge the same problem arises in all its strength as in the domain of desire. The object is always an externality. And will not the detachment which thought maintains toward what it thinks always hinder it from *penetrating into* what it thinks, and leave it irremediably confronted with an impermeable, closed world, of which it can see and know only the surface?

But Balzac was never once disturbed by this problem. Indeed for him this would be the very epitome of a false problem, for in his eyes *the outside is the same as the inside*. The perceptible world is most authentically the intelligible world; or, in any case, it is an adequate representation which the mind can learn to read as fluently as any language: "It is so natural to break open the body to find therein the soul." [212]

Every man is an ensemble of traits, gestures, behavior. He *is* in the color of his eyes, in the curve of his mouth, in the manner of his walk. He is in the protuberances of his skull and in the cut of his clothes. More than that, his belongings, his house, his

family, his business, his relations, the place where he lives, the
environment he haunts, all that human space which he furrows
or fills, all of this, in a sense, is himself; or it is a kind of prolongation and exterior expression of himself which characterizes
him, not only physically, but also spiritually. For where the eye
sees an object, the gaze of the mind sees a sign, and behind this
sign that thing immediately thinkable, an idea: "A hand is not
simply something attached to the body, it *expresses* and *continues* a thought which must be laid hold of and conveyed." [213]
Hence the innumerable material details which Balzac's attention
detects are not there simply for the purpose of arresting the mind
before their visible presence, but rather of constituting, by means
of the resistance which their materiality opposes to the free flight
of thought, a kind of transforming milieu thanks to which the
second sight can penetrate beyond bodies and "read souls."

Thus in Balzac the world of appearances has at the same time
an extraordinary importance and none at all. It is a "material
translation of thought," [214] that is to say, a language. And, as in
the case of any language, its function is to disappear in making
that appear which it expresses.

But what does it express? What does it say, this instantaneous
testimony conveyed to the interior man by physical appearances?

Ah well, if God has impressed, for certain clairvoyant eyes,
the destiny of every man in his physiognomy . . .[215]

I have to admire Gobseck, who, four years earlier, had com-
prehended the destiny of these two beings within an old bill
of exchange.[216]

For whoever would have had a heart firm enough to observe
it, his history was being written by the passions in that noble
clay become mud.[217]

You might have said the bed of a torrent in which the violence of the rushing waters had been attested to by the depth
of their wake . . .[218]

I shall be so bold as to say that I was learning everything
there was to know about her, including a crime. This feeling

was proceeding from a view of the future which was revealed in her gestures, her glances, in her manners and even in the intonations of her voice.[219]

What the physical aspect of the Balzacian personage represents, what the Balzacian glance makes appear, behind the exterior and spatial reality, is another reality, interior and temporal. Everywhere and in everything, man exhibits his past history and his future destiny. In the infinite detail of exterior life there is simultaneously both hidden and revealed an existence which is just as inexhaustibly detailed, the historical existence.

But what is history? If one supposed history to be the "paltry system" which "is restricted to reproducing the facts following the seeming happenstance that makes them succeed one another," [220] history would be a radically anarchical and successive duration. It would decompose into a series of atomic moments, independent one of another, the length of which the mind could neither descend nor reascend. Then past and future would not exist, or would scarcely even be broken pieces of a road the continuity of which was interrupted at every point by the incalculable apparition of contingencies.

It is striking to observe Balzac repudiate with horror any conception of a discontinuous duration. The time of his universe can be neither Cartesian time nor Bergsonian time. Nothing is more repugnant to his mind than the notion of reiterated creation or of heterogeneous duration. Such a duration would be unexplorable, unthinkable. There is no way of comprehending historical facts except in *"seizing upon their homogeneous continuity and their reciprocal generation."* [221] History therefore appears as an uninterrupted series of facts of the same nature which engender one another. Between them there is neither interstice nor hiatus into which could be inserted an event which would not necessarily appertain to the series. There is no possibility of chance. There is rather one single homogeneous continuity, in which everything is linked together before and behind, a *replete dura-tion,* exactly like that *replete space* throughout which the Bal-zacian energy propagates itself in the manner of light:

> Everything is linked together in the real world . . . Every-thing is fatal in human life, as in the life of our planet . . .[222]

> In real life, in society, facts are so fatally linked to other facts that they do not exist without one another.[223]

In duration as in space, there is the same co-ordination, the same "chain of necessary connections." [224] From connection to connection, from facts to facts, in a spatial and temporal nature which is always "a compact whole" [225] and "where all is re-plete," [226] thought can travel. On the roads that go from past to future, from future to past, its motion is that of "a slow vision by which we descend from cause to effect and reascend from ef-fect to cause": [227]

> A mosaic reveals an entire society, as an ichthyosaurian skele-ton implies an entire creation. On all sides everything is de-duced, everything is linked together. The cause allows us to divine an effect, just as each effect permits of remounting to a cause . . .[228]

Thus the mind is capable of seeing things and beings "in their original and consequential ramifications." [229] Future and past are two roads equally open to deductive thought.

But of these two roads the most important, beyond a doubt, is the one that remounts toward the past. For the past is the king-dom of cause. Within it reside the germs of that which is and that which shall be. Comprehending is almost the reverse of existing. Instead of following with the movement of time the descending series of effects, it is to ascend, against the current, along the "concatenation of causes." [230] As of old the alchemists did, it is to "search out motion at its origin," [231] that place where "the subtle motion we call life has its source." [232] All the great thinkers "go from effect to cause." [233]

Thus Cuvier.

Thus also "the illustrious Desplein":

> Was he proceeding by this power of deduction and analogy which is the principle of Cuvier's genius? Be that as it may, this man had made himself the confidant of the Flesh, *he laid hold upon it in the past as in the future, in dwelling upon the present* . . . It is impossible to deny this perpetual observer of human chemistry the antique science of Magism, that is to say the knowledge of principles in fusion, *the causes of life, the life before life, that which is to be, through its preparations for being prior to being* . . .[234]

Thus already that predecessor of Desplein who appears in a novel of youth:

> . . . He came to know so well all the physical springs of our machine that simply by oculary inspection he would discover the symptoms, the course, and the causes of a sickness . . . This perfection of knowledge had regard not only to the body, it applied itself to the mind, and he discerned the cause of our pains and our pleasures, of our passions and our virtues with such superiority . . . that he knew at once what such and such a man lacked in order to be happy . . . , and only by feeling the cranium, the foot, the spinal column, he could tell what in such a given social situation he must do and even say.[235]

Or thus again the examining magistrate Popinot:

> Judge in the same manner as Desplein was surgeon, he penetrated the mind in the same way as the scientist penetrated the body . . . He would fathom a lawsuit as Cuvier would dig into the humus of the globe. Like that great thinker, he went from deduction to deduction before coming to a conclusion and *reproduced the past of the mind* as Cuvier reconstructed an Anoplotherium.[236]

Thenceforth Balzacian duration appears very clearly characterized. As later with Flaubert, it is a movement, at first regressive, which, reconstructing the past, remounts the slope of time and the chain of causes, before consequently redeploying itself in a progressive movement, toward the present and the future:

> . . . The past appeared to him in a distinct vision in which the causes of the feeling he inspired stood out like the veins of

a cadaver of which, by some skillful injection, the zoologists color the slightest ramifications. He recognized himself in this fugitive tableau, he followed his existence therein, day by day, thought by thought . . .[237]

> He saw the fact in its roots and in its products, in the past which had engendered it, in the present in which it was made manifest, in the future in which it was unrolling.[238]

To the eyes of the Specialist (taken in the Balzacian sense of the term), the actual being or fact is comprehensible only as it appears in an historical and posthistorical continuity, each of the points of which is related to generative causes hidden in the past. The psychologist, the novelist, like the examining magistrate,

> is duty-bound to question everything in a man's past . . . He must take account of everything, *seek out the prior thought* . . . , track down the crime or the thought of the crime, morally and physically trace back its course.[239]

Just as behind exterior deeds there are interior beings, so behind these beings are their reasons for being. All actual existences, all present effects are fatally linked in the past with "mysteriously conceived reasons which have necessitated them." [240] Today's action is the result of the *prior thought*. In it alone reside its justification, its warrant, even its ideal reality. Beyond actual and concrete realities, one must go back further and further to an anteriority more and more abstract.

The Balzacian genius cannot simply adhere, therefore, to a discovery of the present, to an invention of the future. There is nothing more anti-Stendhalian than the exigency of thought in Balzac, which forces thought, even in his consideration of things to come, to "perceive and understand them in the germ of causes." [241] Balzac does not know how to evade the need of "reconstructing the past, whether by the efficacy of a retrospective view, or by the mystery of a regeneration." [242] For it is only when one perches upon the height of the past that present and future appear as they must truly be, the result of an intentional life which was predetermining them. But also on the other hand, in proportion as step by step the mind reascends from effects to causes, as it reconstructs in reverse the path which the motivating causality descended, it is oriented toward a more and more barren reality in which "facts are nothing," in which "nothing of us subsists except Ideas": [243]

> Abstraction, Balzac wrote in an early version of *Louis Lambert,* Abstraction is the finest product of thought. It is nothing else than the seed that contains the flowers, the odors, the leafage and the physical system of plants; it can enclose a whole nature in germ.[244]

> There exists a primitive principle! Let us catch it at the point where it acts upon itself, where it is one, where it is principle before being creature, cause before being effect; we shall see it absolute, shapeless, susceptible of assuming all the forms we see it take.[245]

> A grain of rice from which proceeds a creation, and in which this creation is alternately embodied, afforded them a pure image of the creative word and of the abstractive word . . .[246]

> The states which one presents in the world are only reappearances; the reality is the idea! [247]

Thus we see that in the final analysis the retrospective motion of the mind has, for Balzac, an entirely different significance from that which it will have for a Flaubert. For what he seeks to attain is not solely the anterior ensemble of lived experiences which later will constitute the depth and historical density of the Flaubertian being; and we never see him, like Flaubert, abandoning himself to a simple phenomenon of the affective or sensory memory, letting himself be carried back and deposited, in the midst of the past, upon the crest of a wave of sensations and emotions which would then sweep him passively back to the present. The exigencies of Balzacian thought are such that the passage from the present to the past can only occur as a passage from a world of effects to a world of causes. And, even within the causes, the retrospective motion of the mind can never be halted before having attained to a sort of absolute generative principle which precedes, encases, and orders all the historical determinations of man. It is then necessary for Balzac, despite a concrete actuality which by its bulk gives a fallacious impression of objective reality, that we gradually withdraw from this world of appearances in order to rise by a sort of oblique motion, backwards, toward a superior and anterior world, a world that is no longer one of *determinations,* but of *determinancy.* By means of this movement of the mind, reality changes its nature; it is no longer constituted either by exterior aspects, or by individuals, or by the souls of individuals; it now resides no longer in the passions of the soul, if the passions are passively experienced by the soul. All of that appertains only to a world of effects from which we get strangely detached by a regressive operation of more and more abstractness. And nothing is more striking in this regard than the gradual disinterestedness that Balzac and his reader feel for the being and history of the characters as the Balzacian novel advances. If a character advances, on its part, more and more dramatically in accomplishing its destiny, thought, on the contrary, goes farther and farther in the opposite direction, where the causes of its destiny lie. What it *becomes* has less and less importance in comparison with what *makes it become.* And above and beyond all human existence, there appears in its priority an entirely different existence, one of nonhuman, superhuman causal energy, which installs itself in the human in order to realize itself there exteriorly.

Thus, by a sort of withdrawal, the mind reascends to a place of abstraction where only pure energies exist, that is to say, donor forces of life and duration, *the life before life,* before time:

> Effects! Effects! But they are the accidents of life, and not life.[248]

The true life is the life of causes. He who reaches it arrives not only at omniscience but omnipotence. By regressive abstraction he is transported to what Goethe called the Kingdom of the Mothers,

the kingdom where everything *pre-exists,* and which contains all
times, all places, and all forms. He has found "the motion at its
origin"; he has succeeded in "placing himself within the thought
of God in order to become initiate of the ideas of creation." [249]

VIII

The *Effect.* Is this not Nature? And Nature is enchanting, she
belongs to man, to the poet, the painter, the lover. But is not the
Cause, in the eyes of some privileged souls and for certain gigantic
thinkers, superior to Nature? *The Cause is God.* In this sphere
of Causes live the Newtons, the Laplaces, the Keplers, the Descartes, the Malebranches, the Spinozas, the Buffons, the true poets
and solitaries of the second Christian millennium . . . Each human feeling admits of analogies with this *situation in which the
mind abandons the Effect for the Cause,* and Thaddée had
reached this height where everything changes in aspect. In quest
of the inexpressible *joys of the Creator,* Thaddée was in love
equal to the greatest in the annals of genius.[250]
"To be identified with the causes," [251] is finally, therefore, to
be identified with the Cause of the causes, with the "supreme
reason for all the effects of nature," [252] as Claës, searcher for the
Absolute, puts it. Then one carries in his forehead "the last word
of creation," [253] the first and last word, to which comes back, and
from which emanates, the entire creation. One thinks the world,
and in thinking it, one creates it. There is nothing stranger than
this "pride of father and of God," [254] which never ceased to possess Balzac from his youth. One can compare with it only the
pride of another mind no less great in the annals of creative
genius, that is to say, Mallarmé. But whereas the Mallarmean
pride is that of a thought indifferent to its creations and finally
anxious over the one sole void in which it situates them, Balzac's
pride is that of a god passionately attached to his creatures and,
still more, to the providential role he plays toward them. Like

one of his characters, he may say: "I am God." [255] In identifying himself with God, he makes himself and God the first in priority and the first in reason of all actors in *La Comédie humaine.* Hence throughout his work there is continually to be found a divine, royal, or magic-making personage who exerts upon all the others the sorcery of his despotic power. It is Gobseck, "fantastic image of destiny," [256] Vautrin, "taking upon himself the role of Providence" [257] and saying to Rubempré: "You belong to me as the creature to the Creator . . ." [258] It is Godefroid "in possession of a new sense, the sense of an omnipotence more certain than that of despots," [259] or Melmoth declaring: "I am the equal of Him who brings forth light." [260]

It was previously the hero of the *Centenaire,* and the hero of *Falthurne:*

> Look at him . . . possessing himself of all power, *going over the globe,* knowing it in its minutest details; turning his very self into the archives of nature and humanity . . . Such a man *replaces destiny,* he is almost a god *on earth.*[261]

> I am judge and executor . . . The invisible world has submitted to my orders . . . I replace what man calls Providence or chance.[262]

From this celestial kingdom of Causes in which Balzac has situated himself, he exerts a will that has become omnipotent, which, although it emanates from a sort of heaven, reigns nonetheless *over the earth.* "He who lifts the heavy veil with which a jealous power enveloped *the sanctuary of first causes,* that man *masters the earth* . . .—and proceeds as the equal of destiny." [263]

Like the divine creating and preserving power for which it substitutes itself, the Balzacian power appears as a providence which, according as it is considered in its origin or in the field of its action, is revealed as transcendent or immanent. It is the immanence of that action which procures for Balzac the joy of making himself felt in his creation, of using and abusing his creatures, of "penetrating them like an active cause" [264] in such a manner as to "produce in them sortileges against which the poor helots are defenseless." [265] To supersede destiny is even more than this: It is to espouse the particular existence that destiny reserves for each of its creatures. It is at one and the same time to make and to live out their fate, to be the author, and to be the drama. Thus, the god Balzac can become: without ceasing to be cause, the providential concatenation of effects which constitutes the space and duration of human beings. He *is* and he *makes* spaces and times.

Consequently this God intensely enjoys his creation. He is occupied with nothing else. He is "everywhere completely involved" with it. [266] He is perpetually retouching it and enlarging it; he makes it more various and more full. *La Comédie humaine* in its totality dilates, in the same way as any part of it does, by means of a kind of internal swelling, an interior multiplication. In Balzac's work there is a progressive occupation of space, an increasing voluminousness which finds its physical counterpart in the place it occupies in our libraries. There is also an analogous growth in duration. By a constant addition to the incidents that compose it, by a bringing to light of a continually larger quantity of intermediate events, Balzac *lengthens* time and develops all the internal richnesses which it contains. Time and space constitute an interlocking which grows richer and richer in relationship values, in such a fashion that we see not only the whole ensemble of *La Comédie humaine* increase in size, but also, within the four dimensions of space-time, we witness the growth in *stature* of all the characters as they appear and reappear. So much so that space and time end by appearing as an infinite combining, as an original unity which by its motion tends to realize itself mysteriously in an incalculable Number: "You neither know where the Number begins, nor where it stops, nor when it will end. Here you call it Time, there you call it Space." [267] Balzacian Time and Space never halt in their numerical progression. Developing an "immense equation" [268] of which it

seems to have forgotten the roots, the Balzacian providence enjoys losing itself in the magical multiplicity of its creation and
in matching "the incommensurable number of throws that
chance implies." [269]

"There exist, sir, infinite modes, boundless combinations in
movement." [270] No universe, therefore, no plurality of real combinations can exhaust the desire of a demiurge that wishes no
longer simply to manage and mold the real, but to amuse itself
with all the forms of the possible. He who has thought to find
"the motion toward his principle," who has thought to "catch it
at its point of departure," discovers for himself a power which
surpasses even that of the creation of the real. Master of the
principle of life, he has become *"master of imposing upon it the
form which pleased him,"* [271] and consequently of imposing his
own will not only upon the real but upon the possible. Beyond
the realities of *La Comédie humaine,* the god Balzac visibly prolongs the exercise of his providential action among an infinity of
virtual human Comedies, in a fantastic arabesque.

But this creator so occupied with his creation is not solely an
immanent god, he is also a transcendent god. If in the Balzacian
universe there is an incessant, direct, and visible intervention of
the providential power in the affairs of creatures, there is also
another form of the manifestation of this will, which, for being
invisible, is nonetheless efficacious. There is a god Balzac who
brutally penetrates his creatures and installs himself in their
dispossessed minds. There is another god Balzac who, like the
caliph of the *Thousand and One Nights,* loves to exert upon his
universe a nocturnal providence. Sometimes, anonymously, the
latter is incarnate in a town, in a district, in a whole social system:

> A system is an immense being, almost like God. It has its
> providence, its views, its intimate thoughts, its destiny which
> it unceasingly obeys. Men enter its moral world . . .[272]

Again, sometimes Balzacian providence is incarnated in a small
group of beings, "all silent and unknown kings, the arbiters of

your destinies"; [273] and then, like the Thirteen or the Brothers of the Consolation, a secret god, dissembled among several persons, rejoices to see at its feet the world, which is unaware of its action. Finally, sometimes it is a single person who elects another "to be its providence, remaining mysterious itself." [274] There is no pleasure more properly divine than that of anonymously and remotely exerting one's influence upon one's creature, as does the hero of the story *Honorine:* "Watching over her, in her cage, *without her knowing she is in my power.*" [275] The protection of a being, unaware of it, is the subject of *La Fausse maîtresse,* of *Les Vendéens,* of *L'Envers de l'histoire contemporaine.* The ruination of a being, unaware of it, is the subject of *Albert Savarus.*

An occult creative power is thus doubly a power. It is such first of all because it shows its efficacy in duping its creature; it is such also because it triumphs from a distance and seems to descend upon the being like manna from heaven. Apropos of this, there is an astonishing and little-known remark of Balzac's in the *Code des Gens honnêtes:*

> . . . to assist from afar, to succor an orphan without his knowing it, to become a sort of god over him, to conduct him on life's way, to snatch him away from misfortune, is a pleasure more rewarding than any other.[276]

To assist *from afar* is to affirm transcendence. It is to keep oneself at a distance in that anterior and superior place from which all power descends *a posteriori* upon human beings. It is to impute the pre-eminence and predominance of the creative causality.

But also, in the final analysis, by a consequence which the theologies of predetermination can never escape, it is to withdraw from the world all power, and in the same stroke, all reality, all true temporality and spatiality. In the Balzacian novel the same phenomenon invariably happens: we come to believe no longer in the reality of a drama which seems so rigorously contrived. Or rather, assisting at this drama, we end by suspecting that it is the reproduction of another drama which has already been entirely accomplished, mentally, in the coulisses of the mind. Or it is not yet even that: it is precisely that the drama is simply the scenic development of something we cannot call anything else than an Idea. And since the Idea is not only the motivating but the formal cause of this drama, since "perhaps it contains it entirely," [277] as the seed contains the plant, the plant once developed, the drama made explicit risks appearing to the eyes of the spectator and still more to those of the author, as a doublet, and consequently as a useless repetition. If it is true that with Beethoven "effects are so to speak distributed in advance," [278] then what is the good of the symphony? "The music exists independently of its execution." [279] There is thus no longer need of execution.

The Balzacian universe tends, then, to be reimplicated in itself, to be reabsorbed in its Cause; that is to say, to disappear into "the wholly spiritual kingdom of abstractions where everything is contemplated in its principle and perceived in the omnipotence of the results." [280] Thus the Balzacian creation can be reduced to a pure conceptual thought, to a simple mental calculation,

> monstrous science with which you strip all human things of the properties given them by time, space, and form, in order to consider them mathematically under I know not what pure expression . . .[281]

From then on, no more human time, no more history, except "under an algebraic form: we will see abstract man, the Idea instead of the fact." [282]

The Idea of Man, the Idea of the World, simple formula. Instantaneous possession instantaneously annulled. "To see all at a single glance." [283]

In giving himself omniscience and omnipotence, the god-man gives himself as well a world that is exhausted as soon as it is possessed.

—I possess the whole world, says one Balzacian character.

—And I, immediately replies another, I have devoured it.[284]

Beyond the Balzacian world, which with its people and its dramas recedes in the distance and vanishes, there is a solitude of Balzac, a thought which, having transcended the world, can no longer think the world, can no longer think anything:

> This enormous power, apprehended in an instant, was exercised, judged, and consumed in an instant. That which was all, was nothing.[285]

"Arrived at a disgust with all things," [286] through the vision of all things, the mind discovers itself to be "in the horrible isolation which attends powers and dominions." [287] Beyond *La Comédie humaine,* beyond the Balzacian creation, there is a despair of Balzac which is not owing to powerlessness or to defeat, but to an excess of power which, having projected itself upon everything, empties itself, beyond all, into nothingness:

> Thus all at once, in a moment, he could go from one pole to the other, as a bird flies desperately between the two sides of its cage; but after having made this leap, like the bird, he saw immense spaces.[288]

At the very instant when all duration, all concrete space are abolished with the worlds that filled them, at the instant when the human being apprehends himself alone in the face of nothing, this Nothing takes again the form of a space and a duration. For space is the infinite and cavernous distance, behind which all hope of reality has withdrawn, where desire projects itself forward, but which it cannot fly over; and time is the perpetual effort one makes to project oneself there without ever being able to fly from that spot. Ultimate space is made of *separation.* Ultimate time is made of *waiting.*

And the last attitude, in which we must leave Balzac, is once more that of the man of desire; that is to say, of the being who, eternally, projects himself beyond his being:

> I saw a great shadow. Upright and in an ardent attitude, this soul *was devouring the spaces with its glance, its feet remained attached by the power of God to the last point of that line*

*where it was unceasingly accomplishing the painful straining
by which we project our forces* when we wish to take our flight,
like birds ready to fly away. I recognized a man . . . In each
small portion of time, he seemed to experience, without taking
a single step, the fatigue of crossing *the infinite which separated*
him from the paradise into which his gaze unceasingly
plunged.[289]

Chapter VI Hugo

I

> On the plain
> A sound is born.
> It is the breath
> Of night . . .[1]

It is indeed in a vague sort of place that, emerging from a kind of night, there becomes visible this poetry which is, above all, a rumor made up of words and images. From the outset, the poetry of Hugo presents itself as something that vaguely takes shape in the total vacuity of thought. Of course in the youthful verse an already skillful rhetoric applies itself to concealing this void. It develops common places. But a common place is not an authentic place. It is a mental vacuum in which words drift and roll. Hugo will acknowledge it later: with him there is never an initial movement *of* thought; there is only a movement *in* thought; that is to say, within the void which constitutes it, the sudden appearance of a sort of nucleus formed of confused, undulating images that tend to spread out and multiply:

> One sees floating *in space or in one's own brain* something, one knows not what, vague and unseizable as the dreams of sleeping flowers . . .[2]

> Then like an island of shadows drifting on the breast of nights . . .[3]

153

> An idea rises up in my mind, and passes.
> Or some deep line of poetry winds through space,
> As an undulating fish in midst of sleep . . .[4]

This undulating fish that glides about in the "aquarium of night," [5] one must seize if one can. If the prey escapes, others will come by, an infinity of others. They are "floatings of forms in the darkness." [6] They seem to drift in shoals, swimming in a turbid density; in what comprises for Hugo the ecstasies in broad daylight as well as the dreams of night:

> What was I doing there? I no longer know . . . I wandered, I dreamed, I worshiped, I prayed. What was I thinking of? Don't ask me. There are moments, you know, when thought floats as if drowned in a thousand confused ideas.[7]

Nothing yet exists of thought, therefore, except a confused profusion. Before the mind knows what is the matter in hand, it is already a matter of something vast and multiple, of a throng. Thus it is for Quasimodo when he sees the army of vagrants arriving:

> . . . Thick as the gloom was, he saw the head of a column emerge at that street, and in one instant there spread over the square a crowd *of which one could distinguish nothing in the darkness except that it was a crowd* . . . He seemed to see advancing toward him a mist full of men, to see shadows stir in the shadows . . .[8]

> It was a cloud and it was a host.
> It scudded along, it flowed, it rose up like a swell.[9]

Multiple presence, agitated by the "inexpressible movement of the chimera," still anonymous and formless, but a presence which the simple exercise of the visionary power immediately transforms into a plurality of extraordinarily distinct figures:

> There are no mists, there are no algebras,
> Which resist, in the depths of numbers or skies,
> The calm and deep fixity of eyes;
> I gazed at that wall first confused and vague,
> Where the form seemed to float like a wave,
> Where all seemed vapor, vertigo, illusion;

And, under my pensive eye, the strange vision
Became less hazy and more clear . . .[10]

It is thus by a double amplifying movement that Hugolian poetry takes possession of its space. For on the one hand its fig-ures seem endowed with a kind of instantaneous fecundity which makes them proliferate and multiply forthwith; and, on the other hand, as each of these figures becomes more distinct, it divides itself, so to speak, into all the perceptible elements that compose it; "immense shade with thousands of tiny carved leaves"; [11] so that this multitude is as it were interiorly inflated by precision of detail and variety of aspect.

It is at first sight, or oftenest, an infinity of faces:

Now and again upon the livid wall the lightning
Made thousands of faces glitter all at once.[12]

So that the frightening space presented nothing now
Save visages, living flux, living reflux,
A soundless teeming of hydras, men, and beasts,
And the depths of the sky seemed to me full of heads.[13]

Sometimes, as in *Les Orientales,* and indeed nearly everywhere, edifices, Babels, whole silhouettes of cities rise up, curiously etch-ing their contours upon the same depth of emptiness:

There are Alhambras, high cathedrals,
Babels, thrusting their spirals to the skies . . .[14]

Some Moorish city, dazzling, wonderful,
Which, like a rocket expanding in showers
Rends the opacity with its shafts of gold! [15]

Or again there are visions of features, of bodily movements, of limbs, of costumes; then murmurings of all sorts, the sonorous volume of which multiplies and thickens the visible volume of the apparition:

A ray issues forth from the fullness,
And the creation, misshapen multitude,
Appears before me; and I hear noises, footsteps,
       voices . . .[16]

Crowd without name! Chaos! voices, eyes, footsteps . . .[17]

Thus the nebulous core is at once condensed and deployed within a mass and within a number. It is like a sea, a sea of details. Everything is agglomerated into a moving unity which has in no wise the character of a mental construction and which will never be able to attain it. Everything is gregarious. Everything is at the same time distinct and alike, absolutely definite and totally absorbed in the whole. Nothing can be classified, or ordered elsewhere, than at the point of happenstance where it is numbered within the number. Such is the aspect concrete things present when one sees them flung one upon another, piled up pell-mell.

Images pell-mell:

> All of light that the infinite is able to hurl
> At once breaks to pieces pell-mell in the air.[18]

Pell-mell also of the words that express them; for words are things and are images:

> Yes, all of you must understand that words are things.
> They roll pell-mell into the dark gulf of prose . . .[19]

Finally a pell-mell of the whole creation, as it appears from below, for example, to the Devil:

> You cannot imagine the effect, from below,
> This enormous train of disasters has,
> Chaos, plagues, planets, globes, stars,
> Pell-mell . . .[20]

Hence the universe which delineates itself in the eyes of Hugo seems from the first to be reduced by who knows what disruptive force to its dislocated elements. It is less a universe than the colossal and still-smoking residue of some cosmic catastrophe:

> One sees in the air no more than splendid ruins,
> Confused accumulations, glittering heaps
> Of coppers and brasses crumbling upon one another . . .[21]

> Instead of a universe, it was a cemetery;
> Here and there rose up some lugubrious stone,
> Some standing pillar, no longer supporting anything;
> All the truncated centuries lay there; no more linkage . . .[22]

No more linkage between centuries, places, beings, things; and the consequent impossibility of reconstructing them or of setting them in order. A world returned to chaos, to brute, to bulk, to undifferentiated unity. And yet this fallen world has, by very virtue of its shapelessness, an extraordinary stability. Whatever be the collapses and upheavals which never cease to happen, whatever be the vast eddies which incessantly displace things therein, it is none the less true that things persist there, tangible, concrete, with that fundamental capacity things have of occupying place, of making volume, of piling themselves into a heap:

> Like a Babel with approaches obstructed
> By turrets, by belfries, by slender spires,
> Buildings constructed to fit all minds;
> Enormous piling up of stone and intelligence,
> Vast amassment . . .[23]

Hugo's universe is nothing other than that: an immense piling up of perceptible forms, reflected by this other amassment, that of works and of words:

> This is one immense horizon of ideas barely glimpsed, of pieces of work begun, of rough drafts, of plans, of drawings hardly started, of vague lineaments, dramas, comedies, history, poetry, philosophy, socialism, naturalism, *a heap of floating works* into which my thought plunges without knowing whether it will return.[24]

This note relating to the rough copy of 1846 goes as well for the final so-called finished works. For even the totalities of *La Légende des siècles* and *Les Misérables* are still rough drafts. Hugo can never do anything except add and enlarge; add to the multitude of detail, enlarge the mass of the whole. But whatever he adds to it, this totality remains forever sketchy. Inexhaustible cascade of words that fall, incalculable heap of images that pile up, the work of Hugo is a discrete plurality, without dimension, in which nothing is linked to anything else, but in which the Nothing becomes Everything, and the void, mass:

Who then will measure the dark from one end to the other,
And life and the tomb, unheard of spaces
Where the pile of days dies under the heap of nights? [25]

II

It is under the firmament
A kind of strange and mournful heaping up . . .[26]

Dark and moving mass of meditations! [27]

This mass is never anything but a mass. Nevertheless it is a
moving mass. It stirs. It swarms. It grows. And the vast movement that animates it and that continually traverses its formidable framework from one end to the other is not solely an internal movement of growth and the development of parts; it is
a movement of translation by means of which the huge mass
displaces itself and becomes still more huge, because, coming
all the time nearer and nearer, it more and more fills the field
of vision:

And this ominous, heavy mass arisen and flowing toward us,
Dismal, livid, huge, with an air of rage about it,
Rolled on and increased, driven by stormy gales . . .[28]

The monster grew larger and larger without cease,
And I no longer knew what it was. What was it,
A mountain, a hydra, a deep abyss, a city,
A cloud, a shadow, the immensity? [29]

To this enlargement in space there corresponds an analogous
enlargement in time:

I saw suddenly arise, sometimes from the breast of the waves,
Beside the living cities of two worlds,
Other towns with strange façades, unheard of,
Ruined sepulchers of vanished times.[30]

All peoples having for tiers all times . . .
All towns, Thebes, Athens, all the layers
Of Rome upon the heaps of Tyres and Carthages . . .[31]

Time is only then a second space; that is to say an extent in
depth in which all the images of the past are disposed and

amassed and out of which they can be drawn forth by our gaze
like images of space. At any instant from the depths of forgetfulness, there can "pour forth pell-mell like smoke two thousand years of memories." [32] Pell-mell, that is to say torn up out
of chronological order, detached from historical continuity, and
by consequence immediately susceptible of being added to the
actuality without disparity or contradiction. Hugo's universe is
ageless for it indifferently comprises all the ages. Like the "wall
of centuries," with which the *Vision d'où est sorti ce livre* opens,
it is a plane upon which are entangled together figures and
styles that belong simultaneously to all times, and upon which
the play of light and shadow makes now one epoch, now another
appear:

> There were intercrossings of flame and of cloud,
> Mysterious playings of splendor, throwbacks
> Of shadows from one century to another . . .[33]

So Hugolian duration is radically discontinuous, made up of
a perpetually renewed accumulation of anachronistic images between which incongruous meetings occur; and in that respect,
on an infinitely vaster scale, and on the plan of a cosmic and
not an individual history, it presents an unexpected resemblance
to Proustian duration. For, like the latter, it is full of sudden
encounters between epochs which do not follow each other but
which nevertheless touch and even collide with each other. And
actually there are passages in the work of Hugo in which the
typical operation of the "involuntary memory" is most out-
standingly revealed. For example this passage from *Alpes et
Pyrénées*, in which, by means of the miracle of the affective
memory, Hugo suddenly meets on the way into Spain the child
he had been thirty years before:

> It is July 27, 1843, at half past ten in the morning, that, at
> the moment of entering Spain, between Bidart and Saint-Jean-
> de-Luz, at the doorway of a wretched inn, I saw once more
> an old Spanish oxcart. I mean by that the little cart of Biscaye,

with its team of oxen, and the two stout wheels that turn with the axle and make a frightful noise such as one hears a league away in the mountains.

Never smile, my friend, at the tender care with which I so minutely record this memory. If you only knew how charming for me is that din so horrible to anyone else! It recalls blessed years to me.

I was very small when I crossed those mountains and when I heard it for the first time. The other day, as soon as it struck my ear, just to hear it I suddenly felt young again, it seemed to me that my whole childhood suddenly came back to life within me.

I would not know how to tell you by what strange and supernatural effect my memory was as fresh as an April dawn, everything returned to me at once; the slightest details of that happy epoch appeared clear and luminous to me, lighted up by the rising sun. The closer the oxcart approached with its savage music, the more distinctly I saw once more that ravishing past, and it seemed to me that *between that past and today there was nothing . . .*

Bless him, the poor unknown ox-driver who had had the mysterious power to make my thought *radiate* and who, without knowing it, summoned up this magical evocation in my soul!

Is not this sudden radiation of a past until then obscurely buried in the "interior gulf" the same phenomenon that Proust has described in a famous passage? And does not the noisy sound of the axle play the same evocative role as the *madeleine* in the cup of tea? In both cases the retrospective leap is made with the same suddenness and fullness, enveloped by the same feeling of freshness and joy. And if, in the work of Proust, there are other places where the affective resurrection remains incomplete, half sunk in oblivion, by the same token it is possible to find in Hugo recollections which are unachieved or only glimpsed in the depths of time. Does not perhaps the true meaning of the *Tristesse d'Olympio* lie in this imperfect vision, "in a dark coil where all seems to end," of a memory which remains veiled and which one feels to palpitate without the power to awaken it from its sleep?

Here, as many times in Proust, the total radiation of the past has been on the point of being accomplished; but the "mysterious play of splendor" by which the Hugolian memory operates, has not this time succeeded in making it rise up, in making it *radiate*.

For "memory," says Hugo, "is a radiation": [34]

> O memories! treasure growing in the darkness!
> Somber horizon of bygone thoughts!
> Precious glimmer of vanished things!
> Radiation of a past that has disappeared . . .[35]

As in Gautier, as in Nerval, as later in Flammarion and Renan, there is thus in Hugo the belief in the indefinitely luminous life of images. Scattered throughout a universe of shadows where they set up their hearth of light, they cast into this temporal space more or less strong rays which can be caught by the mind. Just as the images of the present dilate themselves, as all sounds reverberate, as everything that occupies a place in the spatial universe tends to become larger or to move up to first rank, so in the extents of duration everything continues to radiate, that is to say, to palpitate, to project light, to reproduce itself, to tend to approach the actual. And the property of the poet is precisely to further by the act of his retrospective vision all this confused movement by which the past strives to become the present again. One always has the impression, in a poem of Hugo's, of a vast vanguard of images, like that of an army on the march toward the actual. As in the thought of Bergson, it seems as if the entire past occupies the whole length of the line of the horizon. But in this case the progress toward the present and toward the future does not possess the Bergsonian character of a continuous glide; indeed on the contrary it is a chaotic outburst, a loose bundle of disparate flashings in which all is confounded and confused: "Our memory, a kind of forest," [36] says Hugo; and in the *Préface aux Contemplations*:

> These are all the impressions, all the memories, all the realities, all the vague phantoms, pleasant or dismal, which

a consciousness can contain, recurring and recalled, gleam by gleam, sigh by sigh, *intermixed in the same cloudy swarm.*

Once again we observe that astonishing relationship in Hugo between clarity of detail and massiveness of ensemble. It is the reason why, disparate as memories may be, and violent as the shock of their reality may be against the reality of the actual, there is no fundamental difference in Hugo's world between what one remembers and what one imagines, no more than between what one imagines and what one sees. All is simply form, and form upon form; and all simultaneously serves, by the same activity, for the edification of the same Babel: a vast structure which unfolds in height as in breadth, in the centuries as in space, but of which each block, that is to say each word and each image, whatever its origin, has the duly assigned present task of supporting the immense ensemble in its actuality:

> It was like a great building
> Formed of accumulations of centuries and places;
> One could not find the sides or the center of it;
> At all heights, nations, peoples, races,
> A thousand human workers, leaving their traces everywhere,
> Labored night and day . . .[37]

A simultaneous labor in which all the imaginations, perceptive, retrospective, prospective, collaborate in the same task: the enlargement and the drawing closer of a nebulous core which now occupies all space and all time, all space-time; "mounting flood of ideas that invades you little by little and that almost submerges the intelligence." [38]

III

And you wish that, under the *pressure* of all these concentric gulfs at the bottom of which I am, bah! I should curl up and roll myself into my ego! . . . You want me to say to all that is: I am not of it! You want me to deny my adhesion to the indivisible! [39]

Thus for Hugo the self is found amongst an engulfing reality. The Hugolian being comes suddenly to consciousness when the formidable mass of things breaks over him and he feels everywhere its moving and multiple contact. "The pressure of darkness exists"; [40]—therefore I exist!

There is nothing more fundamental to the thought of Hugo than this discovery. One can even say that if there is a "thought of Hugo," it is thanks to this discovery. Before the discovery occurred, Hugolian thought was only vision and spectacle. It was that anonymous point of view from which the eye embraces what there is to see. Nothing existed for it except a regarding of the immense field from which the radical objectivity of things unrolls.

And suddenly the object is no longer an object, and the spectacle is no longer a spectacle. How can one describe this situation in which a human being appears all at once to himself, not in the sanctuary of his consciousness, not in a solitary thought which assures him of his sole existence, but in so total an envelopment and penetration by things that he cannot detach himself from them, cannot distinguish himself from them, cannot abstract himself from them? He *is,* but he is *in* things. He is *athwart* things, and things are athwart him. He is, but like a wrestler so tightly entwined with his adversary that the same heat and the same lock seem to animate both of them. There is nothing so different from the state of the spectator one was just beforehand. There is no longer on the horizon a growing mass of external images which one watches approach with the same detachment one has in seeing clouds scud across the sky, forerunners of a storm. Now the storm is here, everywhere, in all the ways of access to me, and in my very self. It is "storm under the skull." [41] One discovers oneself at the center of a whirling world which is an enormous pressure and an enormous presence. One ceaselessly experiences "the obscure thrust of an inexpressible encounter" or "the monstrous weight of the whole." [42] "The incom-

mensurable cosmic synthesis overwhelms and crushes us."[43]
It is like "a sort of seizure of our mind."[44] One is, and one feels
oneself to be, solely in the feeling of a total and forced participation in a reality which encroaches upon us because it is *all* and
consequently also *us:*

> One feels caught. One is at the discretion of this shadow.
> Evasion is impossible. One sees oneself enmeshed, one is an
> integral part of an unapprized All, one feels the unknown
> within oneself fraternize mysteriously with an unknown out-
> side oneself.[45]

There is in the strict sense, therefore, neither individual
thought nor even individual existence:

> The world is an ensemble in which no one is alone.[46]

> All is confounded with all, and nothing exists apart.[47]

No one has lived more intensely than Hugo this primary experience in which there is discovered the solidarity of the self
and the world. The one exists only *with* the other, mingled with
the other. There is no otherness because there is really no
personality:

> Then is this the life of a man? Yes and the life of other
> men too. None of us has the honor of having a life to himself.
> My life is yours, your life is mine, you live what I live . . . Ah!
> madman, you who believe that I am not you! [48]

And so for Hugo, as for Bradley later, there are no *external
relationships.* There is only the internal relationship of an all
to a self and of a self to an all; immediate co-penetration of the
mind and the world; simultaneous presence of anything to
anybody, upon which rests the substantial unity of the real and
the thinkable. In a certain sense, everything I apprehend is myself; and in another sense, everything I imagine is to be found
outside myself, in things, because I bring pressure to bear upon
things as things bring pressure to bear upon me:

> The dream one has within oneself, one finds again outside
> oneself.[49]

The world is then composed not only of what I see in it, but of what I imagine in it, and as a consequence of what my imagination really makes my eyes see in it. I unceasingly dispose within surrounding space the real and visible form of my thoughts, as a thing which I place among things. And therefore I see myself, objectively and subjectively at one and the same time, within myself and in that exterior outside myself:

> And in the lugubrious vision *and in myself*
> *Which I beheld as in the depths of a pale mirror,*
> Boundless life expanded its misshapen branches.[50]

In contemplating the universe, Hugo contemplates himself:

> He fathoms the destinies and contemplates the shadows
> Which our dreams form when thrown among things.[51]

Hence the impossibility for Hugo of regarding himself as simply a self-thinking consciousness and of considering himself, even in his own eyes, as a pure subjectivity. If he never analyzed or poured out his soul, if we never distinguish in him, contrary to other romantics, the feeling of interior solitude and the taste for introspection, it is because consciousness for him is not a thought that withdraws itself, that isolates itself and situates itself within itself, outside the object. Hugo always places himself within the object, or at least *alongside* it. For him all consciousness of being is a consciousness of being in common with something and indeed with everything. He does not set himself apart. He does not belong exclusively to himself. He belongs to an existence that is the cosmic existence.

And in this vast existence he regains all the elements of his own. Not only of his present existence, but of his past existence as well as his future existence. By means of his memory, by means of his imagination, he perpetually encounters, outside himself, a being which he was or will be. If Hugo's affective resurrections are as profound as Proust's, they never involve him, however, in a solitary and internal search for lost time. Time is never lost. It is there, outside, among things. To remember is not to find within oneself, in the presence of a certain object which plays the role of "recollecting sign," an interior world which is that of our memories; it is to see in the object something of oneself which one has placed in it and which one finds there again. For Hugo, if we recognize objects, they also recognize us. Depositories of our states of mind, they know they must return to us one day the deposit we have entrusted to them:

> God lends us for a moment the meadows and springs,
> The great shuddering woods, the deep rumbling rocks,
> And the azure skies and the lakes and the plains,
> To *place there* our hearts, our dreams, our loves . . .[52]

Thus the drama of the *Tristesse d'Olympio* is that for once nature does not restore to us that part of ourself which she had in keeping, and that is because having herself changed, she does not recognize us as her depositor. But inversely one can find in the work of Hugo numerous cases in which this recognition takes place and in which restitution is integral. The instance developed at greatest length relates to the journey to Spain in 1843. It must be cited in its entirety:

> I am in Pampelune, and I should not know how to say what I am experiencing here. I had never seen this town, and it seems to me that I recognize every street in it, every house, every doorway. All of the Spain which I saw in my childhood appears before me here as on the day when I heard the first oxcart pass by. Thirty years of my life are effaced; I become a child again, the little Frenchman, *el nino, el chiquito frances,* as they called me. A whole world that was sleeping awakens within me, lives again and teems in my memory. I thought it was almost entirely blotted out; and now it is more resplendent than ever . . .
>
> I have spent two delightful hours tête-a-tête with an old green small-paneled shutter that opens in two sections in such a way as to make a window if one opens half of it, and a balcony if one opens all of it. This shutter had been for thirty years unsuspectedly in some corner of my thought. I called out: Look! There is my old blind!
>
> What a mystery the past is! And how true it is that *we deposit ourselves in the objects that surround us!* We think

them inanimate, yet they live; they live with the mysterious life we have given them. At each phase of our life we cast off our entire being and forget it in some corner of the world. All that entirety of inexpressible things which was ourself *remains there* in the shadow, *making one with the things upon which we have imprinted ourselves without our knowledge.* Finally one day, by chance, we see those objects again; they abruptly rise up before us and, all at once, with the omnipotence of reality, *restore our past to us.* It is like a sudden light; *they recognize us, they make themselves known to us, they bring us back, complete and dazzling, the consignment of our memories,* and they render to us a charming phantom of ourself, the child who played, the young man who loved . . .[53]

Nothing could be more striking than this passage, first because in it Hugo passes, without being aware of it, from the classic conception of an *internal* memory ("That shutter was in some corner of *my* thought"), to the prelogical and primitive conception of a purely *exterior* memory; and in the next place because this particular theory of memory clearly appears here for what it is, that is to say an application of the more general theory which Hugo was forming of his relations with the universe. Memory is projected into outside objects; in them it lives a semi-objective existence. It is regained *within* this world of objects, inextricably mingled with them and participating in their life. It is *my* memory, but it is mingled, as I myself am, in an ensemble. It is made, of all the world, into all the world.

But this propensity of Hugo's to place memory in the object rather than in the subject, leads to another curious result. The object tends to become subject, that is to say, the center of spiritual life, capable not only of preserving and reflecting thoughts and feelings, but also of producing them in its turn. Things are animate. They simultaneously live the life we have given them and their own life. They think, they suffer, perhaps they even remember obscurely on their own account. Their own recollections are mingled no doubt with our own; so much so that in putting ourselves in communication with them, we become vaguely conscious of this double level. Behind personal memory, then, there appears an historical memory, a cosmic memory. There is always, disseminated throughout the universe, a sort of "legend of the centuries" which adheres to objects and beings, and which, if one observes carefully, reveals, linked to the present image, the image tenfold of a "vertiginous past": [54]

> I stared at the pebbles in the empty road. I gazed at nature, serene as a good conscience. Little by little the specter of things superimposed itself in my mind upon present realities and effaced them like old writing that reappears on a badly bleached page in the midst of a new text; I thought I saw the bailiff Gessler lying bleeding on the empty road, on those diluvian pebbles fallen from Mount Rigi, and I heard his dog barking in the woods at the gigantic shadow of William Tell standing in the underbrush.[55]

From perception the mind passes without transition to the memory of facts and then to the recreative evocation. It is thus impossible to distinguish in Hugo what is the part of memory and what of imagination. From a certain point of view everything is memory, since everything is directly suggested to the mind by the object. Together with its sensory appearance, the object delivers up to him its historical depth. But from another point of view everything is imagination; since any memory, whatever it may be, is immediately covered by new layers of images. Hugo never experiences pure memory or isolated memory. Nothing can remain isolated in the Hugolian universe. And also memory, like the rest, appears at the heart of a tumultuous plurality which changes its perceptible aspect, its affective tonality, and finally invests it with an epic grandeur. The perspective recession enlarges the image instead of diminishing it:

> . . . Objects loom larger in the imaginations of men like crags in mists, in proportion as they move into the distance.[56]

Hugo can never, in the strict sense, remember. He can only imagine, and imagine himself.

IV

And so the whirling universe, at the center of which whirls the thought of the poet, appears now as continuously enlarged and expanded by a genuinely creative operation. It is not only, as previously, a sort of amassing of things which proliferate. It is a world into which there is constantly thrust the alluvial deposit of an imagination that never ceases to invent its forms for itself. It is a creation to which is superadded another creation, that of the mental forms of the mind. Hugo is clearly aware of the fact that the real is incessantly and really augmented, not only by its own fecundity, but by a sort of condensation of dreams into living matter. The universe is not simply a universe of the real, it is also a universe of the possible which realizes itself:

> The Possible is a formidable matrix. The mystery is concretized into monsters. Some fragments of darkness emerge from this mass, immanence, break away from it, detach themselves, roll, float, condense themselves, borrow from the ambient blackness, undergo unknown polarizations, take life, create for themselves out of the obscurity one knows not what form and out of the miasma one knows not what soul, and go forth, larvae, through life. It is something like shadows made animals.[57]

> A chimerical reality appears in the indistinct depths. The inconceivable takes form a few paces away from you with a spectral clarity . . . Cavities of night, things become haggard, taciturn profiles that vanish as one approaches, obscure dishevellings, irritated wisps, livid puddles, the doleful reflected in the funereal, the sepulchral immensity of silence, unknown possible beings, bendings of mysterious branches, frightening torsos of trees, diffuse bunches of quivering grass, one is defenseless against all that. There is no one so fearless as not to tremble and to sense the proximity of anguish. One experiences something hideous, as if the mind were amalgamated with darkness.[58]

There is thus not only what one sees; there is also what one glimpses; and behind what one glimpses, there is that which one fancies. All that is possible *can* exist; all that is imaginable already exists if it is imagined. The enveloping mass is not made up solely of realities, but of possibilities which one has himself simply by the act of his imagination summoned into matter:

> Contemplation becomes vision. One knows not what whirl-pool of the hypothetic and the real, that which can be compli-cating that which is, our invention of the possible deluding even ourself, our own conceptions mingled with the obscurity, our conjectures, our dreams and our aspirations taking form, all chimerical no doubt, all perhaps true . . .[59]

As a consequence, as in the mentality of primitives, which has been rightly compared with that of Hugo, a strange amalgam of the real and the possible takes place. Any line of demarcation disappears between what one dreams and what one perceives:

> One meditates, bewildered by possible things;
> All borders are erased, one sees invisible ones . . .[60]

Everywhere things are seen which are there because they *are;* but everywhere also are detected things which, although they *are not,* are nevertheless also there because there somewhere exists a thought that has dreamed them. When Claude Frollo saw the cathedral transformed first into a crowd of human figures, then into a gigantic animal on the march, it was still only an isolated attack of fever and madness, so intense "that the exterior world was now no more for the poor unfortunate than a sort of visible, palpable, frightful Apocalypse." [61] But precisely this Apocalypse existed solely *for* the poor unfortunate, and within himself. For the Hugo of maturity, on the contrary, each human thought is capable of engendering an Apocalypse for everybody else. Thus when one wanders through a sleeping city, one is surrounded by a crowd of phantoms created by the thought of the sleepers:

> The discomposed thought of those asleep floats above them, a vapor that is both living and dead, and is combined with the possible, which quite likely also thinks in space. *As a conse-quence there are entanglements.* The dream, this cloud, super-imposes its thicknesses and its transparencies upon that star, the mind. Above those closed eyelids within which vision has

replaced view, a sepulchral disaggregation of silhouettes and aspects dilates within the impalpable. A dispersion of mysterious existences is amalgamated with our life by means of this margin of death that sleep is . . .[62]

There is thus added to the dilation of the real the dilation of the dream. The two mingle or become neighbor one to another in an "unfathomable promiscuity," [63] co-penetrate one another in order to form a complicated space which the imagination furnishes with a vertiginous fourth dimension, the "extent of the possible." [64]

But where is this extent? Is it without or within? It is at once external and internal, felt and dreamed. It is the exterior world in which the things that are seem to open up or to draw aside in order to make room for the things that are not; and it is also the "dark inner immensity," [65] in which thought is continually assailed, oppressed, and penetrated by phantoms from without. "All that is in the abyss is in man." [66] There is only one selfsame space without, within, comprised by the same tangle of crisscrossing forms. By dint of everywhere disposing intersection points and meeting places, of laying trajectories crosswise, of ramifying and joining certain growths, in the course of confronting everywhere the ugly and the beautiful, the darkness and the light, the grotesque and the terrible, one ends by delineating, without as within, in thought as well as outside of thought, a penetrable and innumerable entity which has the appearance and the density of forests:

> A forest for thee is a hideous world.
> The dream and the real are mingled there together.[67]

This forest is the world; and it is also thought. World and thought are for Hugo the same entanglement:

> Knowest thou the true, the possible,
> All the *network* of the invisible? . . .[68]

> This *entanglement* of stars and universes . . .[69]

O dark *intercrossing* of gulfs and dreams,
Sleep, white aperture of apparitions . . .[70]

As if all the invisible threads of being
Crossed in my breast which the universe penetrates! [71]

In the strange *forest* one calls thought,
Everything exists . . .[72]

To this cosmic and psychic entanglement there corresponds also an entanglement of words. The Hugolian sentence is constructed under the form of the tangle, the network, or the web. It multiplies the branchings-off, contrives the intersecting of terms and incidents, seeks to create a kind of sonorous and visual volume by the double density of modulations and perspectives. It makes "the verse roar, stormy forest." [73]

But a forest is not composed solely of tree trunks, branches, and foliage. Dense as it may be, there is always depth in its mass and daylight in its foliation. A forest is a lattice. Things pass, and the gaze passes, through its meshes.

Such again is the Hugolian universe. The mass of forms which constitute it do not check the gaze like a curtain. Into the tangle of things the restless gaze, uneasy as to what lies beyond, can on all sides penetrate deeply. Farther off than what one sees, there is always something one merely glimpses; and beyond what one glimpses, there are gaps in which there seems to be nothing, gaps in the void, in which one's gaze is lost:

frightening holes, torn from the infinite, with enormous stars in their depths, and wonderful gleams . . .[74]

Like the gigantic shafts of a temple in ruins,
Allowing glimpses of the abyss between its broken walls.[75]

Behind the amplitude there is a void. Behind number, behind mass, within the depths, in the interstices and amid the thousand apertures of a network-world which cannot succeed in keeping out space, there is this space, a space-gulf: "Such are the precipices we call space . . ." [76]

And once again, as a consequence, everything changes its nature. The tangle of things no longer appears as an edifice, a Babel, as the construction of a world, as the approximation of a plenitude:

> Something unheard of, gigantic, incommensurable; an edifice such as no human eye has ever seen;[77]

all becomes hollow, porous, penetrable; "all becomes uncertain and vague." [78] Everything passes through everything. The world is now nothing more than one vast coming-and-going of atoms in the darkness, a series of ebbings and flowings which range from the infinitely great to the infinitely small:

> The forms of night come and go in the darkness.[79]

> In vast cosmic exchanges, universal life comes and goes in unknown quantities, rolling everything along in the invisible mystery of its effluviums . . .[80]

> Frightening aspects are seen everywhere;
> The ghost vibrio equals the phantom sun;
> A world more profound than the star is the atom;
> When under the thinker's eye the infinitely small
> Is placed upon the infinitely great, it engulfs it;
> Then the infinitely great remounts and submerges it . . .
> All being, whatsoever, is the milieu of the gulf . . .
> This is why man, a prey to so many dark tumults,
> Dreams, and *fingers space,* and desires a point of support,
> Fearing the tragic night round about him . . .[81]

Thus the colossal and massive construction of a universe full of images is broken up. Its scattered elements, whether stars or atoms, roll on, lost in the vacuity of a space more vast and more real than they are. Instead of appearing in one single compact mass which intercepts the horizon and fills up the expanse, they pass at frightful distances from one another,

> Ghost worlds . . . ,
> These, faint, rolling in the gloomy depths,
> Those, almost engulfed in the boundless infinite.[82]

Suddenly, above as below, as in the depths of itself, there is only one selfsame gulf in which everything rises up, floats, revolves, decreases, pales, and is effaced,

> . . . space
> In which the formless floats forever, passes and repasses . . .[83]

There is no longer anything but a space that one vainly fingers in search of a point of support:

> O cistern of darkness! O livid depths!
> Plenitudes are equal to voids.
> Where then is the support? [84]

To the immense effort of the imagination to establish itself in the number, in the plenum, in the thickness and in the whole, there succeeds, in the general dissolution of things, a feeling of vertigo and anguish. One is deserted by the universe. One is alone, teetering at the edge of an abyss.

Among all the effects of contrast which constitute the work of Hugo, there is none more striking than that to be found between the motion by means of which the images first appear, surge up, accumulate, and fill all the horizon; and on the other hand, the movement by which, having passed through thought, they decrease, disaggregate, and are lost in the distance:

> Soon all around me the shadows increased,
> The horizon was lost, forms disappeared,
> And man and thing, and being and mind
> Floated away on my breath; a shudder took me.
> I was alone . . .[85]

> Then, as in a chaos which would withdraw a world,
> All is lost in the folds of a thick mist.[86]

> Everything has but to rise, float and disappear . . .[87]

Such is the double movement, everywhere repeated, in *Les Contemplations,* in the *Légende,* in *Dieu,* in all the great works of maturity. It is already, as Baudelaire was the first to remark, the subject of the *Pente de la rêverie,* which dates from 1830. But it was already the subject of the *Djinns,* which dates from

1828. All the poetic effort of Hugo consisted in trying to condense into a void—the void of thought—a vaporous core of images in order to make out of them a reality, all reality. And at first this attempt seems to succeed. Images concretize and amalgamate themselves, a world is formed in which thought finds, situates, and supports itself. But this imaginary reality soon appears fantastic. Its very fecundity ends by becoming the principal agent of its destruction. For it exists only by a continual invention which always lures thought beyond that which is directed toward what can be. It is like a sort of vicious circle in which it is unceasingly necessary for the imagination to produce new forms in order to shore up those it has already imagined. But the more of them it produces, the more unreal this superabundance appears. There is

So much reality that all becomes phantom . . .[88]

The Hugolian creation ends by resembling the delirium of a demented creature:

The abyss appears mad beneath the hurricane of being . . .[89]

Being is prodigious to such a point—I shudder at it!—
That it resembles nothingness; and All gives at intervals
The same vertigo as Nothing! [90]

It is a chaos that returns to chaos and nothingness, not by deficiency but by plethora. One could say that in its rush toward existence it is incapable of halting at a mysterious and infinitely delicate point of the spiritual universe, the point where thought and image can subsist in themselves, affirm themselves viable and durable. The very fury with which the thought of Hugo wants to realize itself in an avalanche of forms makes it overshoot the mark. He is incapable of stopping this hurrying motion of the fancy which passes within him and throughout him, in order to lose itself in the impalpable. What he says of one of his characters he can say of himself:

His brain had lost the power of retaining his ideas, they passed like waves, and he held his forehead in his two hands in order to stop them.[91]

After the passage of ideas, of images, there is nothing left but a universal void, the very void in which they took shape. Nothing remains except space:

> All flies,
> All passes;
> Space
> Effaces
> The sound.[92]

V

> Come, I shall teach thee all: *There is a gulf.*—
> As if he had said all in this word, the owl
> Paused; then resumed:—When? why? how? where?
> All is silent, all is shut, all is deaf, all withdrawn,
> All lives within the fathomless and fatal twilight . . .[93]

If, in this episode of the poem *Dieu,* Hugo attained the highest summit of his poetry, it is because in no place is his own thought more adequately expressed. Almost everywhere else, as we have seen, this thought either does not exist, or is found engaged with things, hemmed in by forces, grappling at close quarters with a multiple reality from which it cannot distinguish itself; or simply absorbed with the enormous task of fomenting a world. But in the movement of Hugolian thought, there is a moment, a single moment in which this thought is shown naked, disencumbered of its creations, given over to itself. A frightful moment, for it then discovers itself in the void. And it is in this void, in this absence of any image or idea, that the thought of Hugo is made manifest to itself, such as at very bottom it is: no longer creator of images, no longer participator in a cosmic drama, but anxious, terrified thought, conscious of its powerlessness and of the enormity of the questions it asks itself.

No doubt the image of a Hugo "leaning over the crumbling edge of the bottomless problem," somewhere on the coast of Guernsey, or on "the promontory of thought," is marred for us by the final emphasis with which he retrospectively described himself in the pose of the "thinker." But the true Hugo is not this optimistic and sovereign being who "talks with God" and who is represented emblematically in his poem by Eagle, Griffon, Angel, or even Light. Far from that, he is simply the Owl, that doubter, bird of night, the scared creature who in the dark vouches for the immensity of the void and the misery of human thought:

> I am the formidable regarder of the pit;
> I am he who wishes to know why; I am
> The eye the tortured in the torture opens . . .
> This world is the abyss, and the abyss my cave.
> Mournful, I dream in the cavern-universe; and darkness
> Buffets my forehead with its great somber branches . . .
> I have for spectacle, in the depths of these haggard limbos,
> For aim of my mind, for goal of my regards,
> For meditation, for reason, for madness,
> The extraordinary crater of immense blackness;
> And I have become, having neither light nor sound,
> A kind of horrible vase of the night
> Which chimera and dream slowly fill up,
> Aspects of gloom, the shoreless depth,
> And, on the threshold of the void with its indistinct hollows,
> The rugged shuddering of dismal escarpments.[94]

Neither Goya, nor Piranesi, nor De Quincey ever attained to such effects, the very effects which the most modern poetry seeks for. And what is more disconcerting is the fact that Hugo achieves them by the very reverse of his habitual procedure. For image here is simply image. It no longer creates a form. It no longer establishes an illusory reality. It is simply a pure symbol, and *the symbol of nothing*. Hugo attains to the highest poetry, not when he tries to fill his mental space with a forest of pseudo-real forms, but when he succeeds in expressing, by means of forms of which each in its turn acknowledges itself to be hollow and empty, the very reality of the void. Before Mallarmé, Hugo had discovered negative poetry.

A poetry whose descending spiral glides down into a gulf over the edge of which Hugo has for a long time been leaning:

> Reverie is a hollowing . . .[95]

> . . . Vertiginous spirals of the mind returning upon itself, which make thought seem like a snake . . .[96]

> Wells of India! tombs! constellated monuments!
> You whose interior offers to confused glances
> Only a turning mass of stairs and ramps . . .
> Chaoses of walls, of rooms, of landings,
> Where collapses at random a staircase-gulf! . . .
> Before your depths I have often grown pale
> As when looking down into an abyss or a furnace,
> Dreadful Babel that Piranesi dreamed! . . .
> —O dreams of granite! visionary caves! . . .
> You are less profound and hopeless
> Than fate, this den inhabited by our fears,
> Where the mind hears, lost in frightful labyrinths,
> The billows of days with a thousand dull sounds
> Fall to the dark depths of an unknown gulf! [97]

Here again there is revealed in Hugo that poetry which is the inverse of his habitual poetry. For the *turning masses,* the *chaoses* of things were precisely the materials with which he expressly strove to erect the Babels of his positive poetry. But here we find ourselves in the presence of "Babels turned upside down" [98] which plunge themselves into the subterranean world that leads, by degrees, and deeper and deeper, into a negative universe.

A universe over the edge of which one leans, but also perchance one slips off the edge. No theme had haunted Hugo more than that of the swallowing up, or of the fall:

> He had the sensation of someone who loses his footing.[99]

> It seemed to him . . . that he found himself slipping over an incline in the middle of the night, upright, shuddering, recoiling in vain from the extreme edge of an abyss.[100]

> To fall in the silence and the mist forever!
> At first some brightness of luminous pinnacles
> Lets you distinguish your desperate hands.
> One falls, one sees pass frightened forms,
> Mouths open, foreheads bathed in sweat,
> Hideous faces that a glimmer lights up,
> Then one sees nothing more . . .[101]

One sees nothing more because there is nothing more to see.
Hugo's most tragic experience consists in this interior fall of
thought in which one feels oneself progressively removed from
all that once was the object of one's vision—images, figures, perceptible events, concrete things—in such a way that nothing remains perceptible or thinkable except the selfsame place in which
the mind situated all that it saw and thought.

But this place is "the double sea of time and space." When
the mind is stripped of all concrete forms, when nothing remains,
within it or around it, of the universe of figures and movements
which it distributed over the expanse and the duration, that expanse and that duration continue nonetheless to remain in the
mind, as the first and last forms of its intuition, but an intuition
which now can no longer be exercised upon anything else but
itself. It seems that in this supreme experience Hugo had attained
to the "dark underside" of thought, the place where one can,
so to speak, see function naked what Kant calls the *a priori* forms
of human perception. He saw running on no load the fundamental gearing of spiritual activity. A terrifying experience, in
which space is now no more than a yawning gulf, and time
nothing else than a continuous shipwreck.

The experience of space:

> . . . And when my eyes were reopened, I saw
> The shadow; the hideous, unconscious, fathomless
>   shadow,
> Formidable vision of the invisible Nothing,
> Without form, without contour, without floor, without
>   ceiling,
> Where into obscurity obscurity is melted;

No stairway, no bridge, no spiral, no ramp;
The blind shadow unlighted by any lamp;
The dark of the unknown, undisturbed by any wind;
The shadow, frightening veil of the specter eternity;
Who has not seen that has seen nothing of the terrible.
It is yawning space, impossible expanse,
A thing of affright, confusion, and wreckage
That flies through all the senses before the distracted
    eye.[102]

The experience of time:

The abyss was being blotted out. Nothing had form.
The gloom seemed to swell its enormous wave.
It was something submerged, one knew not what;
It was what is no more, the vanished and silent;
And one could not have told, in this horror profound,
If this frightening residue of a mystery or a world,
Like the vague fog in which the dream escapes,
Called itself shipwreck or called itself night . . .
And the archangel knew, like a mast that founders,
That he was the drowned of the deluge of the shadow.[103]

This experience is agony. Pure time and space are what still
subsist when nothing else subsists. But they are also what ceases
to subsist because nothing else any longer subsists. It is what
dies in the last place. Beyond there is nothing. There, one touches
"the place where Everything is no longer": [104] "One is in absence. One feels himself dying. One desires a star." [105]

But as in the extraordinary poem of the *Titan,* in which one
sees the overwhelmed giant, in order to flee from the vengeance
of the gods, plunge himself deeper and deeper into the earth and
suddenly emerge under the open sky of the antipodes, it is in
the depths of his spiritual agony that Hugo discovered his certitude and regained the optimistic energy that allowed him to begin again to create worlds. There is still a page that must be cited
here; it is the passage in *l'Homme qui rit* in which one sees a
hanging on a plain. And this sinister spectacle seems at first to
engender in the mind the same descending and dissolving movement as everywhere else: "One felt around him as it were a

diminution of life going into the depths." Everything is drained and obliterated in the consciousness of something boundless enveloping this central point of vision. But this boundlessness can no longer be conceived as something negative, as a space without forms and a time without events: "The boundless, limited by nothing, neither by a tree nor a roof-top, nor a passer-by, was around about this death. When the *immanence* hangs over us, sky, gulf, tomb, eternity appear *patent;* it is then that we feel the whole as inaccessible, immured. When the infinite opens, there is no closing more formidable." [106] At the moment then when thought, having been stripped not only of all forms but even of the principle of those forms, finds itself in the presence of the total void, it is in this very negation that it suddenly finds an infinite presence and affirmation. It is then that in a kind of sacred horror one has the experience of a "Me-gulf," me, "into whom all the me's fall." [107] Divine immanence is the immanence of a transcendence. It is at once something that opens and something that closes. It is that limitless plenitude which can only be perceived as a limitless gulf.

> The latent me of the patent infinite, that is God.
> God is the evident invisible.[108]

Thus at the depths of the interior void to which one attains by means of a sort of negative theology, in a feeling of inexpressible awe, of "horror of God," [109] one arrives at an absolute evidence. Thought and the universe are in a gulf. But that gulf is God. Consequently all is saved. All is sustained: "The universe hangs, nothing falls." [110]

Nothing falls except in God, toward God. There now remains only to imagine that procession of beings in the abyss, their gradations in spaces, their eternal progress in the divine. Including Satan himself, all creatures infinitely draw near to God across the spaces of the future.

Chapter VII Musset

I

Let us suppose you are returning from a journey . . . *Does not your heart beat faster as you turn the street corner, approach, and finally arrive?* Well! This natural but vulgar pleasure, this impatience for bed and table which you feel for all that is known and familiar to you, suppose now that you experience it for everything that exists, noble or coarse, known or brand new; suppose that your life is a continuous journey, . . . that every inn is your own house, that, on every threshold, your children await you, that there in each bed is your wife; . . . thus it is with the poet; thus it was with me when I was twenty! [1]

The starting point with Musset is this beating of the heart at all the turnings of existence, this bounding from one moment toward another:

. . . Tell us
How a heart twenty years old bounds to the rendezvous.[2]

Life is at first a summons and a dawn. Before it springs forth, there is nothing and no one, except a kind of negative being incapable of doing anything, even of imagining its future pleasures: "Thus I do nothing, and I feel that the greatest unhappiness that could come to a man of intense passions would be to experience nothing at all . . . I need to see a woman; I need a
182

pretty foot and a fine figure; I need to love." [3] A need to love, a
need to live. Life, love are outside one, in the future, in a world
in which there are lovers, in a time when one will be able to
love them. But that world is remote, that time has not come;
nothing happens, and one vegetates, till all of a sudden an
occasion for loving, for living presents itself, and then, in the
feeling of this lightning proximity, a human being suddenly
awakens, becomes animate, feels the beating of its heart, takes
cognizance of itself in the quickening and prodigious stirring
of its desire:

> —Oh! how at this instant the heart of a woman leaps!
> When the single thought in which her soul is engulfed
> Ceaselessly flies and grows, and before her desire
> Recoils like a wave, impossible to seize!
> Then, memory exciting hope,
> The waiting for happiness turns into suffering;
> And the eye probes only a dazzling gulf,
> Like those which in dream Alighieri descends. [4]

Just beyond the instant in which one is, where one is alone,
where one is empty, where solitude and vacuity are conjoined
to form that kind of interior gulf which one calls suffering, there
is another moment, so near one thinks he can touch it, so de-
sirable that it makes the whole fragile bodily armature vibrate
with impatience, a moment which, one is certain, is immediately
going to be filled to the brim with joy and with love:

> To the right, to the left, over there, at the horizon, every-
> where voices call to him. All is desire, all is reverie . . . If one
> had a hundred arms, one would not hesitate to open them in
> the void; one has only to clasp there his mistress, *and the void
> is filled.* [5]

The earliest of Musset's poetry is therefore the presentiment
of a plenitude, the feeling of an imminence; it is a poetry of youthfulness and of youth, a poetry of pleasure or rather of the flight
toward pleasure, which singularly recalls that of the true masters
of Musset, that is to say, the petty masters of the eighteenth

century. But whereas these, a Voltaire, a Bertin, a Boufflers, are fully confident of instantaneously capturing that instantaneous thing called happiness, the poetry of Musset cannot be resigned to awaiting the moment which is going to present him his object. It mounts up, it bursts forth in a kind of smarting realization of not yet being what it is going to be; it is the feeling of mad impatience and of extreme thirst which one experiences at the instant when the cup has not quite yet touched the lips, when one is tortured by the anguish to know if it be certain that desire will be transformed into pleasure. Thus all the thought of Musset is condensed into a sort of temporal interval in which it is possible that the duration will change and the moment transmute itself into another; and it is this anticipation, this piercing hope which gives him a life that is like the beating of a heart, like a leaping forth of being, a rapid and precipitate capturing of the consciousness of self between the time when one was not, or when one had nothing, and the time when occasion and love can bestow everything:

> —Twenty times I have tried to accost her; twenty times I have felt my knees melt at her approach. When I see her, my throat tightens and I choke, as if my heart had heaved up into my mouth.
> —I have experienced that. It is thus when in the depths of the forest a doe patters with short steps over the dry leaves and the hunter hears the bushes slip by her restless flanks, like the rustle of a thin gown, the beatings of his heart seize him in spite of himself; he lifts his gun in silence, without taking a step, without breathing.[6]

The first movement of thought with Musset is thus a passionate dedication of the whole being to a future that is on the point of becoming present. Like the poetry of Vigny, that of Musset is the thought of a human being "always ready to become transfigured."[7] But in contrast to Vignian poetry, it is by no means a pure anticipation of itself, in which one apprehends oneself as one dreams of being, as solitarily one foresees oneself. Here,

on the contrary, the future is an imminent pleasure, dependent
upon a precise object which has already entered the field of
desire and regard. All existence feels itself dependent upon an
immediate future which it must seize in flight. And the heart pal-
pitates at the idea that its beating marks the exact instant which
precedes that of happiness.

II

Love! divine torrent of the infinite source! . . .[8]

Drunkenness of the senses, O delight! yes, like God, thou
art immortal! Sublime flight of the creature, universal communion of beings, delight thrice sanctified, what have they
said of thee, those who have praised thee? they have called
thee passer-by, O creatress! [9]

In the drunkenness of the senses, the human being thus attains
to a creative moment. Each preceding moment existed only as
an imperfect entity, which had no other use than immediately
to carry thought forward toward another moment more worthy
of being lived. Each preceding moment existed only in the painful feeling of a moment that is *other,* toward which it let itself
move in a torrential springing forth, that of duration. But the
moment of erotic drunkenness is of an entirely different kind.
It is not *in* the torrent, it is the torrent itself; it is not that
which eternally hurls itself beyond and elsewhere; it is that
which eternally lives of itself and within itself, that which en-
genders its own existence. The being that succeeds in living in it
abandons itself to an enveloping presence, before and after which
there is nothing to cause regret or foreboding, for there is nothing
any longer there except a circuit of feelings and sensations within
which one is enclosed with another human being. And in this
sense, therefore, love is indeed a movement, but no longer the
temporal movement by which man, beyond the moment, searches
for a perfection of which he cannot bear to feel himself deprived.

An eternal moment, since in it source and end coincide; the moment of love surges up out of time as a pure activity. It asks nothing, it regrets nothing; it has neither past nor future. It is a present that *forgets* time and suspends the course of it:

> Oh! how, absorbed in their profound love,
> They forgot the day, life, and the world! [10]

> I thought I felt time stop in my heart! [11]

Thus, in Musset's eyes, the moment of love takes on an importance beyond any other, and that by reason of its "eternity." This doesn't mean, of course, that it continues forever, identical to itself, replacing the transitory duration of man by a permanent duration, like that of God; though, it is true, Musset will never explain to himself, except by the intervention of infidelity and falsehood, the abrupt termination of the lover's ecstasy and his dropping back into time. But the thing of which Musset will never entertain a doubt—save in the darkest hours when the anguish consists precisely in asking oneself if one has not lived a lie—is the revetment of eternity which these lone hours acquire when the voice of desire is silenced, and when one can forget his temporal condition. Eternal moments, in that they repudiate and erase all others, in that they do not reintegrate common duration, but stay in isolation without being linked, before or behind, to other moments which their refulgence abolishes. Hence, despite the violence of the sensual ecstasy, what Musset essentially remembers of them is the consciousness of a *pause* in time, a resting place:

> It is a pause—a calm—an inexpressible ecstasy.
> Time—that traveler whom an invisible hand,
> From age to age, at a slow pace, leads to eternity—
> Pensive, at the side of the road, pauses and stops. [12]

But this pause, this interior silence, this peaceful dispensation from desiring, which the being who loves enjoys at the instant he loves, if it is a part of the instant, it is no longer the center, the heart, but already the end of it. This pause is no longer an ardent, actual joy; it is a joy that has been thought and is almost over. And it is striking that the two places in which Musset chooses to describe at greatest length the realization of the happiness of loving are those each time when the lover finds himself *after* the night of love "leaving with slow steps" the house of the loved one, and thanking God, not for possessing, but for *having* possessed his happiness.[13]

III

Inevitably, as in the same period Kierkegaard was to demonstrate, the moment in which one loves draws away from the mind which experiences it and only offers an evanescing image which is soon going to become a pure memory. No doubt, with a Musset as well as with a La Fontaine or a Keats, the contemplation of this slow gliding backward is still a kind of rapture. It even seems that in order that man might make the discovery of his happiness, it is necessary that the withdrawing of what is felt create an interior distance in the depths of which sensation becomes perception. But it is nonetheless true that the thought of one's present happiness is a parting thought, and that man dispossessed of his eternity finds himself immediately transported to the after-side of the ecstatic moment, as just before he found himself situated precisely on the fore-side of it. So that for Musset, as for all who place happiness in the erotic moment, happiness is never directly apprehended, never lived interiorly and at his center of being. It is never a present happiness, but a mysterious nonactual presence hemmed in between two moments of extraordinary distinctness: the moment in which happiness is a hope that becomes present, and the moment in which it is a present that becomes memory.

As a necessary consequence, the history of the man who wants to live in the eternal moment, becomes the history of the man who perceives himself always to be withdrawing from this moment. He is going away from his ecstatic moment but continually turning back in order to measure the growing gap that separates him from it. Time becomes a perpetual fissure:

> And I felt a shred of my life
> Slowly rent to pieces.[14]

But the pain which Musset suffers does not consist solely in the consciousness of a moving away and a tearing apart. A past from which one feels himself torn apart is an immediate occasion of great suffering at the end of which there is a hope of healing and pacification. And a past from which one is removed is a sad farewell that one says to himself, up to the moment when the being one was is effaced in the distance in order to give place to the being one is, changed and consoled. But the particularity of the eternal moment is to continue to be eternal, even when it has ceased to be a moment, ceased to be lived. And as at the moment in which it was being lived it was forgetful of all the rest, so in departing from the moment in which it ceases to be lived, it becomes impossible to be itself forgotten:

> Those memories, after I had lost her, pursued me without respite.[15]

> All that past clamored at my ears
> Its eternal oaths of a day.[16]

> Rid me, importunate memory,
> Rid me of these eyes I see always.[17]

The past is not blotted out then, nor cured. Can one even say that it is past, since it continues to exist? It is there, present, though outside of the present, distant without being blurred by distance, ineffaceable memory which never ceases to attest, to aggravate by its negative splendor, the tragic deficiency of the moment which it is not. Such is the strange dividing into two of being and time which Stendhal once called the "repining grief," and which is less the division of time between past and present, than the division of the present itself between a past always present to the mind but no longer lived, and a present which it is necessary to live but which is consumed and unbearable: "The repining over an instant troubles and consumes thee." [18] Thus, for Musset, the actualization of the past has here nothing at all of the characteristics of the affective memory. No doubt it is upon the occasion of a "recollecting sign," the integral revival of experienced sensations and lived feelings. Thus when the hero of the *Confession* casts his eyes on the Luxembourg garden in which he had so often walked in his childhood:

> . . . The garden stretched away before my eyes.
> As a cork which, plunged into water, seems restless under the hand which pushed it down, and glides between the fingers in order to remount to the surface, so something became agitated in me which I could neither vanquish nor set aside. The sight of the walks of the Luxembourg made my heart leap, and every other thought vanished. How many times, playing truant on its little knolls, I stretched myself out under the shade with some good book, full of mad poetry . . . I recaptured all those far-off memories in the leafless trees, in the withered grass of the flower-beds . . . "O my childhood! There you are!" I cried out; "O my God! You are here!" [19]

As has been said, this rising up of the memory is not without resemblance to the famous Proustian episode of the *madeleine*. Yet it differs from it on one essential point. Far from totally invading the present, or of transporting the being who remembers into the epoch which it remembers, the past remains here a distinct apparition. Raised to the same level of duration as the actual being, it remains separated from it by a whole interior distance.

That is seen more clearly still in the passage in which Rolla hears a youthful romance sung by some strolling musicians:

> Ah! how the old airs one sang at twelve years
> Strike straight to the heart in hours of suffering!
> How they consume all! How *far off one feels from them*!
> How one hangs his head finding them so old!
> Are those thy sighs, dark Spirit of ruins?
> Angel of memories, are those thy sobs?

> Ah! how they fluttered, lively fleet birds,
> O'er the gilded palace of childhood's loves!
> How skilled to reopen the flowers of times past,
> And to wrap us in a shroud, they who have lulled us! [20]

The awakening of the past is thus not an awakening of the being. It is not even in a fugitive fashion the recommencement of a lost happiness; or if it recommences and reopens its flowers, it is all in the depths of time, in the distance; so that beholding this strange and faraway resurrection, having become witness of what he was, a being recognizes that he is as different as possibly could be and, comparing himself with his former happiness, apprehends therein the most cruel consciousness of his present unhappiness.

And so Dante was right in saying that the

> greatest grief
> Is simply a happy memory in the days of unhappiness.[21]

A *happy* memory is a *frightful* memory:

> Shall I tell you that one evening, left alone on earth,
> Consumed, like you, by a frightful memory,
> I astounded myself with my own misery,
> And with what a child can suffer without dying? [22]

The contemplation of the past is thus the contemplation of the interior abyss into the depths of which, step by step, one has fallen down all the way to the present. How did one pass from such a height to such a depth, from such a plenitude to such a misery? Existence appears as a progressive denudation, as a rapid ageing: "It seemed to me that all my thoughts were falling like dry leaves." [23] And if one is carried despairingly back, on the one hand, to an anterior epoch of profusion, to a time "when Life was young," in which "Heaven walked and breathed on earth in a people of gods," [24] on the other hand one thereby perceives, and only the more clearly, the moral and physical disgrace of the time which has now become ours. And so the phantom clothed in black, which sets about constantly to accompany Musset in existence, is neither the past nor youth, but "the ghost of youth," [25] that is to say the image of oneself one sees appear when, in solitude, regarding oneself with the eyes of the past, one begins to understand what one has become, "a shadow of oneself" [26] stripped of its youth, its innocence, its power, a sort of tragic caricature of the being which had once lived; "a young man with a fine past," to repeat the terrible remark of Heinrich Heine:

> . . . Yes, I am without strength and without youth,
> A shadow of myself, a trace, a vain reflection,
> And sometimes at night my ghost appears to me.[27]

The eternity of the moment of happiness has become the perenniality of a distant, spectral, accusing conscience, in the face of which the perenniality of unhappiness, of vice, and of misery unrolls itself as a sort of "hideous disguise" [28] or a "Déjanire's robe": [29]

> It is too late—I have got used to my trade. For me vice was a garment, now it is glued to my hide.[30]

For the indelibility of lost happiness there is now substituted the indelibility of the unhappiness experienced because of the waste, the wrinkles, all the blemishes and stains which the sea itself could not wash away, finally the indelibility of the senile and debased image of oneself mirrored in the puddles and gutters of the streets.

Everywhere there are to be found the same wear and tear, the same withering, the same monotony:

> Look at this smoke-blackened old city . . . There is not a paving stone of it over which I have not dragged these used-up heels, not a house of which I would not know the girl or the old woman whose stupid head is forever present at the window; I cannot take a step without retracing my steps of yesterday; well! my dear friend, this town is nothing in comparison with my brain. All the innermost recesses of my mind are a hundred times better known to me; all the streets, all the pot-holes of my imagination, are a hundred times more worn . . .[31]

Then this actual feeling of insolvency, of decrepitude, of leveling becomes distributed over the totality of existence:

> I am more hollow and empty than a statue of tin-plate . . .
> I am older than the great grandfather of Saturn . . .[32]

> I have come too late into a world too old.[33]

> The Earth is as old, as degenerate,
> It shakes a head as desperate
> As when John appeared upon the sand of the seas . . .
> Everything here, as then, is dead with time,
> And Saturn has outlasted the blood of his children.[34]

The world and the self, all is made uniform in the same impotence. It is too late to love again or to be anything, to turn backward or to go ahead. There is now nothing to do but to seek repose, if possible, by dint of fatigue, in the consciousness of the void in which all is resolved.

> Like those mad dervishes who find ecstasy in vertigo, when thought, turning upon itself, becomes exhausted with racking itself, and weary with useless labor, it stops dismayed. It seems as if man is empty, as if by dint of descending into himself, he arrives at the last movement of a spiral. There, as on mountain tops, as in the depths of mines, the air fails, and God forbids him to go farther.[35]

By a different road, but one whose spiral conducts him to the same places, or rather to the same absence of places, it seems that Musset, like Hugo, finally arrives at the consciousness of the fundamental and terminal gulf in which human existence is suffused. When one experiences the latter as an immediate fullness, in the taking leave of which everything comes undone, sinks and disappears into indistinctness, there remains then, in a space stripped of all forms and emptied of every object, only the sole monotonous functioning of a life that is almost dead, reduced to being a mere organic activity, continuing to indicate by the beatings of the heart, in a denuded space, the regular periods of a neuter duration.

The beatings of the blood in the arteries are a strange clock which one feels vibrate only at night. Man, abandoned then by exterior objects, falls back on himself; he hears himself live.[36]

In the general annulment of all desires and all objects, the world, the self seem to have become a sort of anonymous space whose parts are uselessly counted off by duration; "confused dream, succession of uniform days like the motion of the pendulum." [37]

Well, Spark, I am taken with a desire to sit on a parapet, to watch the river flow along, and to set myself to counting one, two, three, four, five, six, seven, and so forth until the day of my death.[38]

IV

Yet I shall have other mistresses, the trees get covered with verdure and the odor of lilacs arises in drifts; everything is reborn and my heart leaps in spite of myself.[39]

So eternal, for Musset, seemed the death of the heart, so unforeseeable its rebirth, finally so nimble, so prompt is the passage from the one to the other and from the past to the future, that it is as if it were supernatural, immediately and irresistibly efficacious, and of a grace coming not from on high but from below, lifting itself up from palpable depths as the odor of lilacs rises in spring. "Love, and thou shalt be reborn." [40] but it is indeed beyond its death that the heart is now reborn. Each of these resurrections is accompanied by a total rejuvenation of the old being, by a gay gesture of forgetfulness throwing off the shroud of the past.

> From the day when I saw thee,
> My life began; the rest was nothing;
> And my heart has ever beaten only on thine.[41]

It seems that the being awakens to life for the first time, or rather that it discovers with rapture the independence of the moment in which it is reborn, over against all preceding moments. Old promises, old hopes, old tears, and even the lot of fallen angel to which one thought himself condemned forever, all that is found, perhaps not abolished, but dropped down, left behind, like a time unloaded on the side of the road. And behold one finds oneself afresh to be desirous, happy, loving, living, carelessly participating, as if one had never lived before, in an utterly fresh time, the adventurous time of love. Doubtless this adventure is the same one which has already more than once lived. And, one knows only too well, it can end only in suffering and death. But beyond suffering and death there are still other loves, and other deaths, and other lives; so that in this mixture of experience and heedlessness, the independence of moments becomes the independence of successive loves and lives, as if the whole ensemble of duration could be constituted by a series of absolute mutations, in which one "gives his heart to each moment" [42] and in which "all dies tonight in order to come to life again tomorrow." [43]

"Man is thus always new." [44] Many times Musset dreamed of organizing his life according to this ceaselessly renewed novelty of feeling. To make of existence the continuity of a discontinuous movement. It is the essence, for example, of childhood: "There's a mad thing to try: to continue to be a child." [45] It is also the essence of the life of Octave: "Imagine a rope-dancer . . . He continues his fleet course from the East to the West. If he looks down, his head swims; if he looks up, his foot slips. He goes quicker than the wind . . ." [46]

But this duration, made of a rapid gliding from moment to moment, is possible only in an existence which would ceaselessly content itself with actual pleasure. Now Célio is not Octave, neither Musset or himself a Marivaux. As we have seen, love is not solely constituted by the actuality of a pleasure even momentarily eternal. It is a mysterious temporal center about which there come to group themselves hopes and memories, desires and griefs which mount up from all the historic depths of the being. The heart is a bush in which, at each step, there sing all the youth, all the different youths which in turn one has received. And if one is perpetually reborn, it is at one and the same time to forget and to remember, to regain life in death, and death in life. To love without ceasing is to be reborn without ceasing; it is also "to die more than once." [47] At each instant it seems that the whole of life is found again, but that it is also lost again. Time "pulls away the ladder behind us as soon as we reach a halting-place; nay, it breaks it under our feet, rung by rung . . ." [48] Musset's existence would therefore appear to be doomed to being a series of systoles and diastoles, of dilations and contractions, if the absolute character of each one of these deaths and rebirths did not furnish an unforeseen hope. For at this point we touch on something than which there is nothing more essential for Musset, something to which he returned with the greatest insistence in his writings, and yet without ever being able to explain himself fully, since, to tell the truth, at this point one perhaps leaves the domain of the explicable. He who remembers, immediately, exclusively, links his recollections to his present situation; thus he colors them with regret, with remorse, with a virulent actuality which profoundly changes their nature, and which renders them narrowly dependent upon this new source of emotions. This is what happens in all the unsuccessful affective resurrections we have seen, in which past and present are measured as two enemy actualities, at once isolated and connected one with another by their very confrontation. But sometimes, on the contrary, memory appears as something purely retrospective, withdrawn from the influence of present existence, liberated by death, forgetfulness, and the renewal of being, representing simply a consummated past, a grief lived through, an existence drawn to a close. Then this remembrance, endowed with its own life at a distance which is no longer a harrowing separation, becomes a simple anterior presence of being to being;

and then all is changed, all is saved. For *to have been* is *to be*. Not actually to be, but anteriorly and eternally to be. Each "fugitive instant which was our whole life" [49] is eternally preserved in its own duration. And the human being who has lived each one of them in its turn is capable, while undergoing the agonies of his actual existence, of preserving and revisiting each of these moments as so many independent possessions of his interior universe. None of them can be taken away from him, or destroyed, or be in the least touched by corruption; "this memory can never be wrested from him," [50] for every one of these possessions is independent of every other, and time is made of this very independence.

Thus it is singular that the point at which Musset finally arrives, and what appears to be his ultimate belief, is the very starting point of Descartes' philosophy. The principle of the independence of the moments of time becomes for Musset a sort of creation reiterated by love. It becomes also an affirmation of the eternity of each moment of life, an eternity at which each moment arrives when, *ceasing to be, it begins to no longer cease to have been.* Each moment enters in its turn into a particular immortality which is *its truth*. It can no longer be either disavowed or denied. It is intact forever.

Chapter VIII Guérin

I

I have arrived at an age when childhood is for me no more than a dream; all the illusions of life have disappeared, and sad realities have taken their place. It is then that one becomes *no longer sufficient unto himself;* it is then that the man who grows pale with fright and who, so to speak, feels his knees give way under him *at sight of life's course* . . . has need of a support, of a succoring arm to sustain him in the terrible trials he must undergo. This need manifested itself to me at the instant when, *casting my gaze upon the future,* I saw myself facing so many dangers all by myself.[1]

Never perhaps has an adolescent more exactly expressed the metaphysical torment of adolescence; that is to say, of the being who finds himself all of a sudden forced to take himself in charge, and who discovers that his destiny depends on the moment in which he is living. Eternal adolescent, "seized by all the ills which a puberty that would never be terminated would most surely engender," [2] Guérin had contracted, from his earliest years and for his whole life, "a meticulous anxiety over all the duties he had to fulfill": [3]

This anxiety follows me everywhere, it lays hold of all my actions in order to ponder the nature of them and *to foresee the issue of them,* so that there is almost no moment in the day which does not bring suffering produced by disquietude and the trembling of a mind incessantly alarmed.[4]

I enter the world, I cast one glance at the course to be taken, and then I look back at myself to determine whether I have enough strength to follow it to the end.[5]

The first moment in which Guérin apprehends himself is thus the precise moment when one sees himself enter the world and time, a moment of passage. A passage from the present to the future, from youth to adulthood. But it is a moment of passage of a very particular kind, since the adolescent who apprehends himself therein asks himself precisely whether the passage will be successfully accomplished, whether the moment in which he lives will be able to lead to and create others. What now appears extremely doubtful is the capacity of the present to constitute the future. On the one hand, the future seems to be the most urgent thing in the world. It is the immediate task to which the being must forthwith devote himself in order to continue to be. On the other hand, the future presents itself as a very uncertain thing; for it may be that it will not come, that it will not *become,* and that, in a way impossible to describe, the present being may fail his future.

But if he fails it, that will be his fault. The anguish Guérin suffers is the anguish each man must suffer in order to be man and because he is man. It is *anxiety,* the most human and temporal of all anguishes. If it were a question simply of being, it would suffice to be an animal, a plant, a stone. But it is a matter of becoming and of making oneself become. Now, at bottom, man feels able to be no more than what he is in the moment when he is. How can one ask him to be yet another, to be something new, to be more and more? At the verge of his next moment of existence he examines his forces. Summoned forth by an immense exigency, he discovers within himself an immense deficiency. Called upon to become the creator of his life and of his being, he searches the depths of himself for some hidden power which will enable him to make his future assured. He sees therein nothing other than a being that clings to his present as one clings like grim death to a buoy. Then he becomes conscious of his powerlessness, of his "inner poverty." [6] He sees himself as he is, "poor, very poor, pitiful and *entirely incapable of a future*." [7]

But if he feels incapable of going forward, he feels himself no less incapable of *turning back*. He who cannot project himself into his future, cannot re-ject himself into his past either. This past is childhood. For the adolescent, arrived at the age "when childhood is now no more than a dream," there exists in the direction of the past only an image of himself that is already half lost in the mists. The past is glimpsed far behind, like a seacoast one left long ago:

> Seven years have slipped past since I left my father's house . . .[8]

He who has left the sites and times of childhood has left them forever. Between them and him there is a void which neither regards nor regrets can succeed in filling. The adolescent who turns his eyes toward a Cayla from which so many places, so many years separate him can no longer distinguish anything other than that far-off image from which he is infinitely remote. The distance traversed, the lived duration cease to be for him a road along which one has passed and along which one could return. The place where one lives, the moment in which one is, are no longer connected with either the time or the place where one was. They are neither the continuation nor the result of it. And the labor of the time which has effected this great difference appears the very inverse of a work of development or prolongation. The whole length of time and distance is reduced to the consciousness of an absolute break and to the impossibility of understanding how what one is can be so different from what one has been:

What a change, what a revolution in ideas and in the reason, is brought about by these years which are like the passage from childhood to adolescence! It is then that one begins to miss that earliest period of life, in which by a happy want of foresight the child enclosed in the present moment never arouses cruel memories in the past or invents evils for himself in the future; he has not yet surmounted the horizon which limits his view; no anxious curiosity persuades him to make inquiries as to what lies beyond . . . But, strange singularity of man! . . . when he is happy, he is unaware of his happiness, and it is only when the first attacks of pain inform him that happiness has vanished that he *begins to perceive it, but already far removed from him,* and that he makes efforts to recapture what has escaped him forever.[9]

It is in vain that for fear of the future one refastens oneself to the past. Between himself and the past Guérin knows there is no continuity, nothing but a void, nothing but the painful consciousness of the "distance between places," [10] and the "effects of absence." [11] Far from supporting and nourishing the present, the past seems abruptly to have weaned it and dismissed it into existence. It is as if one were suddenly deprived of an essential wellspring, or as if time were no longer a horizontal progression, but a vertical falling through space in which one keeps one's eyes focused on a luminous center which withdraws in the distance. Each lived moment becomes that of a diminution of heat and light:

My interior life dwindles each day, I am plunged into I know not what abyss and I must already have fallen to a great depth, for the light hardly reaches me any longer and I feel the cold seize me. Oh! I know very well what drags me down . . . It is the desolating conviction of my impotence, it is that fatal and too true impotence, whose seed I brought here with me, and which has grown so great during these eight months that it has ended by overwhelming me, by overthrowing me and hurling me down to a depth I cannot gauge. Yes, I am falling, that is very sure, for I no longer see what I once saw, I no longer experience what I once experienced.[12]

Thus the sense of the past and that of the present are set against one another, across the intervening distance, like two worlds, of which one is that in which man was capable of experiencing what he experienced, and the other a world in which he is no longer capable of experiencing anything except his own powerlessness. The Guerinian present, as in the case of Musset, is a fallen-down present made up of a decayed past:

> What could be sadder than the present? If the traveler wants to enjoy the spectacle of the countryside, he must not look close around him but away into the distance.[13]

> . . . Could not one say that certain minds preserve a more lively memory of the greatness from which they have fallen? . . .[14]

An inaccessible past, a destitute present, a duration which is a fall. And in the face of all that, the consciousness of a future which must be confronted at all costs. Such is the sense of time that haunts the young Guérin.

A sense of time that becomes tantamount to the feeling of the profound powerlessness of the creature to create a time for himself:

> I am weak, so weak! How many times since grace walked with me have I not fallen like a child without leading-strings! My mind is frail beyond anything one can imagine.[15]

> Sheer misery is my portion.[16]

The Guerinian being is reduced then to the sole consciousness of a moment of life which stumbles, so to speak, between being born and dying. A fundamental feeling, and perhaps more authentically human than that other sense of existence, firmly joined by Descartes to the activity of thought. For in this case the feeling of existence is deprived of any energy of its own. It is characterized by an extreme poverty and is similar in the order of nature to that essential indigence which, in the order of grace, forms the depth of Jansenist piety. It is the state of a being for whom what is essential for being is always on the point of failing. Without past, without future, without duration, feeling to give way and yield under his weight a precarious present which, as soon as it is given, is immediately withdrawn, the Guerinian being discovers himself to be like the neophyte in the ordeals of the cult of Isis who climbed up an iron ladder each rung of which was in turn removed. Nothing supports him except an unsteady actuality encompassed by a void. To sense myself is to have a "sense of *my* weakness." [17] a "feeling of *my* misery and *my* nothingness": [18]

> Finally my mind, tormented by all evils at once, no longer finding anything in the world to which it may attach itself, falls back upon itself, and, finding nothing therein except misery and weakness, it feels itself seized with a sickening disgust for all things. It becomes as it were inanimate . . .[19]

II

"It *becomes* as it were inanimate." The only future existence which might be foreseen and given himself by the being who apprehends himself in his essential weakness is an existence that becomes exhausted, a life that becomes death.

> The idea of the end of all beings ceaselessly presents itself to me.[20]

> . . . In this world where everything passes away and comes to an end, the idea of existence necessarily calls to mind that of death, and to tell the truth I do not know how we can think of the one without thinking of the other.[21]

Thus in the temporal impulse which detaches him from the present and sweeps him along in life, the being who perceives himself in his weakness distinguishes only a final consumption of his forces, a supreme giving-way of existence. To feel oneself live is to feel oneself die. But whereas a Montaigne drew from this reflection the incitement to live more intensely each threatened moment of human existence, how could Guérin find enough resources and interest in himself to quicken the sense of his actual existence? And if he could, what precisely would he vivify except the feeling of a life which becomes death and which, in the very moment he lives it, is dissipated and exhausted? Nothing is more

vain than the wish to isolate oneself in the contemplation of the
little of life one possesses, as one isolates in a tower the princess
unhappily cursed by the bad fairy. To one who sees himself in
his essential weakness, death is not simply the end of life, it is
another name for life itself. To die and to live are the same thing.
Existence is a drop of water that is at once swallowed up by the
sand.

Unless, surely unless, in this failure of all being to continue
to be, some help comes which can only come from elsewhere,
that is to say from above or from outside. Guérin is thus essentially a man who always feels the need of a support, the need of
a helping hand, "in order to keep on living, in order to keep
from sinking into death." He is one "who cannot stand upright
unless someone supports him," [22] and who can only address to
God, as to men and the world, one single petition:

> Maintain my footsteps in this road
> Wherein man so often falls from faintness.[23]

Nothing is more different from ordinary Christian devotion—
the devotion of his sister Eugénie, for example—than the piety of
Maurice. The grace which he implores is not at all that which
wards off supernatural evil and death. It is instead simply the
most natural grace, the continuation of existence. Guérin has
only one prayer: O God, preserve my life. Or rather, as life, as
soon as it is received and lived, is already mingled with death
and is irrevocably perishing, restore me, renew my life, give me
once more

> of that water which is given
> To souls in weakness, and I, needy,
> Fainting, shall grasp alms from this hollow.[24]

The hollow of the stoup of holy water from which the needy
one draws the water of life is already a prefiguration of the pro-
founder hollows to which Guérin will later go to receive the
vivifying water. It is the symbol of a mysterious exteriority from
which alone one can hope for succor. For succor, if it comes to

us, does not issue from us; it must be received from a power other than our weakness. What is deeply interior in us depends on what can only be exterior to us. Guérin also could say of all the human beings he had known, what he said of Lamennais:

> I put my hope in him, I reinforce my failing courage by means of him, and I set to work again with *borrowed strength*.[25]

With borrowed strength one can set oneself to work again, set oneself to live again. A work always rebegun, always about to be interrupted, for everything depends on a prop and a loan which at any moment can fail. And yet this prop is vital, and what one borrows is one's own existence:

> Always a drag, always constrained to *borrow my existence*. The lips of the child that has just been born have strength enough to suck the breast, and I, in the power of young man-hood, haven't enough energy to earn my living, to suck out a little of life.[26]

He who thus discovers himself in his fundamental destitution, thinks himself the only being of his species. For the weakness he experiences he can only experience within himself. Everywhere else, on the outside, he can see only activity and energy. And so Guérin, more painfully conscious perhaps than any man of a deficiency which is that of all men, imagines himself to be a victim or a guilty person. But quite simply he is the one who, in himself alone and for himself alone, undeniably establishes a truth of universal order: that every living thing lives a life which it must perpetually borrow. In order to live, it is necessary first to receive life; and in order to receive life, it is necessary first to find outside of himself, outside of the actuality of his existence, the very source of that existence.

But this source, may it not be the past? Indeed, as we have seen, the past has become absolutely remote. It is no longer part of us, it is away beyond us, like a horizon or a dream. But precisely because it is no longer ourself, can we not find in it that help which can only come from what is outside of us? Can we not turn ourself toward the person we have been as if he were a stranger of whom we would ask alms? Can we not entreat him to give us what he had and what we no longer have? Such, for example, will become the attitude of Proust, who will seek in time past the support of time present. Such, also, and from his earliest adolescence, is Guérin's attitude. If he "lays stress upon his earliest impressions," [27] if he "finds an infinite charm in turning back to his earliest reading," [28] it is because there his "tears well up from the almost exhausted fountainheads of his youth," [29]— tears, but also powers—and because the sources which hardly any longer flow once did flow, and perhaps have not stopped flowing, in a region which is remote, but which is at least virtually present and powerful, the region of the past. As a consequence, across the temporal distances, despite the remoteness, the diminution, and finally, to sum everything up and in the strictest sense of the term, the *alteration* of our being, is it not possible to draw to ourself, like a grace, the influx of that being which is no longer ourself but which, when it was still ourself, was vigorous, energetic, and a dispenser of joy and of strength? In quest of life, Guérin attempts to revive himself by reviving his memories:

> An astonishing thing, the effects of absence on the heart of man; it gives birth to a meticulous passion which nourishes itself on the smallest and least significant objects, so it seems. Everything that recalls those who have been left behind, everything that belonged to them is a treasure in his eyes.[30]

"Treasury of sorrows and secret thoughts," [31] treasury of forces, "which could supply the whole length of the longest life," [32] and which possibly could be established henceforth as a source from which to borrow later on at need. And so Guérin strives unceasingly to make provision from his present and therefrom "to raise up faithful and incorruptible impressions" [33] which will serve as *future memories:*

> Last walk, last visit to the sea . . . With all the power of my attention, I gave myself up to the contemplation of the head-

lands, the crags, the islands, *forcing myself to make as it were a stamp of them and to carry it in my mind* . . . And in order to capture as much as I could of these pleasant spots [34] and as if it had been in their power to give themselves to me, I besought them to engrave themselves upon my mind, to transmit to me something of themselves which would never pass away.[35]

The "meticulous passion" nourishes itself, therefore, on objects, on signs, and on impressions which, despite distance and absence, one day put us again in contact with everything we have left behind.

Now among these objects none has a more magical power of union than the things of nature. There is in the first place by the adult Guérin a rediscovery of nature, not yet in itself and in its own actual efficacy, but as the intermediary of another nature, an *anterior nature,* the nature which was experienced in childhood. For "memories tie their slender threads to exterior, insensible objects which, in appearance, lie outside the heart" [36]— outside the heart that beats now, but not outside the heart that once beat; so that in the nature which in appearance is the most insensible, the most debased, there is always something that "awakens a thousand memories" [37] and makes us "experience anew many a one of our childhood impressions." [38]

All his life Guérin sought in present nature these correspondences and unions with a younger nature. Thanks to them it sometimes seems to him that within him "prodigious relationships" are established between the person he was and the person he is. There is nothing, however, which less resembles the kind of fusion of the past and the present which all the romantics have sought and thought they found in the mysterious operation of the affective memory. It is not a matter here of the total reviviscence that substitutes one epoch for another or joins and mingles them into one identity which confounds the durations. With Guérin the past never ceases to remain past. It never ceases to make its appearance at the very bottom of a retrospective depth which irremediably separates it from the present. Without ceasing to be separated from it by a zone of silence, we can hear its voice, which seems to be aided precisely by the silence and the distance to reach us:

> It is, it is so sweet to hear remount
> From far-off days voluptuous voices
> Returning to enchant us! [39]

A rather sad veil of gray stretches out over my mind as the peaceful clouds do over nature. A great silence is established, and I hear as it were the voices of a thousand sweet and touching memories which *arise in the distance of the past and come murmuring in my ear.*[40]

If they arise in the distance, these memories nevertheless come murmuring in our ear; and, in so doing, they make accessible to us the temporal paths which they have traversed in order to reach us. Distance ceases to be a separation, a difference, the negation of any rapport between that which was and that which scarcely any longer exists. It is now that across which glides to us the image of an anterior life not so poor as ours; an image like that of a sky studded with stars which concentrate their rays and shed their influences upon us from afar. Despite, or even perhaps because of, the distance, we are accordingly susceptible of recognizing the past, of turning our attention to it, of receiving its emanations. We can keep up an assiduous correspondence with it (as with a sister)

> which draws us close together, so to speak, despite the disturbance of places that separate us, and makes us enjoy an interview which is all the sweeter in that the remote distance casts a double interest upon what one receives from a beloved object.[41]

Then temporal distance becomes as it were the most pure milieu through which two beings, one rising and the other descending, approach and meet each other. But can we speak here of mounting and descending? The double movement by which the drawing together of durations operates has no precise direction. One can as easily think of it as an ascension toward life as a plunging toward its origin, as easily the flowing of a spring as the gushing forth of a fountain. Sometimes Guérin seems to his own eyes to be "like the diver who fishes for pearls" [42] and who reascends from the depths to the surface with his prey of memories. Oftener it is at their descent or their rising within him that he assists, and then it is at once the seat and point of arrival of an immense temporal movement by which "faithful memories rally from all sides to one selfsame thought": [43]

> And while I listen, there arrive by thousands
> The pale memories and the vague thoughts,
> Which the slightest accord, on airy wing,
> Brings back to my mind . . .[44]

Six o'clock in the evening. It is the moment when memories return to me by the thousands, like the birds which, at the same hour, swirl in a flock to the rendezvous they have promised themselves in a big poplar tree . . .[45]

Come back, all you memories, sweet emanations of the past, shades of what has vanished, return to my mind, as, at nightfall, the little birds and the bees who had wandered over the countryside fly back to their place of shelter and gather together in it. Come back, all, night has fallen.—Thus I put off my worst regrets . . . I surround them with this murmuring crowd of memories.[46]

Then, through this re-entering into self of all the ghosts of self which one had left behind at all the points of duration, it seems that thanks to their "murmuring crowd" a richer and more vigorous figure of the self is recomposed, a present animated by the concentration of forces which one had scattered along the whole length of the past. One enters upon one's convalescence; one no longer suffers as much of the pain of existing:

When suffering is removed and life remains pale and enfeebled for you, yet still trusting and relishing a calm sensuous pleasure in the very last touches of illness which are disappearing, the most contained mind has a propensity for prolonged and somewhat wandering discourses, mixed with painful memories and a thousand pleasing projects. The first glimmerings of well-being that *re-enter existence* penetrate it charged with languid dreams and sweet and confused images, like so many corpuscles flowing through their breast . . . It is in these moments that *from all sides of my being, as from a calm countryside under a grayish sky and without movement of clouds, there arise restrained and confused sounds, tokens of a life that is returning from afar.* These sounds are produced by my thoughts which, coming out of their painful numbness, tremble lightly with a timid joy and embark upon talks full of *memories* or *hopes*.[47]

Thus from all sides vital forces which have arisen from the farthest regions of the past, arrive, form groups, and converge, not only in order to animate the present but to make it wish for a future. One could say that all duration comes to the aid of a moment that is reeling from weakness. The actual being acquires a life that is brought to him by an infinity of beings, all his anterior selves. It is because they are anterior to him and because he had left them behind along the way that they can now rejoin him and bring him their help. Of himself alone, needy, failing, he was incapable of either living or feeling. Thanks to them, he is suddenly capable of reliving, of refeeling. Such is the law of Guérin, who can never rejoice in the presence of happiness; but hardly has it been removed than he feels "an agitation, an infinite regret, an intoxication of memory, recapitulations which exalt the entire past and which are richer than even the presence of happiness . . . All things are better refelt than felt." [48]

The present, when it is alone, is without force. Nothing ushers it in, and nothing prolongs it. But from the depths of the past, thanks to buried memories, there reascends a throng of primitive feelings which renew our present forces and the feeling we have of them:

It is as it were a regeneration that I experience in the renewal of the emotions of former times, and one feels almost rejuvenated in imbibing after such a long while the springs of the happiness of childhood.[49]

Bathe thyself once more in the memory of the days of independence when thou didst run at thy will over the fields, thine heart bursting with pleasure . . .[50]

The sun has risen for the first time in a very long while in all its beauty. It has opened the buds of the flowers and leaves, and reawakened in my breast a thousand sweet thoughts.[51]

How shall I express what I experienced in plunging myself once more into solitude and into a solitude which recalls to me the country of my sweetest dreams, Brittany . . . I take joy in this resemblance. I apply myself to the study of it, I revive a multitude of charming memories . . .[52]

All is renewed *about me* as well as *in me*.[53]

This is the essential point of the dialectic of life as it is for Guérin. We see that this past which, by a thousand associations, the contact with the present nature restored to him, restores to him in its turn the memory of a younger nature, and that this memory, in bringing back all that past youth into the mind, finally renders the mind capable of finding in the present nature the same freshness as that of the nature of former times:

Sitting down in the sunlight that I might be pierced to the marrow by divine springtime, I experienced once more certain of the impressions of my childhood: I gazed awhile at the sky with its clouds, the earth with its woods; I listened to its songs and its hummings, just as I had then. This *renewal of the pristine aspect of things,* of the physiognomy perceived by our first glances, is, to my way of thinking, one of the sweetest reactions of childhood on the course of life.[54]

Consequently the Guerinian renewal appears as indissolubly linked not only to time but also to space. On the one hand, he who finds himself renewed is a being who owes his actual vigor entirely to the movement by means of which the whole of his past life starts to live again in order to make him live. But on the other hand, at the point of issue as well as at the original point of this re-creation of the being, there is another movement which, this time, takes place no longer within the interior of the being, but between this interior and the outside world. Life not only consists in a recommencement of what one *is,* but also in a renewal of what one *feels.* And what is it that we are able to feel and to feel again, unless it be that exterior life with which formerly, avidly, we communicated, across space, by means of all our senses? The deep experience of time and memory is thus made one, in the final analysis, with the experience of space. The past is a prop only because it is supported in its turn by a force which is authentically spatial and external. At both ends of the line of our life, there is this enveloping, vivifying thing, maker of movement and life, which is called nature. All the existence, past or present, which one discovers in oneself is no more than a borrowing from it.

III

> Each time that we allow ourselves to be penetrated by nature, our mind *becomes open* to the most moving impressions.[55]

> There is no such thing as loneliness for him who knows how to take his place in the universal harmony and *to open his mind* to all the impressions of that harmony.[56]

To borrow, therefore, is *to open* one's being—as one *opens* one's hand to receive alms. It is to allow oneself to be penetrated by influences from without:

> During the six weeks I have spent here, without study, without effort, *letting my mind wander* at will, living in idleness, but in a contemplative idleness *open* to all impressions, I have experienced a tremendous enlargement.[57]

At the very opposite from "the meticulous anxiety" which the being isolated in his weakness experiences when he "compares his strength with the immense struggle of life," [58] now and again for him who gives up hope of founding his existence in himself, there is a deep feeling of quietude and the growth of vital forces. He alone can open up himself to this nutritious affluence who now sets up no barrier, neither any reserve, who, being incapable of giving himself anything, is prepared to receive everything. The quietism of Guérin is of this sort. It offers itself to the impressions of nature in the same way as the quietism of Fénelon surrenders itself to the operations of God. On the one hand as on the other, it is the total renunciation of a being who no longer expects to receive life except from a source upon which he utterly depends and which depends not at all upon him. He has no longer any anxiety, any desire, any thought, nor even any personal feeling. He is now simply a being who opens himself and who opens himself in order to receive being. He is "a borrowing being," [59] a being who borrows being. Now being exists, in profusion, but outwardly. It is simply a matter of letting it flow into oneself like the water from a fountain: *"Let nature flow into one's mind."* [60]

> Then one comes to feel physically almost that one lives *of* God and *in* God: the mind breathlessly drinks of this universal life; it swims in it like a fish in water.[61]

To drink, to let penetrate, to let flow into one's mind. And this existence which one does not possess but borrows, suddenly one discovers it, one discovers oneself within it. One "was wandering here and there, looking for his life," [62] and behold, one all of a sudden finds it, within as without, in oneself as outside oneself, a sort of liquid element, universal and divine, which, from all sides, flows round and inundates us. Or rather, what one then experiences is a feeling of infinite *intimacy*. A force which is not ourselves, which is everywhere and which is everything, penetrates us, and the instant it is within us, it becomes ourself, it is *our* force. The particular intoxication of Guérin is the joy of one who welcomes life into himself. More than that, it is the simplest and most primitive pleasure, that which consists in "sucking the breast," in "drawing sustenance from sap," in "imbibing from the source." The entire activity of the being is concentrated in this instant when one drinks, when one *sucks in* existence:

> If one could identify oneself with spring, could force this thought to the point of believing that one is *drawing into oneself all the life,* all the love fermenting in nature, of feeling oneself to be simultaneously flower, foliage, bird, song, freshness,

voluptuousness, serenity! What would happen to me? There are moments when, by dint of concentrating on this idea and fixedly regarding nature, one believes he experiences something like that.[63]

If, in these moments of "concentration," it seems as if one might become flower, foliage, or bird, it is because one then feels that nature and all of life itself exists by means of the selfsame action that forms our very existence. The being who experiences himself in the instant in which he draws life in discovers himself to be participating in a universal action and in the very generation of things. The simplicity of this action makes for the immense and seizable ubiquity of it. For, being life and all of life, it embraces "the universality of that which is." [64] Whosoever breathes in life can see it simultaneously inbreathed by a whole universe of beings who, like himself, possess being only through and in this universal *aspiration*. Before the consciousness of this action, everywhere the same and everywhere similarly essential, all specific differences are abolished, and there remains only one unique feeling, the presence of a nature at once interior and exterior, endlessly and everywhere imbibing the same "vital energy": [65]

> And the great, ardent, indefatigable worker
> Drew inexhaustibly from the inexhaustible water.[66]

As a consequence, whatever one is, one no longer feels radically different from other people or from the universe. In the very action by which he is, man recognizes himself to be the subject of a universal action. Like all the rest, he is one in whom nature fulfills herself. He participates to the depths of his being in a mystery which makes the puniest plant live and which animates the vast extent of the cosmos. Each drop of life that he drinks contains the infinity of created spaces. And not only the spaces, but also the movement which traverses them. For life is not solely that which "springs from an invisible fountain," it is the stream which, upon leaving that source, descends to beings and things to swell all veins and roll all waves:

> . . . all that rolls round, light, clouds, ravishing sounds, the universal joy circling about a man who spends entire days leaning his back against a tree, and solely occupied in watching nature live.[67]

Outside, before one's eyes, a great, open nature offers the moving spectacle of its activities:

> —*Oh! beautiful spectacle, ravishing thought,* this immense circulation of life which takes place within the ample breast of nature . . .[68]

A spectacle which in a way is redoubled, for to this exterior circulation there corresponds, in the consciousness of the contemplator, a "mysterious circulation of thought in the most lively areas of his mind." [69] Besides the external space in which the eternal torrent "keeps rolling its waves of seed and of life," [70] there is the vast interior field of a thought in which the images "drift with the stream of the secret breathing that moves across all intelligence." [71] There stirs there "all that circulates within me of unknown joys and those hidden transports of which nothing will be lost outside." [72] It is "the silent river of the interior circulation." [73] Within as without, in nature as in man's breast, it is the same "flux and reflux of universal life," [74] an "ineffable movement," [75] perceived at one and the same time by man's looking at things, and by the "interior eye" in the "tabernacle of the spirit." [76]

"Life," said Barbey d'Aurevilly speaking of Guérin, "life, for Somegod, was the general motion of the world strongly reverberating in him . . ." [77]

Consequently in his moments of deep intoxication, Guérin no longer perceives anything except one selfsame motion infinitely recommenced, reverberated. At once witness and actor, through his regard, and through his thought, through his own very existence, he participates in what Guérin's master, Lamennais, called "the eternal development of Creation." [78] Now this development, precisely because it is apprehended here in its persistence and in its ubiquity, appears on the one hand as if it were outside of time and of space. Each moment and each place in which it fulfills itself lose all local and historical particularity, in order thenceforth to be simply the undifferentiated subjects of an immense, eternal creation. Here and everywhere, now and forever, there is only one place and one moment, simultaneously vivified and consumed by "the indefatigable fire whose emanations animate the universe." [79] But, on the other hand, this motion which is apprehended in one place, in one moment forever unique, and of such a kind that the self and the world always receive therefrom life for the first time, is also, contradictorily, a motion that is intensely spatial and temporal. More than that, it is as if in that point and in that moment, the very passage of the vital motion recreated space and duration. At first he who feels the stream of life diffusing itself within him and in the world seems to assist and participate in the double deployment of his being and the universe. There is as it were a simultaneous dilation of the self and of the world which can be sensed in the smallest phenomenon of nature as well as in the slightest shudder of the mind. Between one and the other there occurs a kind of mutual overflowing by means of which the swelling forth of forms or of exterior sounds becomes the interior expansion of the mind. Sometimes it is a storm which, by a maximum of violence, effects this opening out:

> All the sounds of nature: the winds, those formidable breaths from an unknown mouth, which put in play the innumerable instruments disposed in the plains, on the mountains, in the hollows of the valleys, or assembled in a body in the forests; the waters, which possess a vocal range of so enormous an extent, from the purling of a spring in the moss to the immense harmonies of Ocean; . . . finally . . . this continual emission of sounds, this confused noise of elements forever flowing, *dilates my thought* into strange reveries and throws me into states of wonder from which I cannot return.[80]

Sometimes, on the contrary, it is in the stillness of things and of being that one feels life spreading out like an infinite expanse:

> Gray clouds, but lightly silvered at their edges, are spread out equally over the whole face of the sky . . . The winds are still, and the peaceful Ocean transmits to me only a melodious murmur that comes pouring into the mind like a beautiful wave on the beach.[81]

The being who receives life, receives then a life that dilates, a life that creates space. Thought, "swollen by a fresh inundation, flows over the dike and spreads freely over all its banks." [82] One assists at the "deployment of a whole sky which one seems to have within oneself." [83] The interior place in which one "extends oneself as far as the eye can reach," [84] is "a free expanse as vast as the sky." [85] In the same way, the gaze that follows the vital impulse on its course throughout all nature seems to participate with it in the conquest or the new establishment of an exterior space:

> The greenness visibly gains ground; it springs from the garden into the arbors, it dominates the entire length of the pond; it leaps, so to speak, from tree to tree, from thicket to thicket, in the fields and on the slopes, and I watch as it already reaches the forest and begins to spread over the treetops. Soon it will have flowed out as far as the eye can see, and all the great spaces bounded by the horizon will be undulating and rustling like one vast sea, a sea of emerald. A few days more and we shall have all the display, all the unfolding of the vegetable kingdom.[86]

He who lives this experience, "receives into himself the empire of the vastest countrysides and the depth of the sky." [87] Space—exterior, interior—lies at his feet, "a reach of life like a drowsing sea." [88] "You who see," said Barbey to Guérin, "you who see only the great horizons of the world reflected in the mirror of your mind . . . your gaze [is] dilated like that of the eagles, accustomed to embrace immeasurable lines . . ." [89]

It is this invasion of space by one's glance that is sung of in *Glaucus:*

> But the day when, from a lonely mountain peak,
> I saw (it was for me a radiant awakening!)
> The world *traversed by the flames of the sun,*
> And the fields and the streams sleeping in the distance,
> The distance intoxicating my mind and my eyes;
> I wished *to make my gaze equal to space,*
> And possess without limits, leaving no trace in it,
> The width of the fields with that of the skies.[90]

The being who "makes his gaze equal to space" arrives there by a movement of gaze and of mind which reproduces the very movement of life in the universe.

But this movement is more than spatial, it is temporal. What it supplies is life diffused in duration as well as in extent. For Guérin as for Lamennais, time is a dilation of the present. One could say that each moment that comes to birth contains still more than its part of actuality and finds itself already distended with a latent future:

> An innumerable generation is *actually* suspended from the branches of all the trees, from the filaments of the humblest grasses, like children at the maternal breast . . . Future forests imperceptibly sway in living forests.[91]

A half-actual future already forms and stirs within the very precincts of the present. The future is thus no longer the unknown over whose arrival one was apprehensive, the task ahead under the burden of which one was afraid of succumbing. It is not solely that which will be, but that which is already in the process of realizing itself. It is that which one summons up, that of which one has a presentiment, that which is being prepared. It is fulfillment and enlargement. All mistrust falls away and one arrives at "one of those moments of utmost confidence in which everything seems to be disposed according to one's desires, in which the impenetrable future becomes as it were transparent and allows one to catch a glimpse of a thousand felicities; a moment in which one smiles at everything and questions nothing; a moment in which all is wonder and happiness." [92]

Finally there I am, launched in life, provisioned with riches
and courage, and moving with assurance toward the future;
it seems to me that a gleam of light guides me, and I foresee an unknown goal toward which I advance.[93]

Let us sense the vast difference between this "progressive feeling" which, here, "is diffused in the being and fulfills it," and
on the other hand the feeling of total deficiency in respect to
time and the future in which Guérin's dialectic of duration had
taken its start. He who receives the gift of life, receives in effect
the gift of time. From the moment in which he feels that existence
is conferred upon him, he also feels this existence wake and
warm up the future and hatch the future. About him and within
him he participates in becoming. He experiences growth:

Imperceptibly my confidence expands. It is slow to grow,
as the days are; but in the same way as theirs, its development
is vital and diffuses in my breast a fecund warmth.[94]

I am arriving at a critical epoch of my inner life. At a
strange stirring in my ideas, at the almost sudden growth of
several of my faculties, at an acceleration of the movement of
my inner life, I recognize the approach of an evolution which
I have been invoking for a very long time.[95]

Since I saw you, my life is filled as it were with an ever-
growing light.[96]

. . . I shall enjoy nature in following an obscure path to
the heart of growth, in the thickness of the vegetation.[97]

A sense of the duration-growth which, in the first pages of
the *Centaure,* reaches a degree of extraordinary refinement:

My growth took its course almost entirely among the shadows
in which I was born . . . I was uneasy about my strength, I
recognized in it a force that could not remain solitary, and
happening either to shake my arms or to increase my pace
through the wide shadows of the cavern, I forced myself to
discover in the blows I struck at emptiness, and by the passionate leaps I took through it, *toward what* my arms ought
to stretch and my feet to carry me . . .
These disturbances alternated with long absences of any un-

easy motion. Hence I was possessed of no other feeling in my entire being but that of growth and of the stages of life that mounted in my breast.[98]

Never, perhaps, has the triple character of duration been better apprehended in the interior of the instant.

For, on the one hand, it is indeed a matter of a single instant, of a naked instant, similar in its isolation to the hollow of a cavern. He who finds himself there, finds himself without any past, without any definite future. He is in a hollow, a shadow, the pure indetermination of a thought without covering. But it is also this life which ascends, which lifts him up, which carries him along. He is a passage and a current. He is already that toward which his arms must reach and his feet must convey him. Beyond him, a whole temporal movement which is still himself advances toward the broad future, and one has only to follow it, to "order this movement of growth according to the progress of a god." [99] But also, on the other hand, this progress of a god, this course which one is going to follow, emerges in oneself, one feels it rise there. It is like a sort of virginal past, made of potency and impatience, which, given together with being, surges up from pretemporal depths to thrust him in the middle of time toward the future. The being who apprehends himself in this instant apprehends himself beyond instants, in full growth, at full progress; and he is, at one and the same time, he who passes by and he who watches himself pass by, he who follows the march of time, as one travels in the tracks of a being whom one loves, and he who, on the other hand, watches the temporal movement fulfill itself within him and about him.

There is at first something one feels "dawn in the depths of his mind," [100] which "sets out on a journey towards us." It is life. One sees "ascend from the depths of his being vapors that rise up as from a deep valley." [101] Coming from an anterior horizon, laden with seed and with thought, a creative action reaches out to us:

> From the heart of the depths where his infinite grace
> Keeps the stream of being and the treasure of life,
> God with his fecund voice called to awaking
> My soul which was still but a long sleep.[102]

The being who, responding to the call of God, awakens to life, awakens inclined at first, therefore, toward a creative anteriority from which there converge upon him a thousand powers that seek to be actualized. He is "at the center of melodies, the divine mirror on the track of the innumerable images which God has set in motion, flowing array of symbols which we call the universe." [103] He is the "center in which from all sides a thousand currents converge." [104] But he is also each one of these currents, and each one of the particular eddies of which their variations are composed. And he is finally, to the extremity of their drift, the last ripple of the last of their waves:

> Thus I forgot myself in the midst of the waves, yielding to the dragging power of their flow which carried me far and escorted their wild guest to all the charms of the shores. How many times, overtaken by nightfall, I have followed the streams under the shadows which were spreading abroad, laying down in the very depths of the valleys the nocturnal influence of the gods! [105]

> The sea birds left the distant reefs and accompanied the sea, as solitaries the mounting wave of their thoughts, to the most remote cove where the last wrinkle of the waters dies away with a light shudder upon beaches of level sand.[106]

Thus in the prolongation and the infinite enlargement of the instant, there is found achieved the extraordinary spatial and temporal deployment of which Guérin makes us witnesses. Time and space are one selfsame motion which, coming from every side and at all times, passes into the instant and into the place of consciousness, in order to diffuse itself anew into the beyond. The actual being perceives himself as it were invaded from all sides and extending himself in every direction. Like the god Bacchus, eternal youth, he is at one and the same time "deep" and "spread out everywhere." [107] Nature, time, space, all that animates with an immeasurable life the vastly dilated span of a minute of consciousness. Through this point and this moment there passes a creative breath which,

> always renewed, runs through the whole earth, nourishes to its extremities the eternal inebriation of the Ocean, and, impelled into the divine air, moves the stars that revolve without ceasing around the dark pole.[108]

What the present embraces is thus a life at the same time interior and cosmic, which is simultaneously developed in all the dimensions of duration and in all the fields of space; a life that is perceived and lived instantaneously, from one end of its course to the other; "like the flame that shoots from one branch to the other to the very top." [109]

"I alone," said the Centaur, "I alone have free movement, and at my will I transport my life from one end of these vales to the other." [110]

IV

Over the whole length of their course, Guérin's thought accompanies the movement of hours and things. Every hue of the sky, every ray of sunlight, every breath of wind, each particular variation of nature projects in its turn its nuance or its thrill into a mind that seeks to reflect "the universality of that which is."

And at first this gives to consciousness the sense of an absolute continuity. We are here in a thought and in a universe in which everything flows from the same source, in which everything is indwelling in life and in which life is indwelling in everything. As a result it seems that the same continuity prevails everywhere. A continuity of space, which, setting out from all the horizons, converges like as many uninterrupted lines upon the eye of the watcher; and which, setting out from this center untiringly irradiates the horizons. A continuity of time, a perpetual emission of moments, a "monotonous and continuous passage of what-

ever thing that roves [which] possesses the mind and never lets
the eyes turn a moment from the spectacle before them." [111]
A continuity of nature or rather of the incessant work which,
being performed in nature, is performed also in the mind
which is the reflection of it; "continual resumption of a maternal
embrace between nature and the life which she has created and
hidden in us"; [112] it is so close a clasp and continuity that the
motion of one dictates the motion of the other, and their two
movements form one perfect harmony. And so, in Guérin's
language, there is no more significant term than that which expresses this conjoint development:

> . . . I feel rising from the depths of my mind, from the
> first steps I take, a joy of an unaccustomed order and a singular
> vivacity. *In proportion as* I advance into the country, it mounts
> and extends forth . . .[113]

> Like a man who walks through the night, provided with a
> torch, *in proportion as* I advanced, objects seemed to array
> themselves with a sparkle that was altogether lively and
> charming.[114]

> The constellations which rise so pale take on less sparkle
> advancing into the depths of night than my life grew full in
> my breast, whether in power or splendor, *in proportion as* I
> penetrated the fields.[115]

But from this perfect proportion is soon born an inverse
feeling, more and more painful, of disharmony, of rupture, of
discontinuity, of isolation. For he who chooses to "surrender his
footsteps to the leading of the Hours" [116] and to "abandon himself to the gusts of the open air" [117] chooses also—"yielding to
the power of their courses" [118]—to abandon himself by turn to
each of the nuances of duration and the hues of space, and thus
finally becomes "the sport of everything that breathes on
earth." [119]
    No doubt, at first this uninterrupted variation which is the
one of the sky and of the waters, of the moods and of the thoughts,

has by reason of its harmonized double mobility a charm that
Guérin has for a long time felt:

> Each time the sky gives us a serene day
> It is day of pure joy and holiday in my breast;
> For, born on the slopes, my mind is linked
> And with a sweet friendship divinely tied
> To the fields, the woods, the waves, the sun,
> The sky pale or gray, smiling or rosy,
> The divers elements and all of nature;
> And from the intimacy of this pure friendship
> It comes about that *my mind attends the variations*
> *The uncertain winds impress on the seasons,*
> And as often as nature is displayed in festival,
> Then my mind sings and sparkles with joy.[120]

It is joy when nature is on holiday. But then what happens
when the day is gloomy?

> The day is gloomy and I imitate the day. Ah! my friend,
> what are we, or rather what am I, to suffer without respite
> from all things round about me, and *to see my mood follow the
> variations of the light*? . . . The days that are the most even
> and peaceful are yet for me crossed by a thousand imperceptible
> accidents that overtake only me. This mounts to degrees you
> could not believe. And so what is more broken up than my
> life, and what thread is so flimsy as to be more unsteady than
> my mind? [121]

The being who lived the totality of movement becomes he
who lives each of its successive variations. Each in its turn possesses him, and not only possesses him but determines him. And
to the very depths of himself, even to the most intimate feeling
he has of his own existence. In contrast to Maine de Biran,
Guérin cannot preserve the feeling of his being by distinguishing
it from the particular moods which traverse and agitate it. The
person who situates his being, not in his will, not even in *his*
life, but just in plain life, such as he breathes it, finds himself
reduced to never being anything except the one into whom he
has been transformed by life, this life made up of "a thousand
imperceptible accidents" which by turn modify his mind. The

mind then becomes the ever-anxious slave of a master of ever-changing moods. It feels itself "powerless to reject or to moderate the life which is suggested to it." [122]—"The governing of my thought is not in my hands . . ." [123]—". . . Everything makes itself master of me . . ." [124]

There is more to it than this. To the dissolution of the feeling of selfhood, there corresponds an intensification of the feeling of duration. But this feeling is no longer this time that of a continuous duration, apprehended in its entirety, as one creative indivisible flight, always similar to itself in the diversity of its creations. It is on the contrary the feeling of a duration in which nothing any longer survives except this very diversity. Every state of mind, exterior, interior, appears in its turn no more than a fugitive, isolated phenomenon, in which, on the other hand, the totality of existence takes refuge. Being and nature are now no more than the detached beads of a chaplet, a multiplicity which can never be told. Life is scattered like dust every grain of which is a grief:

> I now want one thing only, to live without *being cruelly affected by the slightest portions of time.* But what grounds can support a preoccupation capable of binding up my disquieted senses and freeing me of the *feeling of duration* as sleep does? [125]

A feeling of duration which becomes more anxious still from the fact that the being surrendered to diversity is also a being given up to rapidity. This course which we espouse and which runs in our blood, becomes there

> the unquiet flow
> Of life throughout our ardent nature.[126]

The succession of states which nothing links together takes on the aspect of an agonizing course from the very fact that nothing links them together, that nothing provides a transition between them, that we pass and that we see things pass abruptly from one pole to the other of the affective existence. The feeling of

the duration-growth then becomes the feeling of a monstrous acceleration of movement by which the world and the self find
themselves swept along:

> Since several days, my mind, already so unruly, is seized with
> a restless and somewhat violent mobility which makes it rush
> back and forth from one pole to the other, which no longer
> allows it to stop and sit still at the center of an order of ideas
> or beliefs but *sweeps it rapidly from region to region* and in-
> clines it, in passing, over all the abysses. I savor a strange
> pleasure in *feeling my soul carried away* like that prophet
> whom an angel snatched away by the hair of his head, and in
> *traversing immense reaches at a frightful speed.*[127]

The pleasure then soon turns to dread. For hardly has the
being proudly experienced himself in his feeling of "space ardent-
ly traversed," [128] than that space undergoes before his eyes the
same infernal metamorphosis as duration. It is suddenly no longer
the expanses of which one possesses oneself by "extending oneself
forth in every direction throughout those deserts"; [129] now it is
the desert itself, region empty and naked. The course of the
mind becomes so furious and so swift that it no longer allows it
to "stop and sit still"; it no longer allows man the time to put
substance and life into any point of the regions he traverses. The
latter, empty of self, empty of everything, are no longer anything more than a distance that is soon consumed or an abyss
surmounted in a soaring that becomes a flight of escape:

> My thought has no other guide than an indefatigable in-
> stinct for flight . . .[130]

> The unbelievable rapidity of the flight of life, the mystery
> of our destinies, the terrible questions which doubt from time
> to time addresses to the men firmest in their belief, finally that
> state which so often returns for me, in which the mind, like
> Lénore, *feels itself carried off at full speed toward I know not
> what doleful regions,* all of that had laid hold upon me.[131]

The anguish increases in proportion as the flight of time rushes
forward and as the feeling of the space-abyss is accentuated. The
gulf toward which and into which one is going is no different

from the emptiness one discovers in oneself, or rather between self and self, as if the unrestrained character of the course had caused a split and a growing hiatus between the diverse parts of the being:

> . . . I throw myself impetuously into any new project which can alter my existence; whether someone announces to me a little excursion for tomorrow or whether someone says to me: tomorrow your destinies are going to undergo a great change, I am equally affected, I rush ahead to both these events with the same impatience; a strange activity of thought develops in me. I gnaw quivering at the bit of time which prevents me from seizing at one leap what I devour with my eyes.[132]

Simultaneously, one is he who is already hurled into the future ahead of time, and the one who is left behind in the present. Man is he who "bounds in every direction like a blind force let loose," [133] but also the one who discovers himself to be "tardy in everything" [134] and whose sap runs slow. One is the Centaur, and also that being whom one day the Centaur met and whom he scorned because "his steps were short and his gait awkward." [135] This being was a man. And man is a Centaur, but "reduced to creeping along." [136] On the other hand, he is the one who takes possession of time and space by virtue of the rapidity of his course; on the other, he is the one who "measures space with sadness," [137] because he has been conquered by the march of time. He is the one who flies and the one who crawls, the one who, torn apart, sees hollowed out between the two broken fragments of his being a harrowing temporal distance.

Then it is as if one had committed the gravest fault: which consists in having failed to make our total being benefit from the moving gift of life. Our punishment is the feeling of our abandonment, of our having outdone ourselves. We have been abandoned at the side of the road by the unknown victor in a race which we should have won:

> I outrun myself; my unwieldly and listless will is put out of breath in the pursuit of my mind . . .[138]

The destruction of duration is accomplished in every way: first by the separation of the moments that compose it, then by the splitting of each particular moment.

Nothing remains then but the feeling of living a spasmodic, broken-up life, the life of a being who "draws his breath in short gasps." [139] At every instant it stops to recover itself, and then breaks off again. This is "successionless, convulsive creation, abruptly breaking off every minute . . ." [140] It is the essentially alternated and discontinuous rhythm of cyclothymia:

> In my life there are alternations, contradictions, comings and goings, conflicts between thought and action . . .[141]

> That is my life in brief: an alternation of starts and failures, of transports of the imagination and prostrations of mind, of dreams, crazy by their sheer intensity, and desolating coolings off.[142]

> Yesterday, a thorough attack of fever in thorough form; today, weakness, debility, exhaustion.[143]

> I draw up beautiful moral schemes of life, my courage rises, it seems to me that I am a Stoic. But as soon as I have come home and set myself to the task, I collapse, everything breaks up within me, it is a desolating ruin.[144]

In place of an impetus and a duration, there is now nothing more than a time and a moment that crumble: a life all in fragments made up "of ideas broken, suspended, miscarried." [145] But there is not only the disaggregation of time, there is the dissolution of space. The latter is as it were the issue of the former. He who abandons himself to the movement of time, delivers himself up to "a propensity that *disperses* him over all the regions of the plains." [146] To dilate is to disseminate; and to disseminate is finally to be lost. Already, at the moment of taking leave of his origins and for the first time conveying abroad a power until then "confined without any loss," [147] the Centaur had had the presentiment of this final reduction:

> When I descended from your asylum in the light of day . . . , I felt that my being, until then so stable and so single, was

tottering and losing a great deal of itself, as if it had had to disperse itself to the winds.[148]

At the end of each impetus, then, there is the dispersion of that impetus into the expanses. Each movement of thought becomes by degrees "a bit of floating mist which is going to be dissolved." [149] He who follows the bent of growth, "dissipates his being like the cloud which dissolves and is lost in proportion as it advances into the azure." [150] He "is reduced and is lost as quickly as falling snow." [151] And the mind which thought to take by surprise, in the movement, the secret of nature and of life, sees disappear at the end of the movement, at one and the same time, movement, nature, and life:

> . . . I have thought sometimes that I was going to come upon the dreams of sleeping Cybele, and that the mother of the gods, betrayed by dreams, would relinquish some of her secrets; but I never met with anything but sounds *that became dissolved in the breath of night,* or words as inarticulate as the bubbling of streams.[152]

In place of the feeling of growth, there is now an infinite feeling of decrease. Guérin never ceased to experience it:

> Very young, I sought the dying
> Lustre of declining day.[153]

The being who pursues the experience of life to its end, arrives again, but by a much longer road, at the experience of decay and death. He no longer finds himself immediately assailed and vanquished by the feeling of a fatal impotence. Having this time set out from a feeling of original power, he very soon discovers himself with all of nature drifting toward a terminal point. Death is youth grown old, a long distance traveled, an impetus which little by little, through fatigue, through wear and tear, yields itself up to immobility:

> This last attempt at production, this impotent recurrence of a used-up fecundity, these pale testimonies to a vestige of love and strength . . . presented the idea of a melancholy

spring—the last of the springs, when a decrepit nature will with difficulty make sprout a bit of verdure and will show a glimpse of her supreme and failing smile through the shadows and the cold of an eternal inertia.[154]

Or again it is as if one were departing forever from a being whom one loves:

Meanwhile the darkness is separating us slowly; I am losing you by degrees.[155]

Vanquished thus by time, exhausted by space, life, thought slacken their course, and everything finally stops, fixed in a sort of aridity and stupor:

My head is arid . . . A strange stupor seizes me, I remain motionless, feeling nothing except the heavy, oppressive fixity of life, which seems to have halted in a state of incomprehensible uneasiness, and the beating of an artery which throbs at a spot in my head.[156]

It will soon be eight days since my mental life began to diminish, and the river began to abate, reducing itself by so perceptible a diminution that after some sunny days it was no more than a thread of water. Today I have seen its last drop disappear.[157]

My river is losing itself in the sands.[158]

When the last drop has been steamed out, nothing else remains but a consciousness that is an empty desert. Everything in it is dead, any chance of regaining the source, of communicating with life, has vanished. It is as if one were outside of the world, outside of existence, outside of time and space, like a still lucid corpse that has lost hope of communicating with the living:

. . . This beautiful sun which ordinarily is so beneficial to me has passed over me like an extinct star; it has left me as it found me, cold, frozen, insensible to any outside impression and suffering, in the little of me that still lives, from fruitless and miserable ordeals.[159]

Today I cast nothing but a shadow, all form is opaque and stricken with death. As on a night walk, I advance with the isolated feeling of my existence, among the inert phantoms of all things.[160]

A passage of extraordinary depth which seems to mark the last spiral of Guérin's hell, supposing it were possible to see to the bottom of it. The being who advances into this abyss is revealed therein as simultaneously in an absolute solitude and nevertheless accompanied, not by things, but by the inert phantoms of things. In these limbos where there is no more movement, no more time, no more space, nothing more than a thought uselessly proceeding in a kind of stupor, the image of nature and even the image of life can still be seen, but hideously transformed into specters of death. Nothing could reveal a situation more tragic, an exile more profound, than such a *perversion* of life into death as soon as it crosses the threshold of the mind. We are in the regions of dead life which are inhabited by an existence banished from life, an existence which can be conceived and experienced as a nonlife, as *no longer receiving life.* The being who discovers himself in "the *isolated* feeling of his existence" finds himself in a situation far more horrible than that which he experienced in the feeling of his misery and his nullity. For there is no longer now, it seems, any hope, any recourse. The sole recourse was that in the life outside, in the forces of nature. And thought no longer reaches nature; it reflects it, and this reflection is transformed into a specter. Then, as in the theme of the "unhappy consciousness" of Hegel, one realizes that all thought, all regard, consummate the loss and involve the irremediable negation of life. One "remains isolated, cut off from any participation in the universal life." [161] One remains a thought without object. without power, and without source, without life. One *is,* but one is outside of life, outside of God:

> Through those days, there is revealed in the depths of my mind, in that most intimate and deepest part of my substance, a despair that is quite strange; it is like dereliction and darkness outside of God.[162]

V

My God, how I suffer from life! not in its accidents . . .
but in itself, in its substance, apart from any phenomenon.[163]

Having arrived at this terminal point, thought remains buried
in the consciousness of its isolation, dereliction. "I am alone. I
feel, I experience nothing except *my life*." [164] Only *my* life, that
is to say, only myself without life. Under pain of suffering in-
tolerably, the being, "solitary and excommunicated from nature," [165] must unreservedly renounce any participation in life,
in life spatial, temporal, universal:

Look at what I suffered before resigning myself to the limits
of myself . . .[166]

Resignation is the burrow dug under the roots of an old
oak or in the fault of some rock, which offers refuge to the
fleeing prey a long time pursued. It threads its way rapidly
through the narrow and dark opening, crouches at the bottom,
and huddling itself up and cowering there, its heart beating
at a redoubled rate, it listens to the distant baying of the
pack and the cries of the hunters.[167]

It is in this final sinking down of the being into the hollow
shell of his thought that we must in our turn, it seems, abandon
Guérin. Contraction, withdrawal, folding up the self "around
its own center," [168] that is always the movement by which everything is terminated in Guérin. In the small number of pages
which he has left us, there are very few which do not reflect
"sudden contraction of the being after an extreme dilation." [169]
But what is extraordinary about Guérin's adventure is precisely
that it continues on its course when everything seemed to indicate it had finished it. Indeed, in one sense, it was natural for
it to recommence. It is possible to interpret human life and
human time as an alternating succession of dilations and con-
centrations. After having interred himself in his subterranean
abode, Guérin could yet, indefinitely, "attempt to live," and
this he has done many a time. But that is not the astonishing

thing. The astonishing thing is that, driven to this extreme and terminal point of the human adventure, Guérin should have one day gone *beyond this termination,* should have thrust himself still farther away from life, and that precisely in order to find life. As for Kierkegaard or Lequier, there is for Guérin a sort of transcending of the situation-limit, the discovery of an opening in the wall of the being, a hope that illumines the very depths of despair.

That begins with a question:

> If I sink into your breast, mysterious billows, will there happen to me what happened to those knights who, dragged down to the bottom of lakes, found there a marvelous palace; or like that fisherman in the fable, in falling into the sea would I become a god? [170]

Then the adventure is engaged:

> . . . My thought . . . has little concern with the outside world and sinks itself in the opposite direction.[171]

> (My mind) voluptuously sinks deeper in its motion of flight, it retreats toward places unknown to anyone and to itself, but it is sure of reaching them . . .[172]

> My whole being is a thought; my life draws sustenance from new sources, my imagination faces in new directions.[173]

Finally this word, perhaps the most extraordinary that Guérin has written: ". . . I hope for everything *from the blind side* . . ."[174]

Past the terminal point, into the darkness, Guérin plunges on. He "risks the approaches to an unknown world." [175]

This unknown world is death, or rather it is what lies beyond death. For death is no longer regarded here as pure immobility, negation of life, final point. It is that which is beyond the past life of the being who is dead, but not beyond what sort of future may be reserved to him. It is that which appears in the deepest pit of the mind when "life falls back into nature's breast" [176] and when "the mysteries have re-entered the breast of the gods." [177] Then, "the foreign life which had penetrated it during the day seeping away drop by drop," [178] the mind, withdrawn "into absolute repose," [179] "removed from the action of time," [180] cleansed of all the forms and of all the exterior movements which had imposed themselves upon it, discovers itself, "virginal consciousness," [181] in a point that is situated at both the end and the beginning of all things, in a point which is *between* times, in which are reabsorbed and from which proceed all spaces, a point forever final and forever initial, a dead stop, but also a *punctum saliens,* since from this point life is perceived on both its slopes. The being who succeeds in situating himself in this point, in which one has "the double and mysterious feeling of an existence that subsides and an existence that mounts up," [182] can only "compare his thought [it is almost mad, says Guérin] to lightning that quivers on the horizon *between* two worlds." [183] Now, in this point, the being, detached from nature, detached from his own life, pure consciousness and pure existence, finds himself situated outside of all immanence, and nothing any longer exists for him except the feeling of a personal and universal death, for which there is instantaneously substituted the feeling, this time transcendent, of a naked life, a life that is miraculously conferred to his thought in order that it may recreate for him, at the interior of itself, that world and that self of his which had perished. By means of this spiritual death which each one can live at the end of each moment of consciousness, one sets himself free from the yoke of time and space, one is no longer the prey of a movement that determines us. Removed from the empire of second causes, one "comes upon the cause of the movement," and this cause is the very act, the prime and ever-present act of transcendence: "Dost thou seek the gods, O Macarius, they from whom are issued men, animals, and the principles of the universal fire?" [184] Beyond the living fire which animates the universe, one can thus arrive at the direct consciousness of the creative energy. One arrives at it in "mounting

to the very sources of being"; [185] or rather, in as much as the
interior voyage which one makes in order to arrive there consists
in a stripping by the mind of every mental form and of every
sensuous image, one does not mount to it, one descends to it,
as into a dark and subterranean place "where one sees the sources
re-enter earth's breast." [186] There, in the lowest depths, in a
place where there are no longer any forms, no longer any images,
no longer anything except a naked life which is given, one tastes
that "utterly pure life that flows to us from the breast of the
gods," [187] one is at the junction-point of omnipotence and existence.

A point of arrival which is also a starting point:

. . . Starting point of universal life; there . . . , I hear the
first chant of beings in all its freshness.[188]

For, everything being substituted, the being having broken
with the idea of his anterior existence, it once more becomes
possible for him to form "the most intimate relationships with
the loss which he has sustained." [189] As with Descartes, as with
Mallarmé, to the eyes of him who has abolished all, there is revealed the possibility of remaking all, world and self, time and
space, as a demiurge fashions his universe. He who has placed
himself in the initial moment, in which one sees life "pass
through the pores" and "rush toward the being who calls it," [190]
that being, suddenly become "mighty in his roots," [191] can, from
this point, "secretly govern the whole thought and life," "command all the interior life from its origins, and rule the mind,
as God rules the world, by the knowledge and the possession of
the first principles": [192]

. . . I go on, free . . . , to reconstruct a mind and a world
according to my will.[193]

Thus, commanding all the interior life from its origins, one
"draws near here below to the life of the angels." [194] One is
"admitted into the destiny of the gods." [195] The "engulfed
mortal" [196] is awakened a Centaur.

Chapter IX Mallarmé

> . . . The magic power which
> transforms the negative into being . . .
> (HEGEL, *Phenom.*, I, 29.)

I

Has it been remarked that as early as 1862 Mallarmé gave a very precise definition of his poetry? In an article devoted to a book by his friend Des Essarts, he wrote then as follows:

> The sentiments of Parisian life taken seriously and viewed through the prism of poetry, *an ideal which does not exist through its own dream and would be the lyricism of reality;* such is the intention of the Poésies Parisiennes.[1]

One cannot imagine an "intention" more exactly the contrary of his very own, and it is no doubt for that reason that Mallarmé applies himself to formulating it so precisely. So it will suffice to reverse the terms of it to obtain a perfect definition of Mallarmean poetry. It wishes to express an ideal which *exists* through it own dream and which would *not* be the lyricism of reality.

From the age of twenty then, Mallarmé already knows what his problem is and how it poses itself. It is a question of attaining something which exists only through the dream one makes of it and which is not by any means either a reproduction or a prolongation of present reality. One has to make exist through dream, without any help from the real world, a properly poetic world. There is no possibility, as there was for Baudelaire, of engendering a movement which starts from reality in order to arrive at the verge of the ideal. Reality is not a starting point. It must be suppressed or ignored.

But then how does one attain through dream that of which dream has precisely the need in order to be dreamed? How does one find a starting point?

Thus from the beginning Mallarmean thought finds itself stricken as it were with paralysis. It does not move. It neither takes flight spontaneously, like the poetry of Lamartine or Vigny, nor even artificially, like the poetry of Baudelaire. And if to dream is to imagine, it does not even dream. It situates at an infinite distance an ideal of which it is entirely ignorant, except that the ideal depends upon its dream and it cannot dream it. Then it waits to be able to dream. Instead of a starting point, for Mallarmé there is only immobility and waiting:

> I sink in myself till my ennui mounts . . .

Thus there is no initial movement. There is nothing except a negative state which can be prolonged indefinitely, eternally, like an empty time.

But still, if there is no initial movement, there is this initial situation. In the absence of any movement and any positive duration, there is something that exists or that would exist if it could be dreamed. There is, if you will, not yet a poetry, but the kind of vacancy which is formed in the sky of thought by forgetfulness of the things of the world and by the simple waiting for what has not yet taken place.

The poetry of Mallarmé has thus, in spite of everything, a kind of beginning. It is neither a point nor a movement, it is an initial space.

It is an absolutely virginal space, comparable on the one hand to the whiteness of the sheet of paper on which one will write, and on the other hand comparable to the uniformity of the blue sky. Among the poems of Mallarmé's youth, there is perhaps not a single one which does not have the Azure for its theme. But there is also perhaps not one of them that aims at describing it directly or at seizing upon the positive significance of it. The Azure is the symbol or the presence of an indefinite reality which can only be expressed under the negative form of space or the sky. An ineffable, indescribable presence which seems to get reflected in thought as the sky is mirrored in the water:

> . . . a high gushing fountain sighs toward the Azure!
> —Toward the softened Azure of pale, pure October,
> Which mirrors in great basins its infinite languor . . .

Hardly a faint pretense of movement is made here. No doubt the fountain rises, but this movement of ascension is immediately exhausted, it has only the worth of a sigh, of a sigh *toward* the azure. Nothing exists except in the most purely static relationship of a space to a thought, and of a thought to this space. But from the very fact that it has this relationship, the initial indetermination takes on a new significance. This is no longer simply a space, it is the space *toward which* this sigh rises. It is a positive space, the space of a desire. Besides, between this desire and this place there is another space, a negative space, a void, a distance. The Azure is then that which presents itself beyond its absence, that which affirms itself beyond that which denies it, that which exists beyond that which does not exist. It is a presence, but at a distance. Like an object glimpsed through a window, like a reflection in a mirror. It is in its absence that its presence appears; it is in the void that its fullness is mirrored.

From the beginning, therefore, Mallarmean poetry takes on the aspect of a mirage. A mirage of a very special kind, for that which is found thus situated and contemplated at a distance, this thing and this indefinable place, is neither an object nor an exterior world; it is the very being of him who contemplates. A mirage in which one perceives himself on the horizon, not as he is, not where he is, but precisely as he is not and where he is not. It is the myth of Narcissus and also that of Hérodiade:

> Sad flower that grows alone and has no other excitement
> Than its own shadow in the water viewed with atony.

Detached from the real which it does not notice, but detached as well from an ideal image of itself which it wishes to know, which it situates in the azure, and with which it seeks to be identified at a distance, Mallarmean poetry constitutes itself in a closed circuit. It is the double reflection which, across the void, through the window glass, the two halves of a thought that tries to think itself, exchange:

> For me, Poetry takes the place of love, because it is in love with itself and the pleasure it has with itself rains back deliciously in my mind . . .[2]

Here there reappears the same ascending and descending movement as before, movement reduced to the extreme minimum, since it spends itself and forms again in the void through its own impulsion. This sigh of the fountain in love with the azure; or the reverted image of the movement of divine Charity descending upon the creature while the creature returns it to his creator under the form of love. Mallarmean love seeks its pleasure and its substance in the simplest possible movement, in a desire which rises up, finds itself, reflects itself, and falls back again. It attempts to exist solely in a relationship of exchange from the self to the self, in a purely interior movement in which the given and the rendered back are equivalent; in a perpetual movement.

II

But what if Poetry "in love with itself" should not find itself? What if its pleasure with itself, far from deliciously falling back into its point of departure and arrival, goes astray and never meets with itself in space? Then what happens? What takes place if nothing responds to the movement by which love repairs toward its object, and the latter remains as undetermined as ever?

Then this poetry of love is transformed into that of the most painful desire.

It is so painful a desire because now nothing exists but itself. It is as if it were isolated within itself and so far removed from its object that it no longer knows even what the latter signifies. It is the desire of being other, of being elsewhere, without even the strength to imagine what that other and that elsewhere are:

> To fly! to fly yonder! I sense that the birds are drunk
> From being amidst the unknown foam and the skies! [3]

A desire that does not know where to apply, whom to reach, or even what to ask. Desire reduced to its most elementary essence, that of a need, of a lack. This lack is everything, since now there is nothing except itself in the being, so that the latter has entirely become an indeterminate power of desire, an immense hunger:

> For the lips which the air of pure azure makes ravenous . . .[4]

> And the mouth, feverish and hungry for blue azure . . .[5]

> . . . You know that the sole occupation of a man who respects himself is in my opinion to gaze at the azure while dying of hunger.[6]

If only this "beggar for azure"[7] could ever be diverted from his painful contemplation. But in contrast to Quietism, he cannot forget his own situation, his situation of a mendicant. If he "turns his back on life," [8] he is none the less constantly informed of its presence, if only by the gesture he makes in turning away from it. The more he desires, the more he detests what is not his desire. The more his desire is purified, and in being purified is intensified, the more there is intensified in him the consciousness of the hostile reality which denies the existence, as such, of what he desires. Hatred of life,[9] disgust with the earth,[10] with him-

self, and with sin, such is invariably the inverted form taken by
love for an ideal the celestial reality of which is denied and
affronted by terrestrial reality:

> Modern muse of Impotence . . . , I dedicate to thee these
> few lines of my life written in the clement hours in which thou
> didst not inspire in me the hate of creation and the sterile love
> of nothingness.[11]

Thus the double intensity of love-desire and hate-desire opposes one to the other in a paralyzing conflict, two contradictory
realities which simultaneously exist at a distance and which re-
ciprocally deny each other: the reality in which one lives and
that in which one does not live, the place in which one has
situated one's dream and the place where with horror one sees
oneself surrendered to chance and to ill luck. Between the two
there is an infinite distance made of negation. This position of
radical dualism seems to be a return to Baudelairism, but it is
worse still, because here no positive relationship is possible between worlds which exclude each other. This is a position which
is comparable only to that of a Calvinist for whom the Redemption had not taken place. In the face of a creation which is irremediably defiled, there would rise in an infinitely remote heaven
a transcendence so absolute that no grace could descend from it,
nor any desire be transformed into an endeavor to draw near to
it. And so, from 1863 on, Mallarmé condemns and rejects Baudelairism, not, as it has been said, because of its dualism, but
on the contrary because that dualism is still not radical enough,
for it has not placed a vast enough abyss between two worlds
which no action can link:

> The folly of a modern poet has been to go so far as to grieve
> that "Action was not the sister of Dream." [12]

For Mallarmean Puritanism, therefore, there is no human action possible or permissible. There is only the Dream, because
the dream is not an action, but a sort of passive evasion, a mirage,

in which nothing is joined to anything, in which all distance subsists, in which the supreme principle of the separation of realities is safeguarded. Thus transcendence will not be degraded by any movement to bring the two worlds together:

> My God, what if it were otherwise, what if the Dream were deflowered and lowered, how then should we save ourselves, we unhappy ones whom the earth disgusts and who have only the Dream for refuge? O my Henry, drink of the Ideal. Happiness here below is ignoble.—One should have well-calloused hands indeed to pick it up. To say "I am Happy" is to say "I am base" and oftener "I am silly." To do that one must not see beyond this ceiling of happiness the sky of the Ideal or purposely he must close his eyes. I have done a little poem on these ideas called *les Fenêtres,* I am sending it to you . . .[13]

This little poem, one of the most admirable of Mallarmé's youth, is often neglected by the Mallarmeists because they are of the opinion that therein Mallarmé is still not enough disengaged from the influence of Baudelaire. That is a mistake. Indeed in reality this poem is the first one in which Mallarmé clearly surpasses Baudelairism, but to surpass it he has *to go on beyond it,* to push Baudelairism beyond Baudelaire, and it is in this sense that one can say of *les Fenêtres* that it is a poem authentically Mallarmean because ultra-Baudelairean.

The radical opposition between two worlds of which the one, sad hospital, is the *place where one is,* while the other, the Azure, is the *place where one is not,* forms the subject of this poem. There is no movement from one to the other, except that of the person who stops at once before the transparent obstacle of a window. On one side of this window-glass, the poet; on the other, his image magically transformed into that of an inhabitant of the Azure: "I look at myself and find that I am an angel . . ." Let us not fail to recognize the tragic character of this hypostasis. It is thus that a damned person would see himself in dream in Paradise.

As we read it today in its definitive version, the meaning of

the poem is profoundly changed as the consequence of the changing of a single word:

> I look at myself and find that I am an angel! and I *die,* and I love
> —Be the windowpane the art, be it the mysticity—
> To be reborn, bearing my dream in a diadem,
> In the anterior sky where Beauty flowers!

But in 1863 the poem read: "I look at myself and find that I am
an angel! and I *dream,* and I love . . . to be reborn . . .'' Now,
as we shall see, death will later constitute, in Mallarmé's eyes,
pre-eminently an *action* by means of which one really passes from
one world to the other. In replacing *I dream* with *I die,* Mallarmé
will in 1866 give his poem an absolutely new meaning. There will
then be an action by means of which, from the other side of the
window, one is really born again in the "anterior sky." But in
1863, in the earlier version and for the earlier Mallarmé, it was
entirely different. The dream was not an action, but precisely a
dream and a lie, a lie recognized as such. The poet never ceased
to remain on the wrong side of the mirror; on the other side,
separated from him, was his dream. And the poem consisted entirely in this opposition of two worlds and of two *selves* between
which the transparency of the window interposed an absolute
metaphysical distance.

III

> On account of a woman's hair which has brought to birth in
> my brain the idea of a flag, my heart, seized with a military ar-
> dor, is darting across hideous landscapes and is going to lay
> siege to the strong castle of hope in order to plant there this
> standard of fine gold. But the rash man, after this brief moment
> of madness, perceives Hope to be only a sort of veiled and
> sterile ghost.[14]

Nothing could be more significant than the subject of this poem
written at almost the same time as *les Fenêtres.* In it Hope is
veiled. and is revealed to be the very figure of sterility. This

theme will reappear again and again in Mallarmé's life during the period that is about to follow. There is not a single one of his dreams or his projects in which there is not to be finally revealed the same veiled and sterile specter. Indeed Mallarmé's impotence tends toward a worse despair than Baudelaire's, which is always tinctured with hope and animated by the velleities of action. But what hope is possible when at the turning of every avenue there is always discovered the same perspective of two hostile realities of equal strength which can only neutralize each other? The *ideal existing through its own dream* is only a dream, an absurd dream, for the ideal can exist only in an insupportable contrast with an inverse reality which belies it and which it belies.

As varied as they are vain are the attempts made by Mallarmé to escape from this grief and grievance of seeing "earth and sky mutually hostile." The most brutal, at any rate the most direct of these attempts is that which consists in trying to shatter the translucent partition and to escape from the antinomy by means of the violent negation of one of the two terms:

> Is there a way, my God, who knowest bitterness,
> To smash the glass by the monster affronted
> And escape . . .[15]

to escape out of the real, to get lost on the other side of the glass, in that object of my contemplation which would become an object of union?

But there is no punishment more severe than that which the direct contact with his dream reserves for the mirror-smasher. Mallarmé has the presentiment of it in the same poem, since he adds:

> At the risk of falling throughout eternity.

But he makes a more precise admission of it in a letter to Coppée:

> Two years ago I committed the sin of beholding the Dream in its ideal nakedness,[16]

words identical to those of Hérodiade when she confesses that beyond the accumulated memories in the glass she has now and again distinguished the naked visage of her desire:

> But horror! of nights, in thine inexorable fount
> I have known the nakedness of my disheveled dream.

Between the direct vision of his dream, as it is, where it is, and the feeling of an eternal fall into an abyss, there is no difference. For the dream exists only by reason of the glass, that is to say, the distance, and if there is no longer either glass or distance, there is no longer anything. Except oneself in nothingness. And so there is no graver mistake than that which consists in this confrontation of self with self, all distance being abolished. The direct experience of transcendence has the character of a horrible vision. The being who finds himself in direct contact with this nakedness cannot bear the brightness of it—inhuman, dissolvent, polar—nor can he bear himself.

It is necessary then, at all costs, not to break the glass, to maintain between the ideal and the self the intermediate distance. For this distance is not simply the obstacle which forbids us from approaching it. It is also the protective medium—make-up, veil, or windowpane—which shields us from its mortal contact.

But this protective wall, one must not breach it either in the other direction, and in order to escape again the contradictory presence of two universes, one must not deny, this time, that of the Ideal, to throw oneself in despair upon the enemy world of the Real:

> I cut a window in the wall of canvas . . .

For the punishment reserved for him who yields to the temptation of the real is identical to that incurred by him who wished to force the barriers of the ideal. The torment of the "chastised clown," is to appear as he is, stripped of his rouge and his genius:

> All of a sudden the sun strikes the nudity . . .

insupportable nudity which is the result of the movement toward life, as it is the result of the movement toward the ideal.

Yet there is still, it seems, another recourse, which does not consist any more in shattering the windowpane, in making a breach, in abolishing the wall, but on the contrary in making it thicker, so to speak, in rendering its surfaces so opaque that no communication through it is any longer possible. The more and more insupportable awareness of the existence of a radiant world, whose pure presence at a distance suffices to belie or irremediably to debase the world in which one is and in which one must stay, is easily transformed into a detestation of that ideal which condemns us to endless unhappiness in adoring it. One feels oneself to be the victim of a transcendent exigency which nothing can fulfill. One feels eternally and unrelentingly given over to fixing one's eyes on an object infinitely set apart which he can never approach because he is unworthy, an object unvaryingly similar to itself alone and unvaryingly disallowed by distance to an unvarying unworthiness.

> From the everlasting azure the serene irony
> Overwhelms, indolently beautiful like the flowers,
> The impotent poet who curses his genius
> Amidst a sterile desert of Sorrows.[17]

> The immutable calm of this white blaze
> Makes me hate life and our feverish love . . .[18]

hate life, hate oneself, hate love and happiness. There is there, brought about by the forces of despair, a complete reversal. Hatred of life is transformed into hatred of the Ideal:

> The Azure,
> Seraphic, smiles in the deep windows,
> And I, I detest it, the fine azure . . .[19]

Detestation, denial, which now manifests itself in the desire, no longer to abolish the intermediate space, but to affirm it in its most positive form, to make of this empty extent a space filled in, a solid screen, a wall without window, windowpane, or any opening whatsoever:

> Rise, fogs! Pour forth your monotonous ashes
> With long tatters of mist in the heavens
> Which will blacken the livid swamp of the autumns
> And build, you a *great* silent *ceiling!* [20]

To the crystalline purity of the window glass there now succeeds the opacity of fogs, screens, and ceilings. Thought, in its horror with itself, envelops itself in matter, makes itself matter. But this grayish matter, this thick mental fog in which one is plunged and absorbed, is no different from the polar and translucent purity in which the image of one's dream was dissolved. The temptation of matter and of the "heavy dreamless sleep," [21] the temptation of forgetfulness, is tantamount to the temptation of the insupportable presence. Making an opening or building a ceiling come to the same thing, that is to say, to Nothing.

IV

It is then no less impossible to repudiate one of the two mutually hostile worlds than to establish a direct relationship between them.

One hope remains, however. For if any direct relationship is impossible, does not the very image of the fog suggest to us the possibility of an indirect relationship? The fog, no longer this time conceived as an opaque wall, but as a curtained window, half transparent, at once the conducting and protecting medium through which material things are impregnated with light and in which the luminosity becomes as materially perceptible. Thus space would no longer be entirely a void, nor entirely a plenum, but, as in impressionist paintings, an environment. And thus an exquisitely ambiguous entity, which, in veiling the purity of the dream and the ugliness of reality, would make of them two principles no longer irremediably hostile and exclusive, but in spite of their remote positions joined together by something continuous and almost palpable, along the length of which thought could travel. An entity, again, thanks to the almost chemical power of which it would be possible to transmute one of these principles into the other, to make the ideal into the real, and the real into the ideal. From the time of his youth, in fact, and especially during his sojourn in London, Mallarmé had been struck by the mysterious reconciliation which is operative between the crudity of things and the brutality of light by the operation of sifting and veiling which indeed is that of the fog; the "dear fogs which muffle up our brains": [22]

> I hate London when there are no fogs: in its mists it is an incomparable city.[23]

In the following passage one sees, at the moment it starts to work, this process of idealization which the mist makes reality undergo:

> It was very cold, the grass was wet like the morning—fog after all is dew—and one felt around him an immense amphitheater impalpable but real, behind which were morbidly outlined sparse and beautiful trees; [24]

as, inversely, in the lines already quoted from *Soupir,* there is a manner of *realization* and even humanization of the ideal, owing to the fact that the autumn fog, in veiling the azure, renders it less remote, less inaccessible. It is a *softened azure* and no longer a blazing sky.

This indirect and ambiguous realization, moreover, will not be solely a spatial relationship. It will as well, and indeed oftener, be a temporal one. For, as we have seen, to the simultaneous presence of two spatial worlds, one made of azure, the other of matter, and separated by a void, there corresponded the presence at a distance of two mutually exclusive durations, the one of pure Eternity, the other the perpetuity of a lack and the permanence of an absence. But is there not among all the varieties of duration something analogous to the fog, an equivocal entity, a conducting and transforming medium which might perform the same transitional functions? One of the earliest and from then on one of the most frequent forms under which there is manifested with Mallarmé the very feeling of *time* itself consists in the consciousness of the imperceptible gliding by which things pass, and pass precisely from the reality of the present into the ideality of the past. Or again in the consciousness of the exquisite aerial pause which occurs in the fulfillment of things, when before landing in the present, they are still suspended in air, emerging from the mist of the future, half latent and half imminent: "Suspense over the water where my dream delays the undecided one . . ."[25] Thence proceeds Mallarmé's taste for everything that is still virtual, but also for everything that is in the process of appearing and fading away; his predilection for "faded things,"[26] for "decrepitudes,"[27] for "all that which is summed up in the one word: fall."[28] This love is not due to a naturally "decadent" or "morbid" taste. It has to do with the repugnance of the poet to seize things in their actuality, in the instant when they are nothing other than what they are, that is to say, entirely on one side of the glass. Of better worth to lay hold of them between the instants, in that hollow which is always re-formed in duration when they escape from what they were and when they are not yet what they shall be. The "notion of a defaulting object failing to appear,"[29] such is the temporal mode under which the object to be expressed has the greatest chance of satisfying the Mallarmean dream. Now this mode is that of *Becoming*.

A becoming, however, that one must not necessarily understand in the sense of a horizontal progress in duration, like the Aristotelian, and even the Hegelian, becoming. On the contrary what matters here is, so to speak, a vertical progress which makes surge up the things of the possible, or which, after having brought them into the present and into the real, withdraws them therefrom by a kind of assumption which transfigures them. The passage of things into time, therefore, realizes very exactly what Mallarmé had always sought. It is a *passage through the glass*.

Through the glass of the present takes place the ceaseless passage of the future into the past.

Temporal passage of things, imperceptible operation, fluent and facile—like the spatial passage of light—which makes no breach, which breaks no glass, which compromises nothing, which leaves everything in good condition. An operation as simple as it is perfect, since it is a most natural, though inner, thing, since it shatters nothing and changes nothing, since finally it ceaselessly and painlessly nourishes a reverie that wishes to consist only in a closed circuit, in a perpetual motion like that of a fountain.

Thus of all the joys which Mallarmé experiences, there is none more pure than that which he has in contemplating "that which lives magnificently late through yearning." [30] There is an exquisite pleasure in "being reborn in the anterior sky," a pleasure which consists in recognizing oneself through the windowpane, or in the mirror, in a temporal remoteness analogous to spatial distance. If one can rediscover oneself, it is not despite but because of this distance; it is precisely because the glass is interposed between what one is and what one was: "The phrase reappears, virtual, disengaged from an anterior fall." [31] In a poem written at the age of seventeen, Mallarmé was already very exactly expressing this negative duration, this fall or this hiatus which separates and yet which joins the positive spaces of duration:

> No! yesterday is joined to today
> Only by the fall of a star! [32]

And in the letter to Coppée in which he spoke of the sin he had committed in wanting "to behold the dream in its ideal nakedness," he added that on the contrary what he ought to do was "heap up between the Dream and himself a mystery of music and forgetfulness." [33]—"I need," he wrote at this period, "I need the most silent solitude of mind, and a new kind of forgetfulness in order to hear certain unknown notes sing within me." [34] This new kind of forgetfulness made of absence and negation is precisely the temporal void thanks to which things or beings can be reborn or be made to recognize themselves beyond, in memory. This is a phenomenon that continually repeats itself with Mallarmé. Even in his relations with others he is at his ease only in remembering, in putting space and oblivion between those he loves and himself:

> Truly it is when my friends have left that I begin to be with them, with their memory bordering my Dream, which their veritable apparition sometimes deranges a bit . . .[35]

> . . . It is only after their departure, and when they have become absent once again, that I am with my dear premature guests.[36]

If in his relationships with people, despite his gentleness, Mallarmé will always make felt a constant reserve, let us not judge that to be the effect of timidity or modesty, as in the case of Benjamin Constant or Vigny. The reason is an entirely different one. There is perfect friendship only when one interposes between oneself and others either time or space. Such is the affability, always a little remote, of Mallarmé; it indicates the solicitude "to shed time as an antique balm upon the suddenness of new affections." [37]

"Separated we are together." [38] Logically then, the only perfect relationship becomes that which one has with a being from whom one is separated by an infinite distance, that of death. One entire portion of Mallarmé's work will be devoted to funereal "commemorations." For death is a "removal that acts the part of centuries." He who disappears, reappears, on the other side of death, in a sort of anterior eternity, so remote that he is finally found worthy of all our admiration or of all our love:

> Such as, at last, Eternity changes him into himself . . .

The same transformation takes place in the image of things. Contrary to Proust, memory is not for Mallarmé the total reviviscence of a first impression. It aims to restore neither the shades of the emotion, nor the particular image of the objects which evoked it. It is a notional memory. Of the objects remembered, it simply allows "the pure notion to emanate, without the constraint of a close or concrete recall." [39] Hence the flower which Mallarmé recollects is not at all, as with Proust, such a particular blossom as that of the hawthorn seen on the Méséglise way, but "out of the oblivion to which his voice relegates every contour, in so far as it is something other than the known calyxes . . . , the one absent from all bouquets." [40] The temporal removal has had then not only the effect of putting the object farther off in the perspective, it has detached it from all actuality, even that which is completed, from all contingency, even that which is past: "The reminiscence of the named object bathes in a new atmosphere." [41] An atmosphere which is so new only because the operation of time has finally detached the object from all times, has placed it outside time, in absence.

To remember is to look once again into absence, into emptiness.

Into the emptiness of a mirror.

Thus the faun does, who in order to regain his nymphs, gazes through the luminous skin of the grapes from which he has sucked the splendor:

> Laughing, I lift to the summer sky the empty bunch . . .

It is still in the same nontemporal void that one remembers one's ego and that thus at times one arrives at the pure notion of oneself. One then sees oneself, not as one is, but as one has mysteriously been transfigured by that death one calls the past. As the Mallarmean flower rises in the absence, in so far as it is different from known flowers, so the poet, in the mirror of his thought, can sometimes see appear, on a depth of sleepless night, the very image of his divinized anterior being:

> And thy solitary sister, O my eternal sister
> My dream shall rise toward thee: already such,
> Rare limpidity of a heart that dreamed it,
> I deem myself alone in my monotonous country
> And all, round about me, lives in the idolatry
> Of a mirror that reflects in its sleeping calm
> Hérodiade in her clear diamond brightness.

"My dream shall *rise* toward thee." But is it really rising or descending? Is it even really moving? And this false ascent of the dream, in *Hérodiade,* toward an impossible union with self, has it not for counterpart the no less celebrated lines in which she who seeks herself in her mirror finds herself separated from herself by the same distance, but this time a distance like a deep well over which she leans motionless:

> O mirror!
> Water chilled by ennui in thy frozen frame
> How many times during hours, desolate
> Of dreams and seeking my memories which are
> Like leaves under thine ice in the deep well,
> I appeared to myself in thee like a far-off shade . . .

Now, in this experience, which is the very one Mallarmé goes through, one can no longer speak of temporal movement, and one can no longer discern the perfect happiness there was in feeling the natural gliding of the present into the past through the glass. A present "which outlasts beauty" is confronted from afar by the "vestige of some epoch already accursed." [42] There is no longer any gliding; there is now only a static confrontation of two epochs situated at an absolute distance from one another. Again there appears both the antinomy of the two worlds, and the singular paralysis which follows for him who has the simultaneous experience of them. Of all Mallarmé's attempts to escape his atony, the one which consists in entrusting his dream to the idealizing power of time is the only one which nearly succeeded. It fails, though, like the others, for the same reason as the others, in the same freezing chill, on the same horizon of ice floe and frost.

V

An horizon which from all sides presses its uniform whiteness in upon the poet. In the Mallarmean work, from poem to poem, one watches the Azure, the central theme, gradually grow pale in order to be metamorphosized into a white night. Already in all the early poems of his youth, amidst the sunny blue there stood out at times this frozen whiteness. One saw

> in the azure it gilds
> The sun rise up behind a snowy hill.[43]

Or it was the beauty of the flowers which drew its double origin from a world made of azure and from another made of snow:

> From the gold avalanches of ancient azure, on the prime day,
> And from the eternal snow of the stars
> Of old thou didst detach the great calyxes . . .[44]

But in proportion as the poet's ideal becomes more remote and his contemplation more static, all that remained of blue and solar light in his sky vanishes to give place to polar night. Celestial place, which is not even any longer now that of a Platonic reality, a place in which there is no longer situated anything positive or habitable for thought, a negative desert place, consequently *becomes identical to the distance which separates it from the contemplator.* A place which is no longer that of dream, but of the absence of all dream; a place finally in the reality of which the dreamer has lost all faith, the place of an ideal which no longer exists.

Place of Nothing, pure distance.

The whole distance that separates from Nothing the being who has renounced expressing this Nothing.

Except by silence, that is to say again, by nothing.

Such is the theme of the sonnet on the Swan.

There is no poem in which there could be more completely and more silently expressed, under its two spatial and temporal forms, empty space and empty duration, the impotence of the mind facing nothingness.

At the beginning of the poem there feebly appears the possibility of a redemption:

> The virginal, vivacious, and beautiful today,
> Is it going to . . .

As the poet well knows, each day is a new Today: "Today is not simply the replacing of yesterday, the presaging of tomorrow, but emerges from time, as universal, with a cleansed or new integrity." [45] In every moment that comes to birth there is thus the possibility of *being:* "Unceasingly the hour is as well as never it is . . ." [46] To be is to be possessed of an immediate possession, which admits neither distance nor duration, but a single pure moment and the repose of the being in the object of his possession.

Such is the starting point of this poem—if one can call a starting point that which appears to be in the final analysis the point from which one never starts. Or rather, since it would be inexact to assign here even the appearance of movement to what is exactly the reverse, it is on taking leave of this dreamed point, never reached, that there begins to manifest itself, by a sort of gradually increasing heaviness, precisely the static, paralyzing force which prevents the poem from taking the dreamed flight. For in order to take it, chance or an exterior grace would not suffice; it would be necessary by a positive act, by a blow of desperate strength, *stroke of a drunken wing,* to rend the frozen lake, to shatter the ice. But, as we know, that is impossible. Then there appears, in the place of the dreamed Today, a duration which is the reverse, a naked duration, frozen and uninhabited; a duration which does not flow, which does not advance, a congealed duration; *lake hardened, forgotten.* Or again, it is the vision of a uniformly white and transparent space which extends both out along the surface and into the depths, as if the ice and the emptiness were everywhere blended into the same vitreous substance, null and impenetrable:

> . . . lake hardened, forgotten, which under the frost
> The lucid ice-field haunts with wings that have not fled.

Imperceptibly these translucent walls have covered a whole horizon which is revealed to be that of the past. The dreamed Today is not something before but something behind. He who was wishing is now remembering. He recognizes himself in his memory such as he contemplated himself in his desire; not such as he is, not even such as he has been, but such as he has never been, for not having been able to break this ice, to surmount this distance, to shatter the enchantment of his passive contemplation by the magical action of his song. Nothing appears, then, except an anterior duration in which nothing has happened, and beyond and in the depths of which is situated the image of the magnificent being of whom one was never more than the shadow. Such is Hamlet, "latent lord who cannot become." [47]

Then by a simple change of orientation—the only one possible in this poem in which there is only movement without shifting—to the perspective of the past there succeeds an equal perspective, that of the future:

> All his neck will shake off this white agony
> Inflicted by space on the bird who denies it,
> But not the horror of soil in which the plumage is caught.

A future in which one will continue in vain to oppose his impotent negation to the all-powerful negation that space inflicts, in which one will rediscover the same uniform agony. The anterior horizon and the posterior horizon thus are equivalent, are reunited and are mingled in one selfsame time, in one indifferent selfsame space. Nothing any longer subsists but a moment and an indefinite perpetual place, horrible *soil,* in which one is *caught* —caught in a "dreadful sensation of eternity." [48]

It is the same feeling that is found described in the *Life Of Igitur:*

> —And when I reopened my eyes in the depths of the mirror, I watched the personage of horror, the phantom of horror consume bit by bit what there remained of feeling and grief in the glass, nourish his horror on the last shudders of chimeras and the instability of the hangings, and assume the form in rarefying the glass, of an unprecedented purity,—up to the moment when, permanent, he stood up against the absolutely pure looking-glass, as if *caught in its frost* . . .[49]

In this "absolutely pure looking-glass" he who contemplates himself finally no longer distinguishes anything except a *phantom,* a reflection of self that is more and more translucent, less and less discernible, up to the point that before the motionless contemplator there is no longer any image, no longer anything except an eternal emptiness uselessly offered to an empty duration.

That which "exists through its own dream" has now become that which does not exist, that which does not even dream.

Purity equals nullity.

The sonnet on the Swan is the poem of the being "irremediably dedicated to Nothingness." [50]

VI

But what is Nothingness? It is thought, any thought. There is not a single one of our ideas which is not a lie, there is not one of our dreams which is not a nonreality. Thus a young professor of English tormenting himself on his Tournon pillow is gradually forced by the failure of all his endeavors to recognize that nothing of his thought exists, that it literally does not exist. "We know, captives of an absolute formula, that, indeed, only which is." [51] These words pronounced a quarter of a century later are a sad echo of the anguish suffered in the course of the nights of 1866–1867. During this "frightful year" Mallarmé underwent a metaphysical and moral crisis in which all his beliefs foundered and from which he emerged, like Lazarus, with a new being and with a radically changed conception of the universe and of his art. Nothing existed except what existed. And Matter alone existed. Thought, poetry, the consciousness of self, the presence of God and of the world in the self, all that was a dream, and the dream did not exist. The sky was empty. It was vain to imagine at a distance, in space, a world real yet ideal, the place of Ideas. The latter, pure illusions of the mind, had neither place, nor reality, nor even existence in the spirit. For spirit itself was a lie; and in so far as he was spiritual, the human being himself did not exist.

Such is the conclusion to which had come perhaps the most rigorously idealistic of all the poetic enterprises which had ever been attempted. It ended in the declaration that nothing existed, except "vain forms of matter." [52] Never had a spiritual death been more complete. "I am completely dead," Mallarmé at that time confessed to a friend. [53]

But also three times in letters of this period, he asserts that this death has been conquered and outstripped by him, and that through this death he has forever gained all that had been denied him, all that he had dreamt:

I have died and come to life again with the jewelled key of my last spiritual casket. [54]

. . . After having found Nothingness, I have found Beauty . . . [55]

. . . I am completely dead, and the most impure region into which my Mind might venture is Eternity; my Mind, this habitual solitary of its own Purity, which even the reflected light of Time no longer darkens. [56]

"Such as into himself . . ." How shall we explain this mortal transformation which brings it about that in looking at himself in his mirror, Mallarmé now sees in it only an "impersonal" and almost divine being? "I look at myself and behold an angel! and

I die, and I love . . . to be born again in the anterior sky . . ."
I die, and no longer *I dream:* let us bear in mind this correction
made in the text of the *Fenêtres* at precisely that moment, and
now let us feel all its force. Death—spiritual death—is not that
resigned dream, passively undergone, which had been the cre-
puscular life of Mallarmé up until then; death is an action, a
voluntary operation by means of which one gives existence even
to nothingness.

Death is the only possible action. Crushed as we are between a
real material world whose fortuitous combinations are produced
in us without our having willed them and a false ideal world
whose lie paralyzes and bewitches us, we have only one means
now of preventing ourselves from being delivered up to nothingness or to chance. This unique means, this unique action, is
death. Voluntary death. By its agency we abolish ourselves, but
through it we also establish ourselves. In the moment in which
we give ourselves death, we also give ourselves life. Our very
existence can consist only in an act which lasts a moment. An
act of suicide.

It is this act of voluntary death that Mallarmé has committed.
He committed it in *Igitur.* There is no work of literature in
which there is found perpetrated more completely and more
absolutely in thought the act of abolition and of establishment
of self. The vague dressing-up of the account matters little. What
does matter is that everything in this narrative happens in a moment, that in which the hero, in giving himself death, gives
himself life. It is this single moment that is examined in the two
central episodes, *Le Minuit* and *La Sortie de la chambre.* In the
one, this moment appears not in the action which has filled it,
nor in the person of him who has lived it, but in itself, stripped
of its content, the moment of an action of which one as yet knows
nothing except that it was accomplished in such and such a
place and that, like the place, the meaning of this moment remains; while in the other episode this action finally appears

such as it is in the thought of him who accomplishes it, when he accomplishes it.

In the first episode what is discovered first is a "presence of midnight," not the content of this moment, simply its presence; a presence of *midnight,* however, and therefore of a moment which one knows to be particularly significant, for, in contrast to the other moments of the day, the moment of midnight is confounded with neither that which precedes, nor with that which follows. It is itself, and it "subsists." All the other moments in turn have fulfilled their fugitive destiny. Whether they have disappeared in the "mirror" of thought, whether they have glided to the depths of the mind in order with their heavy forms to occupy there the background of the reverie, one can only say that they have no other than a fortuitous significance and existence; they are appearances and disappearances that have been determined purely by the "infinite hazard of conjunctions."

But it is not the same with this moment of midnight. If it differs from all the others, if it subsists among all the others, that is because it has not been brought or taken away by chance, but is the mind's own creation: "Behold the unique hour which he has *created.*" A moment therefore of unique importance, since it was not determined by a chance which makes and unmakes existence, since it exists through itself, the cause of itself, a moment thus essentially, eternally subsisting, a moment which "makes the absolute present of things."

But what is this moment? As yet we know only the subsisting presence of it. But the very fact that it subsists implies some spiritual place in which it exists. If it *dwells,* it is very necessary that this dwelling place of its existence be situated somewhere— like a poem on a page—and it is this dwelling place of the moment which appears under the form of an empty room; a mental place standing upon the pure indetermination of space, and containing within its limits the thrilling echo of an action of which one still knows nothing, except that it is reflected in an entirely

anonymous thought. But that is already to say that the action
in question is not apprehended in its actuality, but in the reflective
distance of a mind for which it is already completed, despite
the fact the mind imagines it as on the point of being completed.
The mental place which is found described here is therefore not
solely a spatial place, but also a temporal place; it is the place
where there is anteriorly accomplished an action the representation of which is going to be made posteriorly in the consciousness. It is that which is situated between the past in which it took
place and the future in which its reflection will take place. It is
made up, like every poem, of memory and waiting.

Of memory first, and consequently of the past. For this emptiness of the room is that which has been left within it by the
passage of an event which will be remembered later and which
has been accomplished in bygone days: "Anterior place of the
fall of the hour into a narcotic calm of pure *self* a long time
dreamed." But this very purity indicates that the disappearance
of the moment of Midnight is not similar to that of the other
moments and does not gainsay that which remains elsewhere
its presence. If the other moments disappeared, it was in order
to be dissolved in oblivion or to linger in the corners of the
memory. Here, on the contrary, nothing is dispersed or congealed.
The accomplished action entirely leaves the actual, disappears by
reason of its completion, but disappears, not in time, but in
itself. Its disappearance is tantamount to a purification. There
no longer remains in any moment that is going to follow any
other material sign of its apparition except an "opened book"
(opened at any moment, in any "light"), in which its accomplished
apparition persists in remaining foretold. And that doubtless
permits of a great hope, for there is presented to every thought-
to-come the possibility of turning to the book and reading there,
proclaimed, precisely what has been accomplished; so expressly
that it is not presumptuous to expect some future moment in
which the moment that has disappeared will regain its actuality.

Thus, just as a poem which, having one day been written, has the chance of being one day read and relived, "there subsists still the silence of an antique word." But between the past and the future in which it has resounded and will resound, this word subsists presently only as a "virtual light." And so it can never be expressed by a present, but always by a past or a future: "I *was* the hour which *must render* me pure."

An hour which is no more and not yet, but which indefinitely prolongs in each actual moment the phantom of its nonactual presence, so that it only appears as a reflection. It "mirrors itself there," it "makes itself known" at a distance, as that which alone *is,* but which, however, is no more and not yet: "Farewell, night, whom I was, thy very sepulcher, but who, because of the survival of darkness, will be metamorphosized into Eternity."

Withdrawn to the two extremities of duration, but leaving toward the past and the future "panels opened by its nocturnal action," the lived moment waits to be relived.

Waiting and memory: has not all of Mallarmean poetry up to the present been made wholly of that?

But here, for the first time, it is a waiting and a memory that envelop the existence of an *act.*

And since this act has been lived, since it can be relived, nothing hinders making it appear now in its very actuality: such as it *has taken place* in this *place.*

This is the subject of the second episode, in which the moment finally appears in itself, that is to say, as it is lived and thought by a being who gives himself death.

The being who apprehends himself in the moment of "disappearing into the obscurity" of death apprehends himself in a moment situated between a whole past of life accomplished and a whole future of death eternal. And at first this moment appears to him as that of a thought turned anticipatively toward those "future glooms" and being forced to conjecture what its own death will signify for it. But as yet it can conceive this death only in an ambiguous fashion, as the movement of its being, plunging into an "ebony night," a movement ceaselessly attended, so it seems, by the regular beat of a pendulum, by a consciousness of self ever recommenced and always occupied in registering the fall of the moments into the past; as if to live, by thought, his future death were the same thing as to relive by thought the whole series of particular deaths which, in the past, had constituted existence. Thus the consciousness of advancing into the future—even into the future of death—appears identical to the consciousness of "uselessly falling back into himself in the past."

And as a consequence there is revealed to the mind the true nature of duration, the "corridor of time," the "vertiginous and ever-receding spiral," unrolling in the future as well as in the past its ascending and descending continuity, perpetually broken off and begun afresh, projecting as into glittering panels or into endless mirrors the same image of a consciousness that simultaneously perceives itself as appearing and disappearing. Agonizing perspective, in which one feels "oppressed" and "compressed into the mirage" by a "vanishing distinctness," like that of "panels which, although closed, and yet still open, would, in order to arrive at it, in a vertiginous immobility, have been turned for a long time on themselves." Perspective extraordinarily lucid and horrible, labyrinth of smooth walls implacably illumined by a harsh light, "state of self-conscious anguish," from which the mind tries to escape by "prolonging its indefinite flight toward the shadows."

But from the very depth of anguish there surges up a relief or an assurance. For there is no doubt of it, the being whose image is found reflected and multiplied along the whole length of the corridors of time is not a being every time different who, immediate work of the combinations of chance, never rises up into a moment but to be as soon replaced by a being that is radically other. Like scions of the same breed which death strips by turn of their accidental differences in order to make them appear in their specific identity, even so all the moments already lived by the consciousness appear similar and are reduced to a single one, provided that the consciousness remembers only one single thing, the having lived them. Over the whole long line of the past, cleansed by death and by the consciousness of death of any particularity that distinguishes them, they are no longer found to be anything more than the multiple exemplars of one selfsame anonymous type whose ever identical image seems besides to be prolonged beyond death, into the future.

As a consequence the infinite multiplicity of time is brought back to the unity, and all is taken into one "abode" in which one "is in perfect accord with himself"; a unity or accord which is expressed, despite time, through time, by the perfect identity of all the alternative images of self which the consciousness discovers in all points past and future of its conscious existence. And if all these images stand out on both sides, if they manifest their presence here on this side as well as there on that, it is, so it seems, to adduce their multiplied evidence to this unique confrontation; "in order that the last shade should be mirrored within its own self, and recognize itself in the crowd of its apparitions."

And also as another consequence, time past and time future now appear simply as two identical and convergent lines, at the "junction-point" of which the being mirroring himself within himself perceives himself to be existing in a nontemporal moment, "the place of perfect certitude."

> Long, oh! long ago, when thou chimedst in vain, sustaining an atmosphere of absence, thy sound of gold returned to thee, in my reverie and created thee there, jewel of gold, flung in informing me upon your stellar and marine intricacy, the external occurrences of the play of worlds; but I can say, alluding to the memories of a race that thou evokest, that never, upon these surfaces which betoken the multiple and combined plays of the multiplicity of universal thought, never, recapitulation of the universe that you are, jewel of things, hast thou formed *a minute of as magnificent an accord,* and I doubt that *this instant has its equal in the present,* amidst

the inexpressible multiplicity of worlds. *My thought is thus recreated,* but as for me, am I it? Yes, I sense that *this time poured into me renders myself this me,* and I see myself to be similar to the wave of a tranquil narcotic whose *vibratory circles,* coming and going, form an infinite limit which does not attain the calm of the middle.[57]

At this point, and as soon as the consciousness is situated within it, there is no further need of evoking either the future or the past. And indeed how shall we now distinguish the one from the other? How can we still conceive them, except as the negation of the "place of perfect certitude"? Arrived at the "miracle of self," peak of his existence, the being who is wrapped up in this single instant and this knowledge of self, by this very fact "dominates" a past and a future which now and from this point of view seem "finished," "emptied," "exterior." Both before and behind there is now only the "explored lie of the infinite." The being who kills himself becomes pure consciousness of self, and thus escapes the spiral of duration. Past and future are reabsorbed into a unique moment, their end and their negation. As in the philosophy of Hegel, the mind affirms itself and attains its positive reality in a negation of the negation: an instantaneous negation of the temporal negation, which attains to the "notion of itself," abolishes time and at the same stroke the chance which, by dividing the instant, created time:

> Must I still fear chance, that old enemy who divided me into shadows and into created times, both having been equally pacified? and is not this, by the end of time, which brought about that of the shadows, itself annulled?

Upon this summit of the Mallarmean *Cogito,* the being who thinks himself into being founds his existence. He sees himself where he is, in the moment when he is. Existence gathers together into one point, into one instant, into an act of thought. It no longer appears as brought about by that which precedes it, nor drawn ahead by that which follows. "Free at last, sure of itself and disencumbered of all that was foreign to it," it achieves itself in its act: I think myself, therefore I create myself.

An act of creation which is encompassed, before and behind, by negation and silence. Like a poem written on a white sheet of paper at the same time initial and final:

> . . . the white sheet of paper reappears, gratuitous before, certain now, in order to conclude that there is nothing beyond and to authenticate the silence.[58]

It remains then to "dissolve oneself in oneself" in order to authenticate the silence.

Such is *Igitur,* the perfect example of the "philosophic suicide."

VII

The philosophic suicide is thus the sole operation possible. And since it is only a "philosophic" suicide, it can always be repeated. It is the act of negation by which, in any moment and only for that moment, one can lay the foundation of his existence and his thought. The Mallarmean operation is thus comparable to "the internal operation of Descartes." [59] It is *ultra-Cartesian,* in the same way as from another point of view Mallarmé's poetry is ultra-Baudelairean. Mallarmé was conscious of this affiliation. We know through a note written in 1869 that he was then thinking of writing a treatise on language, in which, he said, he would have quoted a page from the *Discours de la Méthode.* Now that must very certainly have been the first page of Part Four of the *Discours,* the famous page that introduces the even more famous *Cogito.* Let us reread it:

> . . . I thought it was necessary . . . that I reject as absolutely false all that in which I could conceive the least doubt, to see if there would not after that remain something in my belief that was entirely *indubitable*. Thus, since our senses sometimes deceive us, I wanted to suppose there was not anything which was such as they lead us to imagine . . . I resolved to *pretend* that all the things that had ever entered

my mind were no more true than the illusions of my dreams. But immediately afterward I was heedful of the fact that since *I wanted to think in this manner that all was false,* it was necessary that I who thought it be something.

And it is then that there appears the celebrated affirmation: I think, therefore I am.

We must feel the full force of the parallel which Mallarmé ought himself to draw between the act of Cartesian consciousness by means of which existence founds itself in thought, and the properly Mallarmean act of consciousness by means of which thought creates existence. On both counts, everything begins by a *fiction,* that is to say by a hyperbolical doubt, by the means of which one *feigns* to abolish the real, all of the real, and thus to produce in and about himself the same *tabula rasa* which would be made by the leveling of death. A doubt which is thus a negation, but a *feigned* and *willed* negation: "I will to think that all is false." By this act of negation or annihilation all is reduced to this single will; and it is in this act of will that the Cartesian being finds himself both thinking and consequently existing. His existence stands out, therefore, against the act of will by which he wishes to annihilate everything, and seems, so to speak, to make his positive presence spring forth from a total act of negation. It is not necessary to carry things much further in order to arrive, as Mallarmé did, at something like this: "By an act of annihilative will, I arrive at an act of creative will."

One can now understand the text of the above-mentioned note of 1869. Immediately before introducing the name of Descartes, Mallarmé says this:

> . . . The *fiction* seems to him to be the very process of the human mind—it is that which puts all *method* into play, and man is *reduced to the will.*

The Mallarmean method is founded on a fiction according to which one wants to believe that that which is does not exist, in order that that which is not, exist.

Now that which is, is matter; that which is not, is thought. Thus one gives an authentic but also fictitious existence to his thought, in fictitiously denying the existence of the real. The act of hyperbolical negation is an act of creation—of creation as it were *ex nihilo*.

In pretending that nothing exists, I make myself and my dream exist.

Twenty-seven years later, in *La Musique et les Lettres,* Mallarmé will ask the question: "Does something like Literature exist?" The gravest question of all, for literature is myself, my dream, my thought. But "we know," says Mallarmé, "captives of an absolute formula, that, truly, only that which is, is." Literature, and the dream, and ourselves are therefore a decoy. The chief thing is nothing. To the question that is posed, there is thus only one true answer possible: No, literature does not exist. However, says Mallarmé, "I reply with an exaggeration, to be sure, of which I forewarn you—Yes, Literature does exist, and *if you wish, alone, differing in this from everything else.*" I can then deny all that is in order to affirm that which is not. Admirable falsehood! ". . . I venerate the act of trickery by which one projects to some forbidden height inhabited by lightning! our conscious lack of that which flashes up above."

This act of trickery, this action particularly appropriate to thought, is the Cartesian doubt carried to its extreme. It is the act by which one escapes the "absolute formula" in *willing* that which is shall not be, and consequently that that which is not shall exist. In order to make his dream exist he must deny the existence of the rest.

It is the whole ensemble of this movement of thought which appears to be described in one of the most admirable of Mallarmé's poems, the sonnet which he published in 1883 in the *Poètes maudits* of Verlaine, under the title *Cette Nuit.* Written long before that date, it has for its subject the agonies and the triumphs of the Tournon nights of 1866–1867.

> When the shadow threatened with the fatal law
> So old a Dream, desire and ache of my vertebrae,
> Grieved to perish under funereal ceilings,
> It folded its indubitable wing in me.

We know what the "fatal law" is, that is threatening with death the old Mallarmean dream. "Captive of the *absolute formula*" according to which "only that which is, is," he is now reduced to being no more than an emanation of one of the "vain forms of matter," a "desire and ache of my vertebrae." From that moment, cut off from the outside, lacking all analogy with the Real, he is condemned to perish "under funereal ceilings" and to fold his wing under the vaults of a Self which itself has no reality.

But already, in this metaphysical catastrophe, a word—a Cartesian word—proclaims the extraordinary about-face that follows. Forced to abjure the reality of his dream and to admit its falsehood, Mallarmé accepts it as such and transforms its negation into affirmation. "I *will*," he wrote in 1866, "I will to give myself this spectacle of matter, having consciousness of being, and, nevertheless, rushing furiously into that Dream which it *knows is not* . . . , and proclaiming before the Nothing which is the Truth, these *glorious lies*." [60] In other terms, by an arbitrary and purely fictitious act, I deny the nonexistence, and I lay down as true what I know to be false. My dream, driven from the real, constrained to fold its wing in me, regains in me, through me, a reality and a place of existence. I resolve that it is *indubitable in me*.

From that point on, there is produced a dramatic about-face whose consequences are going to make the whole Cosmos reel. For I can affirm the existence of that which does not exist only by withdrawing existence from all that which does exist. In order to make my dream exist, I abolish the world.

It is this annihilation of the world by the Mallarmean *fiction* that we witness in the second quatrain:

. . . It is, this mad game of writing, to arrogate to oneself, by virtue of a doubt—the drop of ink akin to the sublime night—some duty of recreating everything, with reminiscences, in order to establish the fact that one is indeed where one ought to be . . .[63]

The inkwell, crystal with a conscience, with its drop, at the bottom, of darkness relating to what something might be.[64]

. . . What is literature, if not this mental pursuit, carried on as a discourse, in order to determine or, with respect to oneself, furnish proof that the spectacle responds to an imaginative comprehension, to be sure, in the hope of being mirrored in it.[65]

Literary creation has therefore an end, and this end is to transform a doubt into a faith; and as this doubt has darkened everything, it is necessary, in order to carry our conviction and substantiate our faith, that that which is created bring with it its own internal light; it is necessary that "it should not tolerate any luminous evidence except that of existing." [66]

Nothing could be less efficacious than a *fiction* which should suddenly claim to be indispensable, "commanding belief in the existence of the person and the enterprise—simply belief, nothing more. As if this faith required of the spectator did not have precisely to be the resultant drawn by him from the concourse of all the arts raising up the otherwise inert and empty miracle of the scene stage setting!" [67]

Thus everything in the Mallarmean work is going to ensure an "obvious display." [68] All concurs in making exist there *fictionally,* but *obviously,* something that does not exist.

But one has to take into account the difficulty and almost the absurdity of such an enterprise. For in order to make exist that which does not exist, it is here impossible to lean upon that which exists. It is not a question here, as in ordinary literature, of inserting into the middle of a *given universe* a fictive element which is going to draw space and duration, solidity and credibility, from this real world into which it is inserted. It is not a question of rendering a lie plausible by situating it within a frame made of true details. Here nothing is any longer true. It is a question of presenting and winning acceptance as a total verity, having *its* space and *its* duration, bearing its own evidence, for something which is nothing and which is sustained by nothing.

The creation of the fictitious (which is pre-eminently the literary creation) thus seems to require the same power as the creation of the real, that is to say a divine power.

And yet Mallarmé declares: It is a "human creation." [69] "The occupation of creating . . . appears supreme and to succeed with words." [70]

The writer who has endured the extreme limit of the drama of human impotence is precisely the one who seems to invest man with an infinite power, that of drawing something out of nothing.

But this nothing out of which he claims to draw something is not the total nothing of the creation *ex nihilo*. It is not an absolute void, it is a sort of unsubstantial world, where, by the operation of the hyperbolical doubt, things have lost their reality, but have nevertheless kept the appearance of it. The drop of darkness of which Mallarmé speaks has thus not completely obliterated things. The latter unabatedly continue to be present to the mind, yet as unreal, to be utilizable yet virtual. They have been reduced to the power of simply suggesting a reality they no longer have. They have become notional.

Let us reread the famous sentence:

> I say: a flower! and, out of the oblivion to which my voice relegates any contour, in so far as it is something other than the known calyxes, there rises up, as idea itself and very sweet, the absent one from all bouquets.

Thus the voluntary operation of the word has the same office as the involuntary movement of time. Relegating to oblivion any real contour, it decomposes the world into its spiritual elements, in order that only "pure notions" may now emanate from it. Everything is now brought round to being simply words and language; and as a consequence there is the infinite possibility of combining them as one wishes, of making them signify —thanks to the combinations of which one is master—no matter what.

In hyperbolically doubting the reality of the world, Mallarmé has not abolished it. He has simply metamorphosized it into a vocabulary: a collection of terms with which it is possible, not, to be sure, to fabricate a new world, but irresistibly to suggest the existence of it by his song:

> For I set up by science
> The hymn of hearts spiritual
> In the work of my patience,
> Atlases, herbariums and ritual-books.

In order to suggest this new existence and to accomplish the fictitious installation of a new world, it suffices patiently to go about disposing the words over which one has command, in a certain order, in a certain hymn. From the arrangement of these terms will be born the conviction that there exists, and indeed that there alone exists, this poetic universe which appears, not within them, but between them, through them, beyond them.

Such is literary creation. It consists in reducing the world to numbers and words in order to make it signify something that it is not. At bottom, that hardly differs from the process of scientific thought.

"What is that good for? For a game." [71]

For "a game, one hardly knows what, which *confirms the fiction.*" [72]

IX

The Mallarmean creation is thus not a creation *ex nihilo*. It is a creation effected by a handling of terms no one of which can claim to express the *being* that is created, but each one of which can in its turn suggest an aspect of it.

Henceforth this creation begins to take leave of virtuality and little by little to take on a manner of existence. A curious existence which seems to consist at first sight in the simple confrontation of terms. Something one does not know appears from a certain point of view, and during a certain moment, to be equivalent to some other thing that one thinks; and then to such another, and to still such another. This is that and then again that; and if this is that, that is this.[73] Everything happens as in a game of charades, but also as in mathematics. One advances by successive identities, each one of which tries, though vainly, to reflect an unknown totality.

> There lies the whole mystery: the establishing of secret identities in a two by two succession which wastes and consumes objects, in the name of a central purity . . .[74]

Thus the terms perpetually confront and replace themselves, exchanging, before extinction, a "reciprocity of proofs." [75] But in some way as they alternate, on the blackboard where their equations succeed each other, one thing remains: the mysterious little term *It is* ($=$), which, whatever are the provisional values that by turn come to be reflected therein, none the less persists in affirming the single positive presence of the *being* which always and everywhere rediscovers itself, compares itself, and reflects itself. *"It is,"* remarked Mallarmé; "the title of an interminable study and series of notes which I have at hand, and one that reigns in the utmost regions of my mind." [76]

Thus already there appears clearly one of the categorical aspects of the Mallarmean creation. It is something which *is;* which is this and that; and again this, and again that. But while each of all the *thises* and *thats* can never be more than momentarily what it is, it is in every moment and always all that they are and beyond all that they are.

Something therefore remains amidst the indefinite succession of terms.

On the one hand, "everything becomes suspense, fragmentary

arrangement, with alternation and opposite terms"; on the other hand, "everything contributes to the total rhythm, which would be in the potential poem with its blank spaces; but rendered, in a fashion, by each pendentive." [77] There is never anything more than the "fictitious or momentary," [78] but as in a sky in which the stars were to enkindle one another at a distance, all these momentary points, "enkindling each other with their reciprocal reflections," tend to form "a virtual trail of fire from precious stones." [79] Thus there is engendered a sort of "chatoyant perpetuity." [80] At first sight this seems to be a movement all but static, something like the multiplied scintillation of a world of diamonds and stars:

> And the gorgeous bath of hair disappears
> In the splendors and shudders, O precious stones!

But as the image of the head of hair seems in the present example to form the natural junction between the static and stellar multiplicity of the jewels, and the fluent multiplicity of the water, thus in all Mallarmean poems, from the chatoyant existence of words and of moments to the pure rhythmic fluidity of the ensemble, there occurs a continuous gliding by means of which the momentary scintillation finds itself ceaselessly prolonged in the temporal vibration. To employ an expression of Poe and Baudelaire, it is "some under-current, however indefinite, of meaning," which moves and sweeps all moments along with it. One perceives in it, at different depths, distinct varieties of duration all of which contribute to establish the temporal existence of the poem and to institute the fiction. There is first each moment in particular, "prismatic subdivision of the Idea, the instant that it appears and that its aid endures"; [81] there is the succession or chain of instants, traced by the "sinuous and mobile variations of the Idea"; [82] and finally there is the "mobile synthesis" [83] of all this complex movement of thought, a synthesis which from beginning to end must keep, by means of the same "impetus of grandeur, of thought, or of emotion . . . the reader going." [84] All of this constitutes a triple temporal reality through which there more and more clearly appears the nontemporal reality of the Idea. "Evidence of the being all identical with itself," [85] which never ceases to affirm itself within the interstices and flight of moments as a permanent, immutable, and total presence which they "simply detail as so many fractions of the infinite": [86]

> Thus launched from self the primary thing which is— simply Verse! attracts no less than it releases for its expansion (the instant they shine and die in a swift blossom, in some transparency as of ether) the thousand elements of beauty impelled to hasten and ordain themselves in their essential worth. A sign! in the central abyss of a spiritual impossibility that nothing can exclusively belong to all, here is the divine numerator of our apotheosis, some supreme mold which is of no effect with regard to any object that exists: but it borrows, in order to sharpen a seal, all scattered unknown layers flowing pursuant to some richness, to forge them.[87]

The Mallarmean poem is thus composed of a spray of small ephemeral durations which engender a continuous duration, through which there appears and in which there is finally made incarnate a nontemporal reality, Fiction. Like a musical accompaniment which at the same time conceals and reinforces the principal theme ("play of sounds strummed all around"),[88] the arabesque which these durations depict, has no other aim than enveloping the Idea in a sort of incessant shimmering which gives it a false air of successive life and makes it appear as if involved in time.

This Mallarmean time, like normal time, is made up of past and future much more than of present. For moments and words never preserve in it their individuality:

> All words mirror themselves in each other to the point of seeming no longer to have their own color, but rather of being only transitions in a scale.[89]

Thus the current that bears them along never allows them the time to be themselves, to be fully significant, to be simply present.

They suggest, they recall. They prepare the words that are going to come, they reflect those which have disappeared. They also constitute—like the acting of the mime as Mallarmé describes it— "a marriage vicious but sacred between the desire and the fulfillment, the perpetration and its memory: here anticipating, there recollecting, in the future, in the past, *under a false appearance of present.*" [90] What they express is never entirely actual: a past that ceases or a future that tarries, a past and future that "intermingle perplexingly." For indeed, says Mallarmé, "there is no present, no—no present exists." [91]

No, the present does not exist, except as a "false appearance" —false or fictitious—and it is in order to establish this fiction of the present that all the suggestions of desire and memory collaborate. Mallarmean time is made of an ambiguous mingling of future and past, of notions which are always forced to confess their nonactuality, but in the midst of which, as at the center of a whirlwind, there is discerned the presence of the eternal Idea, ever contemporaneous with, but still always over the margin of, actuality.

Hence the Mallarmean duration will have a singular and wilfully contradictory character. On the one hand, eliminating all chance, it will present itself somewhat in the manner of the Leibnitzian duration, as a simple successive disposition of the elements that compose it, as the order in which words succeed and reflect each other; but on the other hand, it will assume the character of a true and lived duration, that is to say, a confused movement in which jostle and mingle all the contingencies of life and the determinations of chance. It will claim to express human time in what is more confused, the time of chance.

Mallarmean duration at once denies and affirms the existence of chance.

How can we explain this contradiction which Mallarmé is unable to escape, since his poem, in order to be what he *wills* must be an ordering of which he is absolute master; and since, on the other hand, his poem in order to *be,* must exist under the sole form of human existence possible, under the form of a hazardous enterprise, of a conflict, of an action, of an "existential" tempest?

But Mallarmé's reply is very clear: "All chance must be banished from the modern work and can only be *feigned* in it." [92] The "modern work" is therefore a purposeful disposition of words and notions, in which nothing is left to chance, save a place, and this place is entirely fictitious. There is always in the Mallarmean poem a sort of temporal storm whose eddies seem by turn to incline the mind in opposite directions. This oscillation comes much in evidence in *Un coup de dés:* "One part follows a rhythm of movement of thought to which there is opposed a contradictory design." [93] These contradictions are part of the game. They have no other goal than the play itself, that is to say, to simulate a fiction of duration and life. There is no hazard in the Mallarmean poem, except a fictitious hazard, a "hazard infinitely reduced." [94] As for Boileau, disorder for Mallarmé is an effect of art.

An art which, by means of reminiscences and suggestions of the tempestuous intermingling of the past and the future, consists in creating about that which is never present, which is only eternal and illusory, a fiction of duration. And so, in one sense, the Mallarmean poem consists in this duration. Its apparent lack of coherence, the fact that the mind is obliged to move ceaselessly backward and forward in it, the fact also that in the poem the mind is assailed by turn with contradictory impulsions, all this gives the poem a kind of temporal substance which is formed by the very time it takes the mind to pierce the sense of the poem and live its fiction. But inversely and finally all these "multiple disengagements" [95] can be "recapitulated at a glance," [96] brought back to a "simultaneous vision of the Page." [97] "From the complicated play made by the absent facets," [98] there can suddenly

burst forth a light in which everything is perceived simultaneously, instantaneously:

> . . . lightning flash, instant of resurrection and kisses, mir-
> rored by each jewel in possession of all its fires.[99]

The Mallarmean poem ever strives to make spring up from
duration this "flashing moment." [100] It becomes finally summed
up in this moment. In this moment it is read at one stroke. A
song which then "bursts forth from an innate source," [101]
"launched out of self," [102] is so compact a surge that everything
is therein fulfilled in the same instant, the instant when the act
of its creation and the act of faith in its fiction join together in
the mind. Thus each of Mallarmé's poems is so composed as to
be *finally* read without pause, at one glance, in one single operation of thought; just as are the Cartesian demonstrations in which
the swift flight of the mind, in its conclusions, immediately
reaches a primitive intuition.

The Mallarmean duration strives to reduce itself to the creation of an eternal moment.

X

But there is not only for Mallarmé the problem of the creation
of time; there is the problem of the creation of place.

To create is not only to make sure that a thing be and endure;
it is to make sure that it be in a place and that it take place there.

Just as the thought of Mallarmé is a doubt which a faith replaces, an empty time which fills itself up, a nothingness which
takes the shape of being, so Mallarmean space is to be a void
which fills itself up and which is replaced by the semblance of a
fullness. And that already from the most material point of view:
it is a white sheet of paper on which the pen writes in black.

It is necessary then to consider how this "filling up" is accomplished. Let us think of the poem as a theater. At one end is a

stage, the rest is a hall; a stage still vacant, "magnificent gap" [103] which from a distance, in the void, the desire of the spectator hollows out. And watch how, for example, there appears in this emptiness a human form, that of an actor, a mime, a ballet dancer. What she is matters little, but not what she represents. Where she is matters no more, but not where she pretends to be; and where, before long, by dint of words, steps, or gestures, she will be. The stage has disappeared and in this "void milieu," by virtue of an activity that lavishes itself there, little by little something is delimited which finally takes on the significance of a place; the very place where what happens, happens; the place where what takes place, takes its place.

Such is the magic of the dance:

> When at the rising of the curtain in a gala hall, there appears on the spot as if she were a snowflake blown from where? furious, the dancer: the floorboards, eschewed by leaps or unyielding to toeings, acquire a virginity of site undreamed of, *which the figure isolates, constructs, and decorates* . . . A sorcery which by instinct and exaggeration Loïe Fuller performs, the drawing away of skirt or pinion *establishing a place.* The enchantress forms the environment, draws it forth, and draws it in, from within herself, by means of a silence fluttering with crepe de Chine . . . Behold here, brought back to the Ballet, the atmosphere or nothing, visions as soon dispersed as seen in their limpid evocation. The free stage, at the pleasure of fictions, breathed forth from the play of a veil with attitudes and gestures, *becomes the very pure result.*[104]

Institution of place by the dance, to which there corresponds a similar creation of place by the mimic:

> Just so the Mime performs, whose play confines itself to a perpetual allusion without breaking the mirror: he *installs, in this way, a pure milieu of fiction.*[105]

And so also the poet. For what does he do if, in *placing* black signs on the white sheet of paper, he does not create the place of his dreams? if he does not change a space of nullity into a positive space in which, visibly but fictitiously, what he imagined is localized?

But if what he imagined is realized, it is so at still some distance. As we have seen, the entire thought of Mallarmé has, from the beginning, been less obsessed by the difficulty of installing the place of his dream, than by the impossibility of situating that place elsewhere than in a remoteness from which he finds himself separated by a void. This is the drama of the *Coup de dés,* in which finally "all reality is dissolved" and withdrawn from the *place* of the poem, unless one succeeds in projecting the latter "on some vacant and higher surface":

> *Nothing shall have taken place but place* . . . except perhaps at an altitude so remote that any locality fuses with the beyond . . . , a Constellation, chilled with oblivion and desuetude . . .

Infinite retreat of the dream into the distance, and separation which is equivalent to a negation. All is finally reduced to proving that there is no authentic installation of a poetic universe, unless the place of this universe is identified with the *me* of the poet, and unless what happens in the poem takes place, really place, in the being of him who writes, as well as in the being of him who reads.

Thus everything in the poem must strive to suppress the distance, to identify spectacle and spectator. But this final identification can take place only as the crowning work of all the particular and partial identifications which precisely, as we have seen, constitute the warp and the woof of the poem. If this is that and that is this, if finally everything is intended as an inexhaustible series of successive identifications of one selfsame substance with its attributes, that is because this substance is none other than the very substance of the creating (and perusing) thought. In the last analysis, the poem must be recognized as the "mental place" of him who thinks it, as the site of the mind. In this continuous movement by means of which the Mallarmean poem successively

turns its facets toward us, it is necessary to distinguish an induce-
ment, the offer of a multiple mirror in which there is reflected a
figure with which we must finally identify ourselves. A figure
that is at first entirely mythical, and so distant that we can
hardly believe in its existence. But we watch it perform, confront
itself with itself, authenticate itself by each of its gestures, and
little by little constitute its own type. And, accordingly, we the
more clearly distinguish in it an heroic and deified image, that
of a being in whom we must believe, because it is *ourself*. "Its
motion recapitulates to the self our dreams of sites or of para-
dises." [106] Doubtless this form is not that of our individual personality. It is the "form which No One is," [107] which no one is
individually and concretely; an utterly general form in which
the human type is recapitulated. In order to acknowledge it in
one's own semblance, it is necessary to make the same sacrifice
that Mallarmé had made, and, passing by way of the same spiritual death, to arrive at the same state of renunciation. Mallarmé
once wrote to a friend: " . . . I am now depersonalized, and no
longer the Stéphane you have known,—but rather an aptitude
which the spiritual universe has for seeing itself and developing
itself through what was me." [108]

What the Mallarmean poem proposes to us, therefore, is at
the same time a sacrifice and an identification. By "his death as
so and so," [109] one arrives at being nothing other than this general being in whom the human desire is realized and typified.
One becomes apt at recognizing, no longer outside oneself but
within oneself, him whose figure first outlined itself, unreal and
remote, at a distance, beyond the void, in some mythical place.
That doubt is abolished, that void is filled. One becomes the
place in which the spiritual universe is attested and incarnated:

> Man, then his authentic terrestrial sojourn, exchange a reci-
> procity of proofs.[110]

Is it not so in any communion, and, in particular, in the
liturgical drama and in the lyrical drama? For what appears in

any religious ceremony if not "a mythical presence with whom one comes to confound himself"? [111] And, in the Wagnerian opera, is not the miracle of the music "this penetration, in reciprocity, of the myth and the opera house, by which there is *filled up* to the sparkling of the arabesques and the gold that delineate the limits of the sounding-box, *the vacant space facing the stage*"? [112]

And so the Mallarmean poem can exist only in this "reciprocity." It furnishes the reader with a text which has meaning and even existence only if the reader projects his own thought into it. There is no Mallarmean poem except from the moment when there is no longer on the one side the poem, and on the other a thought, with, between the two, "the vacant space facing the stage." *It is necessary that there should no longer be anything other than one selfsame place,* that in which one selfsame being sees himself and thinks himself, in which he recognizes himself in a spectacle which is none other than "the spectacle of Self." [113]

Thus poem and reader, spectacle and spectator coalesce in one selfsame thought, which is very simply reflective thought. I merge myself and find myself in the perfect moment and in the absolute place in which I create my thought and recognize it for mine. The space, the duration, the universe of my poem, they are myself.

"Myself projected absolute." [114]

Notes

CHAPTER I

1 *Spectateur français,* 1ʳᵉ feuille, *Oeuvres,* éd. Duchesne, t. IX, p. 5.
2 *La Surprise de l'amour,* acte I, scène II.
3 *Spectateur français,* 1ʳᵉ feuille, *Oeuvres,* t. IX, p. 11.
4 Cité par LESBROS, *Esprit de Marivaux,* 1769, p. 29.
5 *Le Don Quichotte moderne, Oeuvres,* t. XI, p. 405.
6 *Spectateur français,* 1ʳᵉ feuille, *Oeuvres,* t. IX, p. 13.
7 *Le Don Quichotte moderne, Oeuvres,* t. XI, p. 323.
8 *La Dispute,* scène XV.
9 *Le Jeu de l'amour et du hasard,* acte II, scène VII.
10 *Le Triomphe de l'amour,* acte I, scène VI.
11 *La Mère confidente,* acte I, scène VIII.
12 *Vie de Marianne, Oeuvres,* t. VI, p. 415.
13 *La Seconde surprise de l'amour,* acte III, scène XI.
14 *Le Paysan parvenu, Oeuvres,* t. VIII, p. 203.
15 *Spectateur français,* 1ʳᵉ feuille, *Oeuvres,* t. IX, p. 6.
16 *Annibal,* acte I, scène IV.
17 *Spectateur français,* 1ʳᵉ feuille, *Oeuvres,* t. IX, p. 10.
18 *L'Ile des esclaves,* scène VI.

19 *La Seconde surprise de l'amour,* acte III, scène XII.
20 *La Double inconstance,* acte III, scène VII.
21 *Id.,* acte III, scène VIII.
22 *Le Prince travesti,* acte II, scène V.
23 *Spectateur français,* 2ᵉ feuille, *Oeuvres,* t. IX, p. 20.
24 *L'Heureux stratagème,* acte III, scène VII.
25 *Les Serments indiscrets,* acte V, scène II.
26 *Le Triomphe de l'amour,* acte II, scène XI.
27 *La Surprise de l'amour,* acte III, scène IV.
28 *La Mère confidente,* acte II, scène VI.
29 *La Seconde surprise de l'amour,* acte III, scène XII.
30 *Spectateur français,* 2ᵉ feuille, *Oeuvres,* t. IX, p. 20.
31 *La Mère confidente,* acte III, scène VIII.
32 *Félicie,* scène IX.
33 *Les Effets de la sympathie, Oeuvres,* t. V, p. 503.
34 *La Seconde surprise de l'amour,* acte I, scène XII.
35 *Vie de Marianne, Oeuvres,* t. VI, p. 294.
36 *Id.,* p. 270.

37 *Cabinet du philosophe*, 3ᵉ feuille, *Oeuvres*, t. IX, p. 563.
38 *Le Paysan parvenu, Oeuvres*, t. VIII, p. 453.
39 *Spectateur français*, 9ᵉ feuille, *Oeuvres*, t. IX, p. 97.
40 *Vie de Marianne, Oeuvres*, t. VI, p. 343.
41 *Id.*, p. 382.
42 *Id.*, p. 317.
43 *Le Don Quichotte moderne*, *Oeuvres*, t. XI, p. 154.
44 *Spectateur français*, 23ᵉ feuille, *Oeuvres*, t. IX, p. 280.
45 *Vie de Marianne, Oeuvres*, t. VI, p. 353.
46 *L'Indigent philosophe*, 2ᵉ feuille, *Oeuvres*, t. IX, p. 455.
47 *La Dispute*, scène I.
48 *Oeuvres*, t. XII, p. 62.
49 *Réflexions sur Thucydite, Oeuvres*, t. XII, p. 98.
50 *Spectateur français*, 17ᵉ feuille, *Oeuvres*, t. IX, p. 196.
51 *Vie de Marianne, Oeuvres*, t. VI, p. 440.
52 *Spectateur français*, 11ᵉ feuille, *Oeuvres*, t. IX, p. 116.
53 *Vie de Marianne, Oeuvres*, t. VI, p. 270.
54 *La Dispute*, scène III.
55 *Arlequin poli par l'amour*, scène I.
56 *Vie de Marianne, Oeuvres*, t. VI, p. 278.
57 *Id.*, p. 333.
58 *La Fausse suivante*, acte II, scène II.
59 *Spectateur français*, 20ᵉ feuille, *Oeuvres*, t. IX, p. 237.
60 *Vie de Marianne, Oeuvres*, t. VI, p. 278.
61 *Spectateur français*, 24ᵉ feuille, *Oeuvres*, t. IX, p. 295.
62 *Le Dénouement imprévu*, scène IV.
63 *Spectateur français*, 4ᵉ feuille, *Oeuvres*, t. IX, p. 33.
64 *Id.*, p. 97.
65 *Le Paysan parvenu, Oeuvres*, t. VIII, p. 145.

66 *Id.*, p. 221.
67 *Id.*, t. IX, p. 332.
68 *Vie de Marianne, Oeuvres*, t. VI, p. 383.
69 *L'Ile des esclaves*, scène VII.
70 *Les Sincères*, scène VI.
71 *La Mère confidente*, acte III, scène VII.
72 *La Double inconstance*, acte III, scène III.
73 *Vie de Marianne, Oeuvres*, t. VI, p. 343.
74 *Félicie*, scène XII.
75 *Vie de Marianne, Oeuvres*, t. VI, p. 491.
76 *L'École des mères*, scène XVIII.
77 *L'Indigent philosophe*, 5ᵉ feuille, *Oeuvres*, t. IX, p. 502.
78 *La Méprise*, scène IV.
79 *Le Petit-maître corrigé*, acte I, scène II.
80 *Le Cabinet du philosophe*, 3ᵉ feuille, *Oeuvres*, t. IX, p. 563.
81 *La Double inconstance*, acte III, scène VIII.
82 *L'Heureux stratagème*, acte I, scène IV.
83 *Le Dénouement imprévu*, scène IV.
84 *Vie de Marianne, Oeuvres*, t. VI, p. 327.
85 *Oeuvres*, t. XII, p. 176.
86 *Spectateur français*, 11ᵉ feuille, *Oeuvres*, t. IX, p. 122.
87 *Oeuvres*, t. XII, p. 35.
88 *L'Indigent philosophe*, 3ᵉ feuille, *Oeuvres*, t. IX, p. 467.
89 *Réflexions sur Thucydite, Oeuvres*, t. XII, p. 93.
90 *Vie de Marianne, Oeuvres*, t. VI, p. 252.
91 *Spectateur français*, 5ᵉ feuille, *Oeuvres*, t. IX, p. 43.
92 *Id.*, 20ᵉ feuille, *Oeuvres*, t. IX, pp. 234–235.
93 *La Double inconstance*, acte III, scène I.
94 *Le Dénouement imprévu*, scène IV.
95 *Les Acteurs de bonne foi*, scène III.

CHAPTER II

1 *Oeuvres*, éd. Gilbert, 2 vol., 1857, t. I, p. 223.
2 Tome I, p. 394.
3 *Id.*, p. 94.
4 *Id.*, p. 443.
5 *Id.*, p. 205.
6 *Id.*, p. 457.
7 *Id.*, p. 36.
8 *Id.*, p. 27.
9 *Id.*, p. 394.
10 *Id.*, p. 67.
11 *Id.*, p. 129.
12 *Id.*, p. 27.
13 *Id.*, p. 93.
14 *Id.*, p. 57.
15 *Id.*, p. 224.
16 Tome II, p. 224.
17 *Id.*, p. 122.
18 Tome I, p. 46.
19 *Id.*, p. 207.
20 *Id.*, p. 62.
21 *Id.*, p. 388.
22 *Id.*, p. 94.
23 *Id.*, p. 30.
24 *Id.*, p. 26.
25 Tome II, p. 139.
26 Tome I, p. 194.
27 Tome II, p. 249.
28 Tome I, p. 485.
29 *Id.*, p. 476.
30 *Id.*, pp. 129–130.
31 *Id.*, p. 129.
32 *Id.*

33 *Id.*, p. 34.
34 *Id.*, p. 130.
35 *Id.*, p. 117.
36 *Id.*, p. 123.
37 *Id.*, p. 94.
38 *Id.*, p. 194.
39 *Id.*, p. 336.
40 *Id.*, p. 414.
41 *Id.*, p. 94.
42 *Id.*
43 *Id.*, p. 433.
44 *Id.*, p. 199.
45 *Id.*, p. 94.
46 *Id.*, p. 457.
47 *Id.*
48 *Id.*, p. 28.
49 *Id.*, p. 456.
50 *Id.*, p. 76.
51 *Id.*, p. 388.
52 *Id.*
53 *Id.*, p. 28.
54 Tome II, p. 29.
55 *Id.*, p. 13.
56 *Id.*, p. 489.
57 Tome I, p. 110.
58 *Id.*, p. 332.
59 *Id.*, p. 418.
60 *Id.*, p. 269.
61 *Id.*, p. 415.
62 *Id.*, p. 329.
63 *Id.*, p. 415.
64 *Id.*, p. 144.

CHAPTER III

1 Chamfort, *Oeuvres*, éd. P. R. Auguis, 1824–1825, 5 vol., t. I, p. 445.
2 Id., *ibid.*, pp. 200–201.
3 Tome I, p. 200.
4 *Id.*, p. 430.
5 *Id.*, p. 409.
6 Tome I, p. 407; t. II, p. 104.
7 Tome II, p. 112.
8 Tome I, p. 350.

9 Tome V, p. 55.
10 Tome II, p. 100.
11 *Id.*, p. 8.
12 Tome I, p. 372.
13 Tome V, p. 211.
14 Tome I, p. 358.
15 *Id.*, p. 366.
16 *Id.*, p. 362.
17 Tome V, pp. 259–260.

18 Tome II, p. 107.
19 *Id.*, p. 73.
20 Tome V, p. 260.
21 Tome I, pp. 357–358.
22 Tome V, p. 98.
23 *Id.*, p. 290.
24 Tome I, p. 372.
25 Tome II, p. 96.
26 Tome I, p. 399.
27 Tome V, p. 274.
28 Tome II, p. 1.
29 *Id.*, p. 141.
30 Tome I, p. 407.
31 Tome V, p. 292.
32 Tome I, p. 407.
33 *Id.*, p. 399.
34 Tome V, p. 282.
35 *Id.*, p. 274.
36 Tome II, p. 56.
37 Tome I, p. 344.
38 Laclos, *Oeuvres*, éd. de la Pléiade, 1943, p. 41.
39 Id., *ibid.*, p. 78.
40 Id., *ibid.*, p. 50.
41 Id., *ibid.*, p. 200.

42 Id., *ibid.*, p. 46.
43 Id., *ibid.*, p. 46.
44 Id., *ibid.*, p. 299.
45 Id., *ibid.*, p. 427.
46 Id., *ibid.*, p. 46.
47 Id., *ibid.*, p. 286.
48 Id., *ibid.*, p. 167.
49 Id., *ibid.*, p. 46.
50 Id., *ibid.*, p. 253.
51 Id., *ibid.*, p. 326.
52 Id., *ibid.*, p. 573.
53 Id., *ibid.*, p. 243; cf. variante, p. 819.
54 Id., *ibid.*, p. 321.
55 Id., *ibid.*, p. 46.
56 Id., *ibid.*, p. 441.
57 Id., *ibid.*, p. 240.
58 Id., *ibid.*, p. 143.
59 Id., *ibid.*, p. 119.
60 Id., *ibid.*, p. 77.
61 Id., *ibid.*, p. 241.
62 Id., *ibid.*, p. 257.
63 Id., *ibid.*, p. 320.
64 Id., *ibid.*, p. 241.
65 Id., *ibid.*, p. 257.

CHAPTER IV

1 *A Fontanes*, 23 novembre 1794.
2 *Carnets*, p. 44.
3 *Id.*, p. 44.
4 *Id.*, p. 55.
5 *Id.*, p. 44.
6 *Id.*, p. 45.
7 *Id.*, p. 209.
8 *Id.*, p. 662.
9 *Id.*, p. 616.
10 *Id.*, p. 391.
11 *Id.*, p. 45.
12 *Id.*, p. 225.
13 *Id.*, p. 44.
14 *Id.*, p. 45.
15 *Id.*, p. 639.
16 *Id.*, p. 178.
17 *Id.*, p. 265.
18 *Id.*, p. 171.
19 *Id.*, p. 233.

20 *Id.*, p. 356.
21 *A Madame de Beaumont*, 27 août 1797.
22 Cité par Tessonneau, *Joubert éducateur*, p. 170.
23 *Carnets*, p. 421.
24 *Id.*, p. 381.
25 *Id.*, p. 276.
26 *Id.*, p. 197.
27 *Id.*, p. 241.
28 *Id.*, p. 160.
29 *Id.*, p. 207.
30 *Id.*, p. 228.
31 *N.R.F.*, 1938, p. 150.
32 *Carnets*, p. 555.
33 *Id.*, p. 499.
34 *Id.*, p. 85.
35 *Id.*, p. 141.
36 *Id.*, p. 295.

37 *Id.*, p. 301.
38 *Id.*, p. 264.
39 *Id.*, p. 204.
40 *Id.*, p. 915.
41 *Id.*, p. 131.
42 *Id.*, p. 200.
43 *Id.*, p. 442.
44 *Id.*, p. 187.
45 *Id.*, p. 183.
46 *Id.*, p. 907.
47 *Id.*, p. 121.
48 *Id.*, p. 451.
49 *Id.*, p. 451.
50 *Id.*, p. 710.
51 *Id.*, p. 293.
52 *Id.*, p. 789.
53 *Id.*, p. 722.
54 *Id.*, p. 885.
55 *Id.*, p. 321.
56 *Id.*, p. 786.
57 *Id.*, p. 376.
58 *Id.*, p. 188.
59 *Id.*, p. 290.
60 *Id.*, p. 742.
61 *Id.*, p. 429.
62 *Id.*, p. 337.
63 *Id.*, p. 648.
64 *Id.*, p. 45.
65 *Id.*, p. 348.
66 *Id.*, p. 786.
67 *Id.*, p. 357.
68 *A Madame de Beaumont*, 20 avril 1799.
69 *Pensées*, p. 4.
70 *Carnets*, p. 596.
71 *Id.*, p. 351.
72 *A Madame de Beaumont*, 20 avril 1799.
73 Cité par Beaunier, *Joubert et la Révolution*, p. 277.
74 *Carnets*, p. 373.
75 *Id.*, p. 824.
76 *Id.*, p. 407.
77 *Id.*, p. 250.
78 *Id.*, p. 446.
79 *Revue d'Histoire littéraire*, 1909, p. 581. Pour l'attribution à Joubert, voir même année, p. 796.

80 *Carnets*, p. 818.
81 *Id.*, p. 493.
82 *Id.*, p. 282.
83 *Id.*, p. 582.
84 *Id.*, p. 368.
85 *Pensées*, p. 299.
86 *Carnets*, p. 66.
87 *Id.*, p. 591.
88 *Id.*, p. 731.
89 *Id.*, p. 457.
90 *Id.*, p. 623.
91 *Id.*, p. 624.
92 *A Molé*, 18 février 1804.
93 *Carnets*, p. 638.
94 *Id.*, p. 463.
95 *Id.*, p. 473.
96 *Id.*, p. 226.
97 *Id.*, p. 874.
98 *Id.*, p. 250.
99 *Id.*, p. 907.
100 *Id.*, p. 83.
101 *Id.*, p. 236.
102 *Id.*, p. 232.
103 *Id.*, p. 263.
104 *Id.*, p. 881.
105 *Id.*, p. 478.
106 *Id.*, p. 582.
107 *Id.*, p. 263.
108 *Id.*, p. 188.
109 *Id.*, p. 134.
110 *Id.*, p. 881.
111 *Id.*, p. 478.
112 *Id.*, p. 263.
113 *Id.*, p. 917.
114 *Id.*, p. 83.
115 *Id.*, p. 142.
116 *Id.*, p. 804.
117 *Id.*, p. 191.
118 *Id.*, p. 168.
119 *Id.*, p. 178.
120 *Id.*, p. 196.
121 *Id.*, p. 558.
122 *Id.*, p. 263.
123 *Id.*, p. 167.
124 *Id.*, p. 427.
125 *Id.*, p. 320.
126 *Id.*, p. 480.
127 *Id.*, p. 456.

128 *Id.*, p. 369.
129 *Id.*, p. 305.
130 *Id.*, p. 456.
131 *Id.*, p. 526.
132 *Id.*, p. 456.
133 *Id.*, p. 212.
134 *Id.*, p. 274.
135 *Id.*, p. 426.
136 *Id.*, p. 513.
137 *Id.*, p. 822.

138 *Id.*
139 *Id.*, p. 44.
140 *Id.*, p. 421.
141 *Id.*, p. 558.
142 *Id.*, p. 513.
143 *Id.*, p. 151.
144 *Id.*, p. 654.
145 R.H.L.F., *cit.*
146 *Carnets*, p. 196.

CHAPTER V

1 *Oeuvres*, éd. Conard *(C.)*, t. II, p. 199.
2 *C.*, t. XXXI, p. 111.
3 *C.*, t. III, p. 37.
4 *Lettres à sa famille*, p. 53.
5 *Sténie*, éd. Prioult, p. 123.
6 *Tableau d'une vie privée*, MILATCHITCH, *Théâtre de Balzac*, p. 85.
7 *C.*, t. XII, p. 552.
8 *C.*, t. XXIV, p. 116.
9 *Oeuvres*, éd. Calmann-Lévy, t. XXIV, p. 240.
10 ARRIGON, *Balzac et la Contessa*, p. 97.
11 *C.*, t. XXVII, p. 307.
12 *C.*, t. XXXI, p. 97.
13 *Id.*, p. 66.
14 *C.*, t. XVIII, p. 134.
15 *C.*, t. XXVI, p. 76.
16 *C.*, t. XXVII, p. 455.
17 *C.*, t. XXIX, p. 173.
18 *C.*, t. XXVIII, p. 393.
19 *C.*, t. XXXI, p. 90.
20 *Id.*, p. 162.
21 *C.*, t. XXXVIII, p. 355.
22 *C.*, t. XXXI, p. 33.
23 *Id.*, p. 162.
24 *Id.*, p. 98
25 *C.*, t. XXVII, p. 101.
26 *C.*, t. XXXI, p. 98.
27 *Avertissement* DU *Gars;* ABRAHAM, *Créatures chez B. . . ,* p. 89.
28 *Le Centenaire*, éd. Calmann-Lévy, p. 286.

29 *Oeuvres*, éd. Calmann-Lévy, t. XXII, p. 402.
30 *C.*, t. XXXI, p. 85.
31 *Id.*, p. 242.
32 *Id.*, p. 334.
33 *C.*, t. XXVII, p. 426.
34 *C.*, t. XXXI, p. 325.
35 *C.*, t. III, p. 37.
36 *C.*, t. XXXI, p. 166.
37 *C.*, t. XXXIX, p. 564.
38 *C.*, t. XXXI, p. 267.
39 *Id.*, p. 51.
40 *Sténie*, p. 19.
41 *C.*, t. VIII, p 74.
42 Première version de *Louis Lambert;* SPOELBERCH, *Histoire des oeuvres de Balzac*, 2ᵉ éd., p. 191.
43 *C.*, t. XXXI, p. 50.
44 *Oeuvres*, éd. Calmann-Lévy, t. XXII, p. 402.
45 *C.*, t. XXVII, p. 343.
46 *A Madame Hanska*, 5 août 1847.
47 *C.*, t. XXVII, p. 24.
48 *Sténie*, p. 6.
49 *C.*, t. XXVII, p. 39.
50 *C.*, t. XXX, p. 86.
51 *C.*, t. XXXIX, p. 460.
52 *C.*, t. XXXI, p. 94.
53 *Sténie*, p. 28.
54 *C.*, t. XXXI, p. 220.
55 *C.*, t. XXXIX, p. 642.
56 *C.*, t. XIII, p. 233.
57 *C.*, t. XXXII, p. 217.
58 *C.*, t. XXXI, p. 93.

59 *C.*, t. XXVII, p. 428.
60 *Id.*, p. 174.
61 *C.*, t. XXXIX, p. 617.
62 *C.*, t. XXXI, p. 181.
63 *Sténie*, p. 6.
64 *Oeuvres*, éd. Calmann-Lévy, t. XXII, p. 402.
65 *C.*, t. XXXIX, p. 194.
66 *C.*, t. XXVII, p. 10.
67 *Id.*, p. 427.
68 *C.*, t. XXXVIII, p. 356.
69 *Album*, éd. Crépet, p. 27.
70 *C.*, t. XXXIX, p. 577.
71 *C.*, t. XXVII, p. 19.
72 *C.*, t. XXXVIII, p. 149.
73 *C.*, t. XXVII, p. 24.
74 *Id.*
75 *Sténie*, pp. 5–6.
76 *C.*, t. XXVII, p. 24.
77 *Id.*, p. 25.
78 *Id.*, p. 17.
79 *Id.*, p. 27.
80 *C.*, t. XXXI, p. 136.
81 *C.*, t. XXXIX, p. 576.
82 *C.*, t. XVII, p. 228
83 *C.*, t. IV, p. 92.
84 *Ibid.*
85 *A Madame Hanska*, 24 mai 1837.
86 *Oeuvres*, éd. Calmann-Lévy, t. XXII, p. 526.
87 DAVIN, *Introduction aux études philosophiques;* SPOELBERCH, *Hist. des Oeuvres*, p. 203.
88 *C.*, t. XXXIX, p. 637.
89 *C.*, t. XXV, p. 197.
90 *Centenaire*, p. 285.
91 *C.*, t. XXX, p. 149.
92 *C.*, t. XXXIX, p. 622.
93 *C.*, t. XVI, p. 414.
94 DAVIN, *Introduction aux études philosophiques;* SPOELBERCH, p. 201.
95 *C.*, t. XXXI, p. 112.
96 *L'Excommunié*, p. 264.
97 *C.*, t. VI, p. 301.
98 *C.*, t. XIII, p. 333.
99 *C.*, t. XXVII, p. 448.
100 *C.*, t. XXIX, p. 269.
101 *C.*, t. XXVII, p. 174.

102 *C.*, t. III, p. 80.
103 *C.*, t. XL, p. 141.
104 *C.*, t. XXVI, p. 240.
105 *Une heure de ma vie,* dans *La Femme auteur*, 1950, p. 248.
106 *Oeuvres*, éd. Calmann-Lévy, t. XXIV, p. 74.
107 *C.*, t. V, p. 125.
108 *C.*, t. XXVII, p. 22.
109 *C.*, t. XXIV, p. 28.
110 *Sténie*, p. 186.
111 *C.*, t. XVI, p. 143.
112 *C.*, t. XXXI, p. 170.
113 *C.*, t. XXVI, p. 57.
114 *Sténie*, p. 133.
115 *Id.*, p. 128.
116 *Id.*, p. 169.
117 *C.*, t. XV, pp. 21–22.
118 *C.*, t. XVII, p. 120.
119 *C.*, t. XXXII, p. 176.
120 *C.*, t. VI, p. 358.
121 *C.*, t. XXXII, p. 152.
122 *C.*, t. XXXVIII, p. 366.
123 *C.*, t. XXXIX, p. 621.
124 *C.*, t. VI, p. 341.
125 *C.*, t. XIII, p. 132.
126 *Id.*, p. 377.
127 *C.*, t. VI, p. 162.
128 *Sténie*, p. 49.
129 *C.*, t. XVI, p. 413.
130 *C.*, t. XXVIII, p. 126.
131 *C.*, t. XXVII, p. 84.
132 *C.*, t. XVI, p. 146.
133 *Id.*
134 *Id.*
135 *C.*, t. XXIX, p. 152.
136 *C.*, t. VI, p. 323.
137 *C.*, t. XXXI, p. 298.
138 *Id.*
139 *C.*, t. VI, p. 322.
140 *Id.*, p. 358.
141 *C.*, t. VIII, p. 151.
142 *C.*, t. XXII, p. 400.
143 *C.*, t. XXI, p. 66.
144 *C.*, t. VI, p. 154.
145 *Id.*, p. 358.
146 *Id.*, p. 323.
147 *C.*, t. III, p. 62.

148 *Falthurne*, éd. Castex, p. 9.
149 *C.*, t. XXVI, p. 31.
150 *C.*, t. VI, p. 316.
151 *C.*, t. III, p. 244.
152 *Album*, p. 9.
153 *C.*, t. XXXI, p. 47.
154 *C.*, t. XXVIII, p. 156.
155 *C.*, t. XI, p. 27.
156 *C.*, t. XXII, p. 337.
157 *C.*, t. XVI, p. 348.
158 *C.*, t. XXVIII, p. 277.
159 *C.*, t. XVIII, p. 268.
160 *C.*, t. XVII, p. 267.
161 *C.*, t. XVIII, p. 268.
162 *C.*, t. VI, p. 111.
163 *C.*, t. XXVIII, p. 249.
164 *C.*, t. XXXIX, p. 662.
165 *C.*, t. XXXI, p. 220.
166 *C.*, t. XVIII, p. 393.
167 *C.*, t. XV, p. 188.
168 *C.*, t. XVIII, p. 376.
169 *C.*, t. XV, p. 59.
170 *C.*, t. I, p. 240.
171 *C.*, t. III, p. 63.
172 *C.*, t. XIV, p. 178.
173 *C.*, t. XVII, p. 127.
174 *C.*, t. XVI, p. 227.
175 *C.*, t. XXIX, p. 53.
176 *C.*, t. XVI, p. 101.
177 *C.*, t. I, pp. 413–414.
178 *C.*, t. XIII, pp. 281–282.
179 *Sténie*, p. 55.
180 *Vicaire des Ardennes*, p. 183.
181 *C.*, t. XIII, p. 397.
182 *Id.*
183 *C.*, t. XXXI, p. 150.
184 *Vicaire des Ardennes*, p. 352.
185 *C.*, t. XIII, p. 321.
186 *Id.*, p. 328.
187 *Id.*, p. 324.
188 *Id.*, p. 328.
189 *Id.*, p. 331.
190 *Id.*, p. 331.
191 Laure SURVILLE, *Vie de Balzac*.
192 *C.*, t. XXX, p. 376.
193 *Id.*, p. 328.
194 *C.*, t. XXXI, p. 120.

195 *C.*, t. XXVII, p. 189.
196 *Id.*, p. 198.
197 *Id.*, p. 287.
198 *C.*, t. XL, p. 140.
199 *C.*, t. XXXI, p. 114.
200 *Ibid.*
201 *C.*, t. XXVII, p. 278.
202 *Id.*, p. 78.
203 *Id.*, p. 38.
204 *C.*, t. XXXIX, p. 662.
205 *C.*, t. XXXI, p. 98.
206 *C.*, t. XL, p. 136.
207 *C.*, t. XXVII, p. 116.
208 *C.*, t. VIII, p. 237.
209 *C.*, t. XXVII, pp. 38–39.
210 *C.*, t. V, p. 390.
211 *C.*, t. XXXII, p. 357.
212 *Album*, p. 20.
213 *C.*, t. XXVIII, p. 9.
214 *C.*, t. XXXIX, p. 168.
215 *C.*, t. XVIII, p. 130.
216 *C.*, t. V, p. 411.
217 *C.*, t. XXVII, p. 392.
218 *C.*, t. XXXI, p. 12.
219 *C.*, t. V, p. 425.
220 *C.*, t. XXXVIII, p. 427.
221 *Id.*
222 *C.*, t. XVIII, pp. 132–133.
223 *C.*, t. XVI, p. 145.
224 *Falthurne*, p. 32.
225 *C.*, t. XXXI, p. 24.
226 *C.*, t. XXVIII, p. 18.
227 *C.*, t. XXXI, p. 78.
228 *C.*, t. XXVIII, p. 112.
229 *C.*, t. XXXI, p. 167.
230 *C.*, t. XVIII, p. 133.
231 *C.*, t. XL, p. 136.
232 *C.*, t. XXX, p. 328.
233 *C.*, t. XXXIX, p. 625.
234 *C.*, t. VII, p. 84.
235 *La Dernière fée*, pp. 5–6.
236 *C.*, t. VII, p. 122.
237 *C.*, t. XXVII, p. 256.
238 *C.*, t. XXXI, p. 167.
239 *C.*, t. XL, p. 235.
240 *C.*, t. VIII, p. 368.
241 *C.*, t. XVIII, p. 131.

242 *C.*, t. XXXI, p. 94.
243 *Id.*, p. 166.
244 Spoelberch, p. 192.
245 *C.*, t. XXX, p. 330.
246 *C.*, t. XXXI, p. 219.
247 *C.*, t. XVI, p. 269.
248 *C.*, t. XXVIII, p. 9.
249 *Album*, p. 42.
250 *C.*, t. IV, p. 29.
251 *C.*, t. XIII, p. 391.
252 *C.*, t. XXVIII, p. 186.
253 *Ibid.*
254 *C.*, t. IV, p. 29.
255 *C.*, t. XXX, p. 375.
256 Première version de *Gobseck.*
257 *C.*, t. VI, p. 337.
258 *C.*, t. XII, p. 547.
259 *C.*, t. XX, p. 356.
260 *C.*, t. XXVII, p. 279.
261 *Centenaire*, p. 252.
262 *Id.*, p. 230.
263 *Falthurne*, p. 11.
264 *C.*, t. XXXI, p. 220.
265 *Id.*

266 *C.*, t. VI, p. 357.
267 *C.*, t. XXXI, p. 288.
268 *C.*, t. XXI, p. 416.
269 *C.*, t. VIII, p. 68.
270 *C.*, t. XXXI, p. 232.
271 *C.*, t. XXX, p. 330.
272 *C.*, t. XXXIX, p. 109.
273 *C.*, t. V, p. 397.
274 *Album*, p. 119.
275 *C.*, t. IV, p. 347.
276 *C.*, t. XXXVIII, p. 99.
277 *C.*, t. IV, p. 265.
278 *C.*, t. XXXVIII, p. 55.
279 *Id.*, p. 54.
280 *C.*, t. XXVII, p. 428.
281 *C.*, t. XXXI, p. 207.
282 *C.*, t. XL, p. 177.
283 *C.*, t. XXXI, p. 167.
284 *C.*, t. XXXVII, p. 469.
285 *Id.*, p. 356.
286 *C.*, t. XXXI, p. 198.
287 *C.*, t. XXVII, p. 257.
288 *Id.*, p. 358.
289 *C.*, t. XXXI, p. 36.

CHAPTER VI

1 *Orientales*, xxviii, *les Djinns.*
2 *Les Misérables*, II⁰ partie, 1. 3, 5.
3 *Légende des siècles*, liv, *Vision de Dante.*
4 *Carnets de Victor Hugo*, 9 mars 1856.
5 *Travailleurs de la mer*, Iʳᵉ partie, 1. I, 7.
6 *Ibid.*
7 *Le Rhin*, lettre XX.
8 *Notre-Dame de Paris*, 1. 10, 4.
9 *Légende des siècles*, liv, *Vision de Dante.*
10 *Id.*, *Vision d'où est sorti ce livre.*
11 Préface de *Cromwell.*
12 *Légende des siècles*, *Vision d'où est sorti ce livre.*
13 *Dieu*, I, I.
14 *Feuilles d'automne*, xxvii.
15 *Orientales*, xxxvi, *Rêverie.*

16 *Dieu*, II, ii.
17 *Feuilles d'automne*, xxix, *la Pente de la rêverie.*
18 *Légende des siècles*, ii, *le Sacre de la femme.*
19 *Contemplations*, 1. I, viii.
20 *Carnets de Hugo*, 1856.
21 *Chants du crépuscule*, xxviii, *Au bord de la mer.*
22 *Légende des siècles*, *Vision d'où est sorti ce livre.*
23 *Les Rayons et les ombres*, xxxv.
24 *Note du 19 novembre 1846.*
25 *Année terrible*, février, v.
26 *Dieu*, I, ii, *les Voix.*
27 *Chants du crépuscule*, xiii.
28 *Légende des siècles*, liv, *Vision de Dante.*
29 *Dieu*, I, i, *l'Esprit humain.*

30 *Feuilles d'automne*, xxix, *la Pente de la rêverie.*

31 *Légende des siècles, Vision d'où est sorti ce livre.*

32 *Alpes et Pyrénées*, 10 septembre 1839.

33 *Légende des siècles, Vision d'où est sorti ce livre.*

34 *Obsèques de Mme Paul Meurice.*

35 *Contemplations*, 1. 2, xxviii, *Un soir que je regardais le ciel.*

36 *Dernière gerbe, Dialogue avec l'esprit.*

37 *Feuilles d'automne*, xxix, *la Pente de la rêverie.*

38 *Le Rhin*, lettre XXVIII.

39 *Post-scriptum de ma vie, Choses de l'infini.*

40 *Les Travailleurs de la mer*, IIe partie, 1. 2, 5.

41 *Les Misérables*, Ire partie, 1. 7, 3.

42 *Les Travailleurs de la mer*, IIe partie, 1. 2, 5.

43 *Post-scriptum de ma vie, Contemplation suprême.*

44 *L'Homme qui rit*, Ire partie, 1. 2, 6.

45 *Les Travailleurs de la mer*, IIe partie, 1. 2, 5.

46 *Dieu*, II, vii.

47 *Id.*, I, ii.

48 Préface des *Contemplations.*

49 *William Shakespeare*, Ire partie, 1. 5, i.

50 *Légende des siècles, Vision d'où est sorti ce livre.*

51 *Contemplations*, 1. 3, iii. *Saturne.*

52 *Les Rayons et les ombres*, xxxiv, *Tristesse d'Olympio.*

53 *Alpes et Pyrénées*, ii août 1843.

54 *Contemplations*, 1. 3, xxx, *Magnitudo parvi.*

55 *Alpes et Pyrénées*, 10 septembre 1839.

56 *Littérature et philosophie mêlées, Journal d'un jeune Jacobite de 1819.*

57 *Les Travailleurs de la mer*, IIe partie, 1. 4, 2.

58 *Les Misérables*, IIe partie, 1. 3, 5.

59 *Post-scriptum de ma vie, Contemplation suprême*, iii.

60 *Toute la lyre*, 1. 3, i, *Effets de réveil.*

61 *Notre-Dame de Paris*, 1. 9, i.

62 *L'Homme qui rit*, Ire partie, 1. 3, 4.

63 *Les Travailleurs de la mer*, IIe partie, 1. 2, 5.

64 *William Shakespeare.*

65 *L'Homme qui rit*, IIe partie, 1. 3, 8.

66 *Id.*, IIe partie, 1. 4, I.

67 *Les Voix intérieures*, x, *A Albert Durer.*

68 *Toute la lyre*, III, xxxiii.

69 *Religions et religion*, iii.

70 *Dieu*, I, i.

71 *Les Quatre vents de l'esprit*, III, xlvi.

72 *Id.*, lvi.

73 *Contemplations*, I, viii.

74 *Post-scriptum de ma vie, De la vie et de la mort.*

75 *Légende des siècles, Vision d'où est sorti ce livre.*

76 *Post-scriptum de ma vie, Choses de l'infini*, i.

77 *Notre-Dame de Paris*, 1. 9, i.

78 *Feuilles d'automne*, xxix.

79 *Contemplations*, 1. 6, xiv.

80 *Les Misérables*, IVe partie, 1. 3, 3.

81 *Légende des siècles*, xlii, *A l'homme.*

82 *Contemplations*, III, xii, *Explication.*

83 *Toute la lyre*, IV, viii.

84 *Dieu*, II, vii.

85 *Les Feuilles d'automne*, xxix, *la Pente de la rêverie.*

86 *Les Rayons et les ombres*, xxxv, *Que la musique date du XVIe siècle. . .*

87 *Contemplations*, III, xxx, *Magnitudo parvi.*

88 *Légende des siècles*, iv, *le Titan.*

89 *Contemplations*, III, xxx, *Magnitudo parvi.*

90 *Dieu*, II, vii.

91 *Les Misérables*, Ire partie, 1. 7, 3.

92 *Les Djinns.*

93 *Dieu*, II, ɪɪ, *le Hibou.*
94 *Id.*, II, ɪɪ.
95 *Post-scriptum de ma vie, Promontorium Somnii.*
96 *Quatre-vingt-treize*, ɪ. 6, 2.
97 *Les Rayons et les ombres*, XIII.
98 *Contemplations, Ce que dit la bouche d'ombre.*
99 *L'Homme qui rit*, IIᵉ partie, ɪ. 4, 7.
100 *Les Misérables*, Iʳᵉ partie, ɪ. 7, 3.
101 *Légende des siècles*, ʟɪᴠ, *Vision de Dante.*
102 *Ibid.*
103 *Fin de Satan*, I.
104 *Légende des siècles*, ɪᴠ, *le Titan.*
105 *L'Homme qui rit*, IIᵉ partie, ɪ. 9, ɪ.
106 *Id.*, Iʳᵉ partie, ɪ. ɪ, 5.
107 *Dernière gerbe, le Grand être.*
108 *William Shakespeare*, Iʳᵉ partie, ɪ. 2, ɪ.
109 *Dernière gerbe, le Grand être.*
110 *Les Travailleurs de la mer*, IIᵉ partie, ɪ. 2, 5.

CHAPTER VII

1 *Le Poète déchu, Oeuvres en prose*, éd. de la Pléiade, p. 328.
2 *Portia, Poésies*, éd. de la Pléiade, p. 75.
3 *A Paul Foucher*, 23 septembre 1827.
4 *Don Paez, Poésies*, p. 30.
5 *Confession d'un enfant du siècle, Oeuvres en prose*, p. 106.
6 *Les Caprices de Marianne*, acte I, scène ɪᴠ; *Théâtre*, éd. de la Pléiade, p. 156.
7 *Lettre à Lamartine; Poésies*, p. 340.
8 *Le Saule, Poésies*, p. 156.
9 *La Confession d'un enfant du siècle, Oeuvres en prose*, p. 201.
10 *Don Paez, Poésies*, p. 31.
11 *Lettre à Lamartine, Poésies*, p. 337.
12 *Le Saule, Poésies*, p. 157.
13 *Le Saule, Poésies*, p. 157; *la Confession d'un enfant du siècle, Oeuvres en prose*, p. 202.
14 *Nuit de décembre, Poésies*, p. 321.
15 *La Confession d'un enfant du siècle, Oeuvres en prose*, p. 129.
16 *Nuit de décembre, ibid.*
17 *Souvenir des Alpes, Poésies*, p. 466.
18 *Lettre à Lamartine, Poésies*, p. 342.
19 *La Confession d'un enfant du siècle, Oeuvres en prose*, p. 162.
20 *Rolla, Poésies*, p. 295.
21 *Le Saule, Poésies*, p. 145.
22 *Lettre à Lamartine, Poésies*, p. 337.
23 *Le Poète déchu, Oeuvres en prose*, p. 326.
24 *Rolla, Poésies*, p. 281.
25 *Nuit de décembre, Poésies*, p. 322.
26 *Lorenzaccio*, acte III, scène ɪɪɪ; *Théâtre*, p. 106.
27 *La Coupe et les lèvres, Poésies*, p. 184.
28 *Lorenzaccio*, p. 105.
29 *Id.*, p. 126.
30 *Id.*, p. 105.
31 *Fantasio*, acte I, scène ɪɪ; *Théâtre*, p. 191.
32 *Lorenzaccio*, acte V, scène ᴠɪ; *Théâtre*, pp. 148–149.
33 *Rolla, Poésies*, p. 282.
34 *Id.*, p. 283.
35 *Confession d'un enfant du siècle, Oeuvres, en prose*, p. 269.
36 *Id.*, p. 161.
37 *Emmeline, Oeuvres en prose*, p. 404.
38 *Fantasio*, acte I, scène ɪɪ; *Théâtre*, p. 193.
39 *A George Sand*, Iᵉʳ mai 1834.
40 *Nuit d'août, Poésies*, p. 327.
41 *La Coupe et les lèvres*, acte II, scène ɪɪɪ; *Poésies*, pp. 184–185.
42 *Sonnet, Poésies*, p. 463.
43 *Nuit d'août, Poésies*, p. 326.
44 *Id.*, p. 324.

45 *A trente ans, Oeuvres en prose*, p. 953.
46 *Les Caprices de Marianne*, acte I, scène IV; *Théâtre*, p. 155.
47 *Lettre à Lamartine, Poésies*, p. 340.

48 *Le Roman par lettres, Oeuvres en prose*, p. 308.
49 *Souvenir, Poésies*, p. 413.
50 *Id.*, p. 415.

CHAPTER VIII

1 *Oeuvres*, éd. Bernard d'Harcourt, Les Textes français, 1947, 2 vol., t. II, p. 19.
2 *Id.*, I, p. 233.
3 II, p. 16.
4 *Id.*
5 II, p. 29.
6 I, p. 204.
7 *Id.*
8 II, p. 11.
9 I, p. 11.
10 II, p. 19.
11 *Lettre à Eugénie*, 7 novembre 1829, DECAHORS, *Maurice de Guérin*, Bloud, 1932, p. 125.
12 *Oeuvres*, t. I, p. 175.
13 *A son père*, 28 septembre 1828, DECAHORS, p. 86.
14 *Oeuvres*, II, p. 22.
15 I, p. 144.
16 Paroles de Guérin (Somegod) dans l'*Amaïdée* de BARBEY. BARBEY, *Oeuvres*, éd. Bernouard, t. IV, p. 164.
17 I, p. 144.
18 II, p. 18.
19 *Id.*
20 II, p. 17.
21 II, p. 26.
22 II, p. 30.
23 I, p. 35.
24 I, p. 90.
25 II, p. 65.
26 I, p. 203.
27 I, p. 143.
28 I, p. 144.
29 *Id.*
30 DECAHORS, **p. 125.**
31 *Oeuvres*, **p. 226.**

32 *Id.*, p. 226.
33 *Id.*
34 *Lieux*. Je corrige le texte. Toutes les éditions ont *liens*.
35 I, pp. 196–198.
36 II, p. 75.
37 I, p. 157.
38 I, p. 160.
39 I, p. 96.
40 I, p. 177.
41 II, pp. 18–19.
42 II, p. 64.
43 II, p. 191.
44 I, p. 92.
45 I, p. 180.
46 I, p. 230.
47 I, p. 234.
48 II, p. 347.
49 II, p. 334.
50 I, p. 212.
51 I, p. 147.
52 I, p. 208.
53 II, p. 84.
54 I, p. 160.
55 I, p. 156.
56 I, p. 154.
57 I, p. 212.
58 II, p. 212.
59 L'expression est de Fénelon. Cf. *Oeuvres*, éd. Gaume, t. I, p. 96.
60 I, p. 151.
61 I, p. 154.
62 I, p. 254.
63 I, p. 167.
64 II, p. 346.
65 I, p. 171.
66 I, p. 106.
67 I, p. 212.
68 I, p. 158.

69 I, p. 215.
70 I, p. 107.
71 I, p. 224.
72 I, p. 222.
73 I, p. 245.
74 I, p. 248.
75 I, p. 151.
76 I, p. 151.
77 *Amaïdée*, p. 173.
78 *Esquisse d'une philosophie,* éd.
  Renouard, 1840, t. IV, p 141.
79 I, p. 21.
80 I, p. 192.
81 I, p. 195.
82 I, p. 217.
83 II, p. 207.
84 II, p. 173.
85 I, p. 214.
86 I, p. 169.
87 I, p. 14.
88 I, p. 8.
89 *Amaïdée*, p. 145.
90 I, p. 138.
91 I, p. 171.
92 I, p. 269.
93 II, p. 163.
94 I, p. 248.
95 I, p. 211.
96 II, p. 258.
97 I, p. 250.
98 I, pp. 3–5.
99 I, p. 19.
100 I, p. 210.
101 I, p. 235.
102 I, p. 53.
103 I, p. 225.
104 I, p. 158.
105 I, p. 6.
106 I, p. 253.
107 I, p. 13.
108 I, p. 16.
109 II, p. 262.
110 I, p. 7.
111 I, p. 235.
112 I, p. 248.
113 I, p. 212.
114 I, p. 223.
115 I, p. 13.
116 I, p. 18.
117 I, p. 249.
118 I, p. 6.
119 I, p. 169.
120 I, p. 128.
121 II, p. 353.
122 I, p. 17.
123 I, p. 225.
124 II, p. 141.
125 II, p. 364.
126 I, p. 105.
127 I, p. 218.
128 I, p. 7.
129 I, p. 6.
130 I, p. 225.
131 I, p. 193.
132 II, pp. 161–162.
133 I, p. 8.
134 I, p. 155.
135 I, p. 6.
136 *Id.*
137 *Id.*
138 I, p. 219.
139 II, p. 222.
140 II, p. 206.
141 II, p. 190.
142 II, pp. 158–159.
143 II, p. 345.
144 II, p. 205.
145 I, p. 254.
146 I, p. 22.
147 I, p. 7.
148 I, p. 5.
149 I, p. 224.
150 I, p. 250.
151 I, p. 11.
152 I, p. 9.
153 I, p. 55.
154 I, p. 252.
155 II, p. 285.
156 I, p. 234.
157 I, p. 222.
158 I, p. 236.
159 I, p. 175.
160 I, p. 223.
161 I, p. 217.
162 I, p. 168.
163 I, p. 238.

164 I, p. 230.
165 I, p. 218.
166 *Amaïdée*, p. 170.
167 I, p. 205.
168 I, p. 217.
169 I, p. 217.
170 I, p. 220.
171 II, p. 179.
172 I, p. 222.
173 II, p. 201.
174 I, p. 226.
175 I, p. 229.
176 I, p. 252.
177 I, p. 12.
178 I, p. 8.
179 I, p. 5.
180 I, p. 243.

181 II, p. 148.
182 I, p. 245.
183 II, p. 340.
184 I, p. 10.
185 I, p. 247.
186 I, p. 245.
187 I, p. 5.
188 I, p. 224.
189 II, p. 191.
190 I, p. 221.
191 I, p. 237.
192 I, p. 244.
193 I, p. 223.
194 I, p. 259.
195 I, p. 22.
196 I, p. 136.

CHAPTER IX

1 *Oeuvres*, éd. de la Pléiade, 1945, p. 249.
2 MONDOR, *Vie de Mallarmé*, N.R.F., 1941, p. 238.
3 *Brise marine*, *Oeuvres*, p. 38.
4 *Oeuvres*, p. 40.
5 *Id.*, p. 32.
6 *Propos sur la poésie*, p. 55.
7 *Oeuvres*, p. 28.
8 *Id.*, p. 33.
9 *Id.*, p. 1427.
10 MONDOR, p. 92.
11 *Oeuvres*, p. 261.
12 MONDOR, p. 92.
13 *Id.*, p. 92.
14 *Id.*, p. 92.
15 *Les Fenêtres*, *Oeuvres*, p. 33.
16 MONDOR, p. 257.
17 *L'Azur*, *Oeuvres*, p. 37.
18 *Tristesse d'été*, p. 1427.
19 *Hérodiade*, p. 48.
20 *L'Azur*, *Oeuvres*, p. 37.
21 *Angoisse*, p. 35.
22 *La Pipe*, *Oeuvres*, p. 275.
23 MONDOR, p. 96.
24 *Id.*, p. 77.
25 *Le Nénuphar blanc*, *Oeuvres*, p. 285.

26 *Frisson d'hiver*, p. 272.
27 *Le Phénomène futur*, p. 269.
28 *Plainte d'automne*, p. 270.
29 *La Musique et les Lettres*, *Oeuvres*, p. 647.
30 *Villiers de l'Isle-Adam*, *Oeuvres*, p. 496.
31 *Le Démon de l'analogie*, p. 272.
32 *Sa fosse est creusée*, p. 5.
33 MONDOR, p. 257.
34 *Id.*, p. 179.
35 *Id.*, p. 276.
36 *Id.*, p. 287.
37 *Remémoration d'amis belges*, *Oeuvres*, p. 60.
38 *Le Nénuphar blanc*, p. 285.
39 *Oeuvres*, p. 368.
40 *Id.*
41 *Id.*
42 *Le Phénomène futur*, *Oeuvres*, pp. 269–270.
43 *Sa fosse est creusée*, *Oeuvres*, p. 5.
44 *Les Fleurs*, p. 33.
45 *Oeuvres*, p. 376.
46 *Id.*, p. 334.
47 *Id.*, p. 300.
48 *Id.*, p. 440.

49 *Id.*, p. 441.
50 *Id.*, p. 694.
51 *La Musique et les Lettres, Oeuvres,* p. 647.
52 MONDOR, p. 193.
53 *Id.*, p. 237.
54 *Id.*, p. 212.
55 *Id.*, p. 211.
56 *Id.*, p. 237.
57 MALLARMÉ, *Igitur* (fragment inédit). Numéro spécial de la revue *les Lettres*, t. III, 1948, p. 24.
58 *Oeuvres*, p. 387.
59 *Id.*, p. 319.
60 MONDOR, p. 193.
61 *La Musique et les Lettres, Oeuvres,* p. 647.
62 *Oeuvres*, p. 296.
63 *Id.*, p. 481.
64 *Id.*, p. 370.
65 *Id.*, p. 648.
66 *Id.*, p. 295.
67 *Id.*, p. 542.
68 *Id.*, p. 307.
69 *Id.*, p. 870.
70 *Id.*, p. 369.
71 *Id.*, p. 647.
72 *Id.*, p. 380.
73 *Id.*, p. 429.
74 *A Vielé Griffin*, 8 août 1891.
75 *Oeuvres*, p. 545.
76 *A Vielé Griffin*, 8 août 1891.
77 *Oeuvres*, p. 367.
78 *Id.*, p. 296.
79 *Id.*, p. 366.

80 *Id.*, p. 536.
81 *Id.*, p. 455.
82 *Id.*, p. 648.
83 *Id.*, p. 304.
84 *Id.*, p. 381.
85 *Id.*, p. 648.
86 *Id.*, p. 333.
87 *Id.*
88 *Id.*, p. 870.
89 MONDOR, p. 227.
90 *Oeuvres*, p. 310.
91 *Id.*, p. 372.
92 *Id.*, p. 230.
93 *Id.*, p. 328.
94 *Id.*, p. 442.
95 *Id.*, p. 309.
96 *Id.*, p. 286.
97 *Id.*, p. 455.
98 *A Gustave Kahn*, 8 juin 1887.
99 *Oeuvres*, p. 615.
100 *Id.*, p. 495.
101 *Id.*, p. 872.
102 *Id.*, p. 333.
103 *Id.*, p. 294.
104 *Id.*, p. 308.
105 *Id.*, p. 310.
106 *Id.*, p. 545.
107 *Id.*
108 MONDOR, p. 237.
109 *Oeuvres*, p. 370.
110 *Id.*, p. 545.
111 *Id.*, p. 396.
112 *Id.*, p. 393.
113 *Id.*, p. 370.
114 *Id.*, p. 434.

Index of Names Cited